LEGENDS OF JUDEA AND SAMARIA

LEGENDS OF

JUDEA AND SAMARIA

THE SACRED LAND: VOLUME 2

ZEV VILNAY

The Jewish Publication Society of America

PHILADELPHIA

CONTENTS

XXI. CITIES IN THE SOUTH

XXII. BEERSHEBA AND ITS VICINITY

XXIII. THE NEGEV AND ITS PEOPLES

B. SAMARIA

XXIV. IN THE MOUNTAINS OF SAMARIA

ILLUSTRATIONS

JUDEA

BETWEEN JERUSALEM AND BETHLEHEM

1 / WHERE THE PROPHET ELIJAH RESTED

A Greek monastery stands out conspicuously on the main road from Jerusalem to Bethlehem. Its monks have named it after Elijah the prophet—*Mar Elias* in Arabic. The hill nearby is also named for him—Elijah's Hill (in Hebrew, *Givat Eliyahu*). Opposite lies Ramat Rachel, a suburb of Jerusalem.

According to tradition, the monastery is built on the very spot where Elijah rested when he fled from the wrath

FIG. 1. MONASTERY OF ELIJAH THE PROPHET (1972)

of the king of Israel to Beersheba and to the Wilderness of Sinai: "And when he saw that, he arose, and went for his life, and came to Beersheba."

At the entrance to the monastery is a rock in which there is a slight depression. This is said to be the mark left by Elijah's body when he reclined on it. A pilgrim who visited this spot in 1586 drew a picture of the monastery and of the holy rock (fig. 3).[1]*

FIG. 2. WAY FROM JERUSALEM TO BETHLEHEM (1586)
On left is Jerusalem and Tower of David (A), Jaffa Gate, and (below) Pool of Sultan (B). From Jaffa Gate road starts south to Bethlehem. By its side is tree (C) named after Judas Iscariot. To west is building (D) named after Saint Simeon. On side of road is Well of Star (E). Nearby are site named for prophet Habakkuk (F) and monastery of prophet Elijah (G). Close to it is rock with impression of prophet's body (H). Nearby is tower named after Jacob the patriarch (I). Also shown are tomb of Rachel (L), village of Beit Jalla (M), named Rama by pilgrims, cistern (N) named after King David, Church of Nativity (O), nearby village of Beit Sahur (P) and Shepherds' Field (Q), Mount Herodion (S), and Wilderness of Judah (T), spreading toward Dead Sea.

* Superior numerals refer to Sources of the Legends.

2 / THE WELL OF THE STAR

"Now when Jesus was born in Bethlehem of Judea in the days of Herod the king, behold, wise men [magi] from the East came to Jerusalem, saying, 'Where is he who has been born king of the Jews? For we have seen his star in the East, and have come to worship him.' . . . And he [Herod] sent them to Bethlehem, saying, 'Go and search

FIG. 3. MONASTERY OF ELIJAH THE PROPHET (1586)
"Monast. S[aint] Heli." This drawing shows monastery (A), Rock of Elijah (B), house of Habakkuk (C), and Well of Star (D).

diligently for the child.' . . . When they had heard the king they went their way; and lo, the star which they had seen in the East went before them, till it came to rest over the place where the child was. When they saw the star, they rejoiced exceedingly with great joy."

It is said that when the wise men approached Bethlehem one of them went to a well in order to draw water. Looking down the well, he saw the star reflected from the surface of the water.

On the way from Jerusalem to Bethlehem there is an old neglected well which was called by the Arabs *Bir en-Nejm*—Well of the Star (fig. 4).

This well was also known as *Bir Kadismu*, a corruption of the Greek *kathisma*, meaning "seat." It is said that Mary rested here on her way from Jerusalem to Bethlehem.

Theodosius, who visited the Holy Land in the time of the Byzantines, in 530, wrote: "There was an imperial governor called Urbicius, who was governor under seven emperors. . . . Now there is a place three miles from the city of Jerusalem where Saint Mary got down from her

FIG. 4. WELL OF STAR
This well is on Jerusalem–Bethlehem highway, next to olive plantation.

ass as she was going to Bethlehem and sat down on a rock and blessed it. This stone did the governor Urbicius cut and fashion in a square shape like an altar, intending to send it to Constantinople. But when he came to the gate of Saint Stephen [in Jerusalem] he could not move it any farther, a stone which one yoke of oxen were drawing. And when they saw that they could by no means move it forward, it was brought back to the sepulcher of the Lord, and there an altar was made out of the rock, and at that altar men communicate. . . . However, it is behind the sepulcher of the Lord."

An English traveler in 1506, describing his way to Bethlehem, recorded: "We came to the place where the star appeared even to the three kings . . . and a little farther we came to an old church where the prophet Elijah was born."[2]

3 / THE FIELD OF THE PROPHET HABAKKUK

In the Middle Ages there was, on the way from Jerusalem to Bethlehem, a field which was named after the Judean prophet Habakkuk. And it was told that one harvest day Habakkuk went out to his field to bring food to the day laborers who reaped the corn. He gave them their part and left some for himself. A voice came from heaven and said: "Go and bring this meal to Daniel, My servant, who is in the land of the Chaldees in the den of the lions!" And Habakkuk said: "O my Lord, who will lead me there in this time, for the way is very far?"

Suddenly an angel came and seized him by the tuft of hair on his head and carried him with the food in his hand and brought him to Daniel in the den. Daniel ate and drank together with Habakkuk, and after that the angel took Habakkuk and brought him back to his place before the harvesters finished their meal (figs. 5 and 6).

An English traveler recorded his journey from Jerusalem

FIG. 5. ANGEL WITH HABAKKUK IN DANIEL'S DEN
A Christian drawing.

FIG. 6. ANGEL WITH HABAKKUK IN DANIEL'S DEN (1743)
A Jewish drawing.

to Bethlehem in 1506: "And thereby is a place where the angel took up Habakkuk by the front and bore him to Babylon, and set him in the den of lions, where Daniel the prophet was, and refreshed him with meat and drink."

A pilgrim who passed this way in 1681 has left a drawing of the ruins of an old building named after Habakkuk which stood on the side of the road (fig. 7).[3]

FIG. 7. RUINS OF HOUSE NAMED FOR PROPHET HABAKKUK (1681)

4 / THE FIELD OF THE PETRIFIED PEAS

Between Jerusalem and Bethlehem the Christian University of Notre Dame stands on a conspicuous hill named, in Arabic, *Tantur.*

A stretch of land in this vicinity was once covered with small round pebbles that looked like peas; hence in the Middle Ages Christian pilgrims called it *Campus Cicerum* —Field of Peas.

This plot, it was said, produced the same lentils for which Esau "sold his birthright to Jacob."

A Christian legend says that Jesus once passed this field

when fresh ripe peas were growing there abundantly. Being hungry, he asked the owner for some to allay his hunger.

The owner said mockingly: "Those are not peas, they are pebbles." And immediately the peas turned into pebbles.

Another version tells us that Mary and Jesus were once passing by this field; they saw a man sowing peas and said to him: "What art thou sowing, friend?"

The man answered impudently: "I am sowing stones."

Then Jesus replied: "Thou wilt reap stones."

When the time for this man's harvest came, he found in his threshing floor stones which looked like peas; hence the Arabic name: *Jurun el-Humus*—Threshing Floor of Peas.

The English traveler of 1734, C. Thompson, repeated the same story with a variation: "Then on our left we are shown a piece of ground, where they pick up small round stones exactly resembling peas, concerning which they have a tradition that the blessed Virgin, going from Bethlehem to Jerusalem, found a man sowing peas, and begged a handful of him to relieve her hunger, which the rustic refusing to give her, and telling her they were nothing but stones, his words were immediately verified, all his peas being miraculously petrified in an instant."[4]

5 / THE FIELD OF FLOWERS—CAMPUS FLORIDUS

Near Bethlehem was a field known by the Latin name *Campus Floridus*—Field of Flowers.

The Englishman Sir John Mandeville wrote in 1322 about "Felde Floridus"—Field of Flowers: "That is to say, the field flourished; for a fair maiden was blamed with wrong and slandered, that she had committed fornication, for which cause she was condemned to be burnt in that place; and as the fire began to burn about her, she made her prayers to our Lord, that as truly as she was not guilty, He would by His merciful grace help her, and make it known to all men. And when she had thus said, she entered into the fire, and immediately the fire was extinguished, and the fagots that were burning became red rosebushes. And those that were not kindled became white rosebushes, full of roses. And these were the first rose trees and roses, both white and red, that ever any man saw. And thus was this maiden saved by the grace of God. And therefore is that field called the field that God flourished, for it was full of roses" (fig. 8).[5]

FIG. 8. FIELD OF FLOWERS, DESCRIBED BY SIR JOHN MANDEVILLE
From Cotton Manuscript in British Museum.

6 / THE BIRTHPLACE OF BENJAMIN

In bygone days a ruined house stood along the way to Bethlehem, near the tomb of Rachel. The Arabs called it after her son: *Kaser Binyamin*—Castle of Benjamin.

Legends tell us that this is the spot where Benjamin was born, as recorded in Genesis: "And they journeyed from Bethel; and there was still some way to come to

Ephrath; and Rachel travailed, and she had hard labour. And it came to pass when she was in hard labour, that the midwife said unto her: 'Fear not; for this also is a son for thee.' And it came to pass, as her soul was in departing— for she died—that she called his name Ben-oni; but his father called him Benjamin. . . . And Jacob set up a pillar upon her grave; the same is the pillar of Rachel's grave unto this day."

Benjamin is the only son of Jacob who was born in the land of Canaan and therefore his descendants enjoyed the privilege of having the holy of holies set up in their portion, in Jerusalem.*[6]

7 / THE HOUSE OF JACOB THE PATRIARCH

Christian pilgrims of the Middle Ages mention a house which stood by the side of the road leading from Jerusalem to Bethlehem, near the tomb of Rachel. The house was called the Tower of Jacob, and legend recounts that the patriarch lived here, next to the tomb of his beloved wife.

A pilgrim in 1681 saw the remains of this edifice and left a drawing of it (fig. 9).[7]

8 / THE WELL OF DAVID IN BETHLEHEM

At the entrance to Bethlehem from the northern side there is a cistern for collecting rainwater. It is named after King David; in Arabic it is called *Bir Daud*—Well of David. Tradition holds that this is the same well from which water was brought to David while he fought the Philistines in these surroundings. As the Bible relates: "And David was then in the stronghold, and the garrison of the Philistines was then in Bethlehem. And David longed, and said: 'Oh that one would give me water to drink of the well of Bethlehem, which is by the gate!'

---

* See *Legends of Jerusalem*, p. 75.

FIG. 9. RUINS OF HOUSE OF THE PATRIARCH JACOB (1681)

And the three mighty men broke through the host of the Philistines, and drew water out of the well of Bethlehem, that was by the gate, and took it, and brought it to David; but he would not drink thereof, but poured it out unto the Lord. And he said: 'Be it far from me, O Lord, that I should do this; shall I drink the blood of the men that went in jeopardy of their lives?' "

To this day the Well of David stands by the side of the highway leading to the Church of the Nativity.[8]

9 / THE MILK GROTTO IN BETHLEHEM

Jesus was born in Bethlehem, on a site over which the Church of the Nativity now stands. An anonymous pilgrim of the twelfth century wrote: "Every year in the middle of the night, at the hour when Christ was born, all the trees around the city of Bethlehem bow their branches down to the ground toward the place where Christ was born, and when the sun rises, gradually raise them up again."

Near the Church of the Nativity is the Milk Grotto, now a Catholic place of prayer (fig. 10).

Once the family of Jesus sought shelter here, and a drop of Mary's milk fell on the wall of the grotto. For many centuries both Christians and Moslems have believed that the rock of this cavern can increase the milk of nursing mothers. To this day round cakes mixed with the dust from the rock are offered to pilgrims.

The German pilgrim Ludolphus, who sojourned in the Holy Land during 1350, wrote of the Milk Grotto: "In her fear Mary chanced to let fall some of her milk upon a stone in that place, which milk is there even to this day. The milk oozes out of the stone like moisture and is a milky color with a tinge of red. Even though the milk is wiped off, it is restored again in the same quantity, and no more. This is the milk which may be seen, and is shown in many different churches; for it is taken away hither and thither by the pilgrims."

Another German pilgrim who was in Bethlehem in 1498 mentioned the Milk Cave and added, strangely enough, that Jewish women also used to visit it: "Close behind this monastery is a cave in which our blessed Lady hid with Christ, her son, when Herod caused all the innocent children to be massacred. In this cave one finds white earth like unbaked lime. If pregnant women, who wish for quick delivery, take a spoonful of this earth mixed with wine or water they are said forthwith to be delivered. If women at childbirth find their milk run dry and partake of it, then forthwith the milk is said to return. This earth is fetched by the heathen and Jewish women, who put great trust in it."

W. Lithgow, a Scottish pilgrim in 1612, made sure that his own sovereign would benefit from the wonderful properties of the Milk Grotto's earth: "Not only available to Christians, but likewise to Turkish, Moorish, and Arabianish women who will come from far countries, to fetch of this earth. . . . I have seen the nature of this dust practiced . . . of which earth I brought with me a pound weight and presented the half of it to our sometimes gracious Queen Anne of blessed memory."

Mark Twain, who visited the Milk Grotto in 1867 noted that it is "a cavern where Mary hid herself for a while before the flight into Egypt. Its walls were black before she entered, but in suckling the Child, a drop of her milk fell upon the floor and instantly changed the darkness of the walls to its snowy hue. We took many little fragments of stone from here, because it is well known in all the East that a barren woman hath need only to touch her lips to one of these and her failing will depart from her. We took many specimens, to the end that we might confer happiness upon certain households that we wont of."[9]

FIG. 10. BETHLEHEM (1845)
At left is large Church of Nativity, near which is Milk Grotto. In background is Mount Herodion rising south of Bethlehem, on border of Wilderness of Judah.

II
IN THE VICINITY
OF BETHLEHEM

1 / THE FIELD OF BOAZ AND RUTH

In the period of the Judges, in ancient Israel, the famous love idyll of Ruth the Moabite was enacted on one of the fields of Bethlehem. On that field the beautiful Ruth met Boaz, "a mighty man of valor."

During the Middle Ages pilgrims came to visit the field, which was named after either Ruth or Boaz. To this day it is shown next to the village of Beit Sahur, where the Field of the Shepherds of Christian tradition is also located.[10]

2 / WHERE IS ANCIENT RAMAH?

Opposite Bethlehem, on the steep ascent of a mountain, stands a townlet called, in Arabic, Beit Jalla. This supposedly is ancient Giloh, the birthplace of Ahithophel the Gilonite, King David's famous counselor.

Between Bethlehem and Beit Jalla lies the tomb of Rachel. The prophet Jeremiah, lamenting the destruction of Israel, cried out: "A voice is heard in Ramah,/Lamentation, and bitter weeping,/Rachel weeping for her children." In accordance with this verse, pilgrims identified Beit Jalla, which overlooks Rachel's tomb, with the Ramah of Jeremiah.

Beit Jalla is inhabited by Christians, and many churches adorn the town. Henri Maundrell, an English traveler in 1697, tells of his visit to Beit Jalla: "It has a peculiar feature. No Moslem can survive there more than two years. Because of this belief, whether true or not, the Christians have the place to themselves, without being troubled by others. No Moslem wishes to risk his life and remain in this place to test the correctness of this belief." Another English pilgrim, R. Pococke, repeated the same story in 1738 and added: "Three[or] four of the inhabitants of the village became Moslems and remained to live in the village."[*][11]

3 / THE POOLS OF SOLOMON

On the road from Bethlehem to Hebron there are three pools known as Pools of Solomon—in Latin, *Piscina Salomonis*. It is said that King Solomon built these pools, and in his Book of Ecclesiastes he refers to this achievement: "I made me great works; I builded me houses; I planted me vineyards; I made me gardens and parks and I planted trees in them of all kinds of fruit; I made me pools of water, to water therefrom the wood springing up with trees."

These gardens and orchards were around the pools, and the crusaders called them *Hortus Salomonis*—Garden of Solomon. The Latin *hortus*—garden—was corrupted into the name Artas, which now designates a small village hidden in the mountains of Bethlehem near the Pools of Solomon (fig. 11).

It is told that King Solomon used to go out from his palace in Jerusalem to refresh himself at the waters of the

[*] See legend XIII:3.

Spring of Eitam which is near the pools (see below).[12]

FIG. 11. POOLS OF SOLOMON (1880)
Three pools, one below the other, and Turkish fortress, near
Bethlehem–Hebron highway.

4 / SOLOMON'S TEMPLE AND THE SPRING OF EITAM

On the side of the highway from Bethlehem to Hebron,
close to the Pools of Solomon, emerges *Ein Eitam*—Spring
of Eitam, named after the town which stood in the vicinity, in Judah's inheritance. Today nothing is left of the
city but ruins on top of a nearby mound.

From the Spring of Eitam water streamed to the Temple
of Jerusalem through an artificial channel. The sages explain: "*Ein Eitam* is higher than the Temple by twenty-
three ells." Legend tells us that at first the intention was
to build the Temple close to *Ein Eitam*, on the top of the

high mountain which overlooks the beautiful countryside. Later it was decided to erect it on the summit of Mount Moriah, according to Moses' blessing of Benjamin: "and He [the Almighty] dwelleth between his shoulders." Indeed, the most sacred part of the Temple, the holy of holies, stood in the inheritance of Benjamin.*[13]

5 / THE SPRING OF EITAM AND THE HIGH PRIEST

On the eve of the Day of Atonement, before entering the holy of holies, the high priest immersed himself in the ritual pool built in the Temple area, above the Water Gate, to which the water flowed from the Spring of Eitam.

Since the Middle Ages there has been in Jerusalem a subterranean pool located in the vast covered underground construction known today as Wilson's Arch. It was a Jewish belief that the waters of this pool flowed from the Spring of Eitam and therefore it was named for it.

In 1211 a Jewish pilgrim at the Western Wall recorded: "And there is . . . a large hall . . . and here the priests come through a vaulted passage to the Spring of Eitam, where there was the ritual bath."

There was mention of the same pool in the writings of a Jerusalemite rabbi: "As the Mohammedans were engaged this year . . . 1845, in clearing a space near the West Wall, they came accidentally to a large subterranean cave, and a spacious and ancient structure, in which is a large reservoir of this Eitam aqueduct, whence the water passes into the tubular box. Sultan Solomon conducted this Eitam water also to the buildings on the west side of the Temple Mount."

After the Six-Day War the removal of the earth and debris around it caused the pool to disappear, and the site was cleaned for use as a prayer place.[14]

* See *Legends of Jerusalem,* p. 75.

6 / THE CLOSED GARDEN AND SEALED FOUNTAIN

In his youth King Solomon sang the praises of his beloved: "Behold, thou art fair, my love; . . ./Thy hair is as a flock of goats,/That trail down from mount Gilead. . . ./ Thy neck is like the tower of David . . ./A garden shut up is my sister, my bride;/A spring shut up, a fountain sealed . . ./Thou art a fountain of gardens,/A well of living waters."

Legend reports that God the Almighty called Israel by seventy different names, two of which are "a closed garden" and "a sealed fountain."

Christian pilgrims of the Middle Ages thought they had found the "sealed fountain" (in Latin, *signatus font*) by the Pools of Solomon. This is the name they gave to a small spring flowing next to the pools close to the Bethlehem–Hebron highway. Today the Arabs call it *Ein Saleh* —Spring of Saleh, a proper name common among them.

Not far from the Pools of Solomon and the "sealed fountain" lies the Arab village of Artas, on the site of Solomon's enchanting gardens. Next to the village there is a big convent of nuns. It is named the Sealed Garden—in Latin, *Hortus Conclusus*—according to the verse in the Song of Songs.*[15]

7 / THE POOLS OF SOLOMON AND RACHEL'S SON

An old Arab legend relates that when the caravan of the Ishmaelites descended to Egypt carrying Joseph in their midst, they passed by the tomb of Rachel, his mother. When Joseph saw the tomb, he threw himself down from the back of his camel and said: "Oh, mother, lift up thy head and behold what calamity has befallen thy son!"

The Ishmaelites went on their way, and only when they reached the Pools of Solomon did they realize that Joseph

---

* In Spanish the monastery is named Notre Dame dalli Orto and in French, Notre Dame du Jardin Fermé.

was not among them. They retraced their steps to look for him and found him prostrate on the tomb of Rachel, his mother (fig. 12). Therefore the Arabs call the Pools of Solomon *el-Marja*—the Return—because from here the Ishmaelites returned to seek for the lost Joseph.[*16]

FIG. 12. JOSEPH ON HIS MOTHER'S GRAVE
This illustration is from manuscript found in monastery of Santa Katherina in Sinai, preserved in British Museum in London.

8 / THE SPRING OF EITAM AND THE EUPHRATES RIVER

According to tradition, the waters of the Spring of Eitam run through subterranean channels to Babylon, to the great Euphrates River, and likewise the waters of the Euphrates flow right into the Spring of Eitam. It is said that the fish which went into exile to Babylon with Israel swam from the Spring of Eitam to the Euphrates.

The sages tell us: "Seven hundred different kinds of pure fish and eight hundred different kinds of locusts, as well as innumerable birds, went with Israel into exile to Babylon. And when they [Israel] returned [to the land], all returned with them except the fish called *shibuta*. And how did the fish go into exile? Through the abyss they

* *Reja* is the Arabic word for an artificial pool in which rainwater is collected.

went and through the abyss they came back."

According to another version it is the fish called Spanish colias which did not return: "The amount of water from Babylon caused the water to stream back to the Spring of Eitam. And whereas the spine [of the Spanish colias] is soft, it could not hold the current and be pushed back."

Rashi, the well-known medieval commentator, added: "The slopes of Babylon return the waters which flow upon them to the fountain of Eitam. And how is this done? Through channels and ladders which are hidden under the bed of the Euphrates and by these ladders the waters stream back to Eretz Israel [the land of Israel] and flow again in the fountains and the fish returned through the same ladders."

The ancients believed that there was a connection between the waters of Eretz Israel and those of the Euphrates. Therefore they thought that when the Euphrates flooded its banks in Babylon, it was proof that a great rain had fallen in the land, which they also called Maarava: the Western—for Eretz Israel lay to their west. They said: "The quantity of water in the Euphrates River is a witness to the many rains in Maarava." According to the words of Rashi: "The Euphrates is a witness that it runs from Eretz Israel to Babylon and feeds on its rainwater. And the people of Babylon know when rain has fallen in the mountains of Eretz Israel, and they rejoice in their brothers' happiness."[17]

9 / EL-KHADER—THE EVERGREEN

Close to the Pools of Solomon lies the small Arab village of el-Khader. Here there is a Greek church dedicated to Saint George (*Mar Djirius* in Arabic), often called el-Khader: the Green One, a nickname that he shares with Elijah the prophet, for both remain evergreen in the memory of the people.

It is believed that Saint George of Lod was imprisoned in this place, and the chain that bound him can still be seen (fig. 71). People stricken with disease, mainly the insane, are brought here to be cured, and the more violent are fettered with the same chain. Even today Arab mothers bring their sick children here, and when they approach the shrine they lift up their voice in a singsong: *"Alek aschraf es-salam ya Khader el-akhdar*—May the noblest peace be upon thee, O thou greenest of all the greens!"

In the Church of Saint George there also was shown a stone, venerated by the people, of which the following story was told. While officiating at the holy communion, a Greek priest once carelessly spilled a few drops of the sacred wine. These seeped through his foot and fell on this stone. Because of this it received a supernatural curative power which benefited every sick person who happened to kneel on it.

It is told that even the tsar of Russia heard of the wonderful virtues of this stone and he sent a man-of-war to bring it to him. In solemn procession the stone was carried to Jaffa. But Saint George did not allow it to be transported farther. Every time the boat carrying this precious treasure moved some distance from the shore, el-Khader brought it back to the land with his spear.*[18]

10 / MIGDAL EDER AND THE MESSIAH

According to legend the Messiah was born on the day of the destruction of the Temple, in the vicinity of Bethlehem, the birthplace of King David, whose descendant he must be.

The Aramaic translation of the Bible fixed the site at Migdal Eder, a place mentioned in Jacob's wanderings: "And Israel journeyed, and spread his tent beyond Migdal Eder."

* See legend XIII:13.

This belief is based on the prophecy of Micah: "And thou, Migdal Eder, the hill of the daughter of Zion,/Unto thee shall it come;/Yes, the former dominion shall come,/ The kingdom of the daughter of Jerusalem."

On the name Migdal Eder—Tower of the Flock—the sages comment thus: this name was given through divine inspiration because when the Messiah comes, the Almighty shall redeem Israel—his flock—from this place.

Migdal Eder stood in the vicinity of Bethlehem, on the border of the Wilderness of Judah.[19]

11 / WHERE DOES THE MESSIAH COME FROM?

The Song of Songs exclaims: "Hark! my beloved! behold, he cometh,/Leaping upon the mountains, skipping upon the hills."

" 'Hark! my beloved,' " say the rabbis, "that refers to the voice of the King Messiah whose name is Menahem— the Consoler. He will come from Birat Malka, near Bethlehem of Judea."

It is impossible to determine the location of Birat Malka, a name which means "Capital of the King." Maybe it stood at the site of the ruin called in Arabic el-Bira—the Capital, near the Pools of Solomon, on the highway to Hebron.

A different version locates the birth of the Messiah in a place called Birat Araba—Capital of Arava—near Bethlehem of Judea. This spot is unknown too. Possibly it was on the site of a ruin named in Arabic el-Charib, in the vicinity of el-Bira, mentioned above.[20]

III

THE ANCIENT CITY
OF BEITAR

1 / BEITAR IN ITS GREATNESS

In the mountains of Judea, near Jerusalem and Bethlehem, nestles the Arab village of Battir, by the side of the railway line running down the hills to Lod (Lydda). It stands on the site of ancient Beitar (or Bether), which gained fame during the revolt of the Jews led by Bar-Kokhba—Son of Star—against the Roman emperor Hadrian and his legions (fig. 13).

Ruins of a fortress known to the Arabs as *Khirbet el-Yahud*—Ruins of the Jews—have remained on the top of the hill, amid the present-day houses of Battir.

After the destruction of Jerusalem, Beitar was for a time an important Jewish town. Our forefathers relate: "There were four hundred synagogues in the city of Beitar, and in every one there were four hundred teachers of children and each one had under him four hundred pupils. And when the enemy entered there they pierced them with their staves and when the enemy prevailed and captured them, they wrapped them in their scrolls and burnt them with fire."

FIG. 13a. ARAB VILLAGE OF BATTIR (ANCIENT BEITAR) IN MOUNTAINS OF JUDEA

וויא דיא רואיין דיא שטאט ביתר מיבר ווארין האבן · אונ' האבן פיל
טויזינט פון דיא יהודים דר שלאגן :

FIG. 13b. IMAGINARY ILLUSTRATION OF BEITAR DURING SIEGE OF ROMANS (1743)

Above, in Yiddish, appear words "How the Romans overcame the city of Beitar and killed many Jews."

Rabbi Gamaliel adds: "There were five hundred schools in Beitar, and the smallest of them had not less than three hundred children. They used to say: 'If the enemy comes against us, with these styluses we will go out and stab them!' When, however, [the people's] sins did cause the enemy to come, they enwrapped each pupil in his book and burnt him, so that I alone was left."

It was said that "the brains of three hundred children [were dashed] upon one stone [when Beitar was subdued]."

"It happened that sixty men were going to the camp of Beitar, and an idolater came from the fight and stated: 'Alas for sixty men who were on the way to Beitar, for they died, I buried them, and their wives were permitted to marry again.' "21

2 / WHAT CAUSED THE DESTRUCTION OF BEITAR?

What was the cause of Beitar's downfall? "The cause of its downfall was the axle of a chariot."

It was the custom at Beitar to plant a cedar tree when a boy was born; a pine tree was planted at the birth of a girl. When a youth wedded a maiden, their own trees would be cut down and used as supports for the wedding canopy. And should any tree be sickly or rot or perish, it was a bad sign for the person in whose name the tree had been planted.

Once one of Caesar's daughters passed by Beitar and the axle of her chariot wheel broke down. Her men cut down a cedar of Beitar and prepared another shaft from it. The inhabitants of Beitar, greatly enraged, attacked the princess and her retinue, who went to Caesar and told him: "The Jews have rebelled against thee, Caesar." Then the army of Caesar went up against Beitar, took it and destroyed it.22

3 / BAR-KOKHBA—THE HERO OF BEITAR

At the head of his troops Bar-Kokhba fortified himself in the fortress of Beitar. He was also called Bar-Kozibah, after his birthplace, Kozibah, in the mountains of Judea.

Rabbi Akiba, who put his faith in him, proclaimed him the savior of Israel. To do him honor he interpolated his name in a verse of the Torah and said: "Do not read, 'There shall step forth a star [*kokhba*] out of Jacob' but 'There shall step forth Kozibah out of Jacob.'" After Bar-Kokhba's defeat, it was said that he was called Bar-Kozibah because he disappointed (in Hebrew, *kazab*) the hopes of Israel: Do not call him *kokhba* (star) but *kozibah* (false).

Each man who came to join Bar-Kokhba's forces had to cut off a finger of his left hand to prove his courage and stoutness of heart. But the sages sent a message to Bar-Kokhba saying: "How long will you cripple Israel?" He answered: "How else can I prove them worthy to join my army?" They told him: "Whoever can uproot a cedar tree while galloping on horseback is capable of joining your army." And so Bar-Kokhba had two hundred thousand men with fingers missing and two hundred thousand men who could uproot cedars. When they went forth to battle they would say: "Lord of the universe, neither aid nor hinder us!"

And what did Bar-Kokhba do? With his knee he threw catapult stones on to the enemy and slew many of their men.[23]

4 / THE FATE OF BAR-KOKHBA

Among the slain in Beitar the Romans found the headless corpse of Bar-Kokhba, which was entwined by a great snake. When it was brought to Hadrian he exclaimed: "If his God had not slain him, who could have overcome him!" Later the corpse disappeared, and no one knows where Bar-Kokhba is buried.

In 1333 Rabbi Isaac Heilo told the following about a certain place called Maon, in the vicinity of Hebron. "One day during prayer a wall of the synagogue collapsed and there issued from the spot great flames of fire, which illuminated the whole district. The stars, exceedingly beautiful in appearance and shining brightly, arranged themselves in letters till the following words appeared: 'Here lies hidden Bar-Kokhba, the king, the Messiah.' "[24]

5 / EMPEROR HADRIAN DESTROYED BEITAR

Emperor Hadrian and his Roman hosts besieged Beitar for three and a half years. Of trumpeters alone he had eighty thousand pairs, and each of them trumpeted for many cohorts. But he could not take the fortress until a certain Samaritan showed him a secret entrance to the town.

The Romans entered and slew the inhabitants till their blood ran from the doorways and gutters and water pipes, and horses swam in blood to their nostrils. And the blood flowed down to the valleys carrying large boulders with it. It rushed through the watercourses for four miles out, and then out to sea.

There are two brooks in the Valley of Yadayim, relate the sages of Israel, each going a different way. When they were filled with the blood of the slain after the war, the sages reckon, they had two parts of water to one of blood.

The heathen made their vineyards fertile with Jewish blood for seven years, needing no manure.

The wicked Hadrian had a vineyard eighteen miles square, the length of the side being as long as the distance from Tiberias to Sepphoris, and he fenced it with the corpses of the slain Beitar fighters.[25]

6 / IN MEMORY OF THE MARTYRS OF BEITAR

Beitar was destroyed on the ninth day of the month of Ab (Tisha be-Av in Hebrew), the most tragic day in Jewish history. The sages say that on Tisha be-Av our forefathers were prohibited from entering the promised land, for the First and Second Temple were destroyed on that day and on the same day Beitar was conquered and razed and its area plowed.

For a long time the slain of Beitar were left exposed in the open field, and it was forbidden to bury them until a new emperor came to the throne and gave the order to that effect.

The sages tell us that after the burial of the martyrs of Beitar, a new prayer was introduced into the Jewish liturgy: "Our Father, our King, . . . our Father, the Shepherd of Israel, the King who is good and does good"— "is good" because the bodies of the martyrs of Beitar did not rot, "does good" because they were finally buried.

The fifteenth day of the month of Ab, when the slain of Beitar were finally put to rest, was a good day in Israel.[26]

7 / BEITAR AND ITS NEIGHBOR KOBI

Some distance from Beitar and the fortress of Bar-Kokhba, on the heights of a mountain, there stood an Arab hamlet named Kabu. In ancient days the Jewish village of Kobi was on this site.

At the time a road ran from Jerusalem to Beitar and to Kobi and thence to the land of the Philistines and their cities Ashkelon and Gaza. Several times the Philistines tried to climb up this way to Jerusalem to fight Israel.

There is a tale that David once fled from the Philistines into the mountains along this road. While chasing a deer David came by chance into the land of the Philistines. Ishbi, the brother of Goliath the Philistine, recognized him and exclaimed: "This is the one who killed my brother!" The Philistines took David, bound him hand and foot, and laid him between the two stones of an olive press. A miracle came to pass: the stones were softened and did not crush David between them.

A dove saw David's plight; it stretched its wings and flew to Abishai, son of David's sister, Zeruiah, and told him of David's mishap. Forthwith Abishai ran, freed David of his bonds, and took him out from between the stones of the olive press. And both escaped to the land of Judea. Ishbi the Philistine saw them fleeing together and cried out: "Now they are two, and they shall slay me!" and started to pursue them. When David and Abishai reached the site where Kobi was later established, the Israelites they met at this spot exclaimed: "*Kom bi!*" Aramaic for "Let us arise [against Ishbi and kill him]."

And when David and Abishai came to the place where Beitar was to be founded they said: "We two [in Aramaic: *bitrai*] cubs, shall we be able to kill a lion?"—and they arose together against Ishbi and slew him.

This is how the names of Kobi and Beitar originated.[27]

IV
HEBRON—THE CITY OF THE PATRIARCHS

1 / HEBRON IS KIRYAT ARBA

Hebron is one of the oldest cities of the world. It gained prominence in the lifetime of our forefathers and has retained its renown today mainly as their burial place.

It was in Hebron that the God of hosts was revealed to Abraham—"the beloved of the Almighty."

Why was the city called Hebron? "This name," say the sages of Israel, "is made up of the contraction of two Hebrew words: *haver naeh*—agreeable friend; this designates Abraham, who was the first agreeable friend of God." God had said to Israel: "The seed of Abraham, My friend." The Arabs call the city *el-Khalil*—the Lover or the Friend; that is Abraham's title in the tradition of Islam. His full name is *Khalil er-Rahman*—Friend of the Merciful.

In the Holy Scriptures Hebron is also called by the Hebrew name of Kiryat Arba—City of Four. Why was Hebron called Kiryat Arba? Because of the four couples who lie buried there in the Cave of Machpelah: Adam and Eve, Abraham and Sarah, Isaac and Rebecca, and Jacob and Leah (figs. 14 and 15).

Others explain that it is called Hebron and Kiryat Arba because the soul of everyone who is buried there ascends to heaven and *unites* (in Hebrew, *mithaber*) with the *four* (in Hebrew, *arba*) groups of angels of the divine Presence.[28]

FIG. 14. HEBRON IN MOUNTAINS OF JUDEA (1850)
On right is building over Cave of Machpelah and its two minarets.

FIG. 15. SEAL OF JEWISH COMMUNITY IN HEBRON (c. 1868)
On seal is imaginary representation of building standing over Cave of Machpelah. Hebrew inscription mentions other name of Hebron, which is Kiryat Arba—City of Four—after four patriarchal couples buried there: Adam and Eve, Abraham and Sarah, Isaac and Rebecca, Jacob and Leah.

2 / THE FIELD OF ADAM

God the Almighty created Adam, the first man on the earth, out of the dust, as it is written in the Book of Genesis: "Then the Lord God formed man of the dust of the ground." And God said to him: "In the sweat of thy face shalt thou eat bread, till thou return unto the ground; for out of it wast thou taken; for dust thou art, and unto dust shalt thou return."

Legend tells us that he was called Adam from the Hebrew word *adamah*—dust of the ground. The dust out of which God created Adam was taken from a field in Hebron, which was known to the pilgrims in bygone days. Rabbi Yaacob son of Nataniel, who visited the Holy Land at the end of the twelfth century, wrote about the field: "And there is the place from which dust Adam was created; for that reason its soil is taken for building houses, and there is never a want of it, and the field is always filled up."

Many Christian pilgrims mention the Field of Adam and call it, in Latin, *Ager* or *Campus Damascenus*—Field of Damascus, after the steward of Abraham's house, Eliezer of Damascus.* They tell of its great holiness, and how its dust is dearer than balsam and tastier than candy.

Fettelus, the archdeacon of Antioch in Syria, wrote in 1130: "In Hebron is shown the field from the soil of which they say Adam was formed. . . . Those dwelling near that region dig in the field and take its soil for sale in some parts of Egypt and Arabia, where it is needed, as it is used in different places as spices [for medicine]. The field we have mentioned, however deeply and widely it is dug, yet at the close of the year, by divine dispensation, it is found

---

* An *Ager Damascus* was also shown in Damascus, Syria, as the English traveler Henri Maundrell mentioned in 1697: "The first place we came to was the *Ager Damascus*, a long, beautiful meadow, just without the city on the west side . . . and [it] is taken notice of because of a tradition current here that Adam was made of the earth of this field."

to be completely renewed. The soil of this field is of a red color, wherefore the Hebrews have a tradition that Adam was of a reddish color."

The German pilgrim Burchard, who came to the Holy Land in 1280, wrote: "A bow-shot west of the Cave of Machpelah is the Field of Damascus, where Adam was formed from clay. As a matter of fact, this field has exceeding red earth, which can be molded like wax. I took a good quantity thereof away with me. So do the other pilgrims and Christians who visit these places; moreover, the Arab Saracens carry this earth on the backs of camels to Egypt, Ethiopia, India, and other places and sell it for a very precious price. Yet there seems to be only a small hole dug in the place. It is said that at the end of the year, however big the hole may have been dug, it is miraculously filled up again. I forgot to inquire about the truth of this, but I can say this much, that when I was there the hole was a small one, so that four men could scarce have sat therein and was not deeper than up to my shoulders. It is said that no beast attacks him who carries any of that earth, and that it saves a man from falling."

An Italian pilgrim of the year 1347 tells of Adam's field in Hebron that "the Moslems of Egypt buy this soil at a high price and chew it as if it were a sweet."*29

3 / THE CAVERN OF ADAM AND EVE

In the Middle Ages there was shown in Hebron the cavern where Adam and Eve lived after they were driven out of paradise (fig. 16).

An English traveler in 1506 described the sights of Hebron: "And in the same vale is a cave in a rock where Adam and Eve dwelled when they were driven out of

---

* According to the sages of the Talmud, "it has been taught that . . . the dust of the first man was gathered from all parts of the earth: Adam's trunk came from Babylon, his head from the land of Israel, his limbs from other lands." (See *Legends of Jerusalem*, p. 69.)

paradise, and there they begot their children, and the form of their beds appears yet in the said cave and the said cave is about [thirty] feet every way."

An Italian monk who visited the Holy Land about 1485 said of the city of the patriarchs: "And there is the cavern in which Adam and Eve lived and wept over their sin for a hundred years. And one can still see their beds cut out in the rock and the cavern is called in Arabic *Magharat et-Tahatein*, that is, Cavern of the Two Beds."[30]

FIG. 16. SANCTUARY OF ADAM
Footprint of Adam is marked by letter "a."

4 / THE FIELD OF ABEL'S DEATH

In the Middle Ages there was shown in Hebron the field where Cain killed Abel, his brother, as it is written: "And it came to pass, when they were in the field, that Cain rose up against Abel his brother, and slew him."

Adam and Eve mourned the death of their son Abel for

a hundred years; and their eyes shed so many tears that the Valley of Hebron was called Valley of Tears (in Latin, *Vallis Lacrimarum*).

Adam and Eve learned from the raven the secret of burial: "And Adam and his mate [Eve] sat crying and mourning him, at a loss what to do with Abel, as they knew not of burial. A raven appeared on whose hands one of his kind had died, and in front of them he scratched the ground and lay his still companion in the earth.

"Said Adam: As doth the raven, so shall I do!

"Forthwith he dug in the ground and lay in it Abel's corpse. And God the Almighty, pleased with the raven's helpfulness, bestowed upon his kind good reward in this world."

An English traveler in 1506 described the sights of Hebron: "Thereby is the place where Cain slew his brother Abel; and not far thence is the cave where Adam and Eve bewailed the death of their son Abel for a [hundred] years. And therefore it is called in some place of Scripture Vallis Lacrimarum."*31

5 / THE HOUSE OF ABRAHAM

In Hebron there was shown the house where Abraham the patriarch lived, not far from where he was buried in the Cave of Machpelah. The Jewish traveler Benjamin of Tudela, who visited Hebron about 1173, related: "On the confines of the field of Machpelah stands the house of our father Abraham, who rests in peace, before which house there is a spring, and out of respect to Abraham nobody is allowed to construct any building on that site."32

---

* Some travelers visiting Damascus, Syria, were shown the place of Abel's death on Mount Kassiun, rising west of the city. An anonymous pilgrim related that Damascus was built by Eliezer, Abraham's servant, on the place where Cain slew Abel, wherefore the name Damascus—in the Bible Dameshec, a contraction of the two Hebrew words *dam*—blood —and *shacco*—to soak; i.e., the field that was soaked with blood. Saint Jerome attributes this tale to Jewish tradition.

6 / THE SYNAGOGUE OF ABRAHAM

*"Let us be grateful to our forefathers
for revealing to us the place of prayer."*

Many years ago the Jewish inhabitants of Hebron were very few in number, there being only nine men. On Sabbaths and festivals the Jews from the neighboring villages would come to Hebron to pray.

Once on the eve of the Day of Atonement, nine men came to the synagogue to pray, and they awaited the villagers. But these did not come, as they had all gone to Jerusalem. The men were in great trouble, for they were unable to pray, being only nine, while the requisite number for formal prayer is ten, *minyan* in Hebrew.

When darkness approached, they grieved deeply, but lo, as they lifted up their eyes they saw an old man approaching and they rejoiced greatly. When he came to them, they offered him food before the fast, and he answered that he had already eaten on the way. So they began to pray and thus passed the Day of Atonement.

At the end of the fast they quarreled with one another, for each wanted to take the stranger to his house. At last they cast lots, and the lot fell to the cantor of the community, who was a pious and upright man and an interpreter of dreams and visions. So the cantor took the stranger to his house in great joy. When he reached his home and was about to ask his guest to enter first, he turned and found that he had vanished. Greatly troubled, he searched for him everywhere but could not find him.

On the same night the stranger visited him in a dream and said: "I was your guest yesterday, and I am Abraham your father. I saw your plight and came to complete your number, so that you might pray together according to the commands of the Lord."

FIG. 17. SYNAGOGUE OF ABRAHAM THE PATRIARCH—HEBRON (1932)

The cantor related his dream to the men of the community, who rejoiced greatly, and from that time they called the synagogue the House of Abraham Our Father (fig. 17).*³³

7 / JEWISH PENITENTS IN HEBRON

At the beginning of the sixteenth century the saintly Rabbi Malkiel Ashkenazi was the head of the Jewish community in Hebron. Rabbi Yeshaya Horowitz tells of the self-mortifications the rabbi and his congregation underwent as they mourned the destruction of Jerusalem and its Temple: "And this is the custom of the holy community of Hebron, may it be rebuilt and restored soon, in our days. Every year, as I was told by the great rabbi, the wise, the perfect, the pious, the humble, our master Rabbi Malkiel Ashkenazi, may his memory live forever in the world to come.

* For a similar legend, see *Legends of Jerusalem*, p. 189.

"First the penitent scourges himself as he sees fit, three or four times, more or less; then he unbelts his clothes and when he is naked, he is covered from head to foot with a coarse sack; then he is laid on the ground and pulled and dragged back and forth by three or four strong young men; meanwhile the rabbi or the cantor walks up and down proclaiming loudly: 'Thus will be done to the man who angered his Creator, thus will be done to the man who offended his Creator. Woe to us on the Day of Judgment, woe to us on the Day of Wrath.' And the people look on and weep."[34]

8 / THE MIRACLE AT HEBRON

"He who sees a place where miracles were
wrought for Israel, should say: 'Blessed is He
who wrought miracles for our fathers.'"

Many years ago a cruel Moslem sheik reigned over Hebron. One day he summoned the chiefs of the Jewish community and said to them: "Know that ye must bring me fifty thousand piasters within three days. And should ye fail, your end will be a bitter one. I shall enslave half of you and burn the rest."

The Hebron Jews were poverty-stricken and their souls shrank within them in fear when they heard this terrible decree. The rabbi ordained fasts and supplications, and all the congregation—men, women, and children—went to the Synagogue of Abraham and prayed and wept with all their hearts and souls throughout the night.

That same night the ruler had a dream. Three old men stood over him and demanded fifty thousand piasters; should he not produce that sum they would at once slay him. Terror-stricken, the sheik quickly left his bed and with trembling hands took from his treasure chest a purse filled with gold and silver coins, which he gave them.

Meanwhile the Jews were praying and prostrating themselves before the holy ark in the synagogue, and the beadle sat at the narrow, lowʾ ghetto gate, mournfully thinking of the plight of his community. Suddenly he heard a noise before the gate, and fear seized him, for he thought the messengers of the ruler were already come. But to his astonishment he saw the hand of a man tearing a hole through the gate, and as he gazed upon it in awe and wonderment it threw him a purse.

The beadle opened the purse and beheld gold and silver coins; he bore it with great joy to the elders of the synagogue. They opened it and found fifty thousand piasters, the sum their ruler had demanded from them. Then they understood that the hand of God had wrought this miracle, and they rejoiced greatly.

Three days passed, then the soldiers burst into the ghetto and demanded the money. The rabbi handed the purse to them. They brought it to their lord, who recognized the purse he had taken out from his treasury to give the three elders of his dream; he understood that God had aided the Jews, and cried: "Behold, the Guardian of Israel neither slumbers nor sleeps."

The Jews of Hebron appointed the fourteenth day of the month of Kislev as a day of joy and gladness to commemorate the miracle. This festival of theirs they called *Takka Purim*. *Takka* is the Arabic name for a small lattice, and the reference is to the lattice torn in the ghetto gate, whereby the hidden hand forced its way and threw the purse.

For many years one could see the hole in the lattice of the gate, and when a new door was prepared for the ghetto, a perforation was made in it in memory of the miracle of *Takka Purim*, and thus it remained until the Jewish quarter was destroyed in the riots of 1929.[35]

9 / PURIM OF HEBRON

At the beginning of the nineteenth century Ibrahim Pasha, son of the ruler of Egypt, reigned over Palestine. He ruled with a heavy hand, and when he imposed exorbitant taxes upon the inhabitants they rebelled—among them the Arabs of Hebron—in 1834.

Ibrahim Pasha gathered twenty thousand men and went up to attack Hebron. He captured it and allowed his men three days in which to loot and plunder at will. Many of the Arabs fled to the ghetto and took refuge in the Jewish houses (fig. 18).

FIG. 18. ENTRANCE TO GHETTO OF HEBRON (1932)

The Jews were denounced for harboring the rebels, and the pasha's angry soldiers came and wished to storm the ghetto as well. But as they neared the Jewish houses and prepared to burst into the narrow courtyards and twisting alleys, a miracle occurred. A sudden order came from the pasha that the ghetto should be left undisturbed.

Joy came once again to the Jews and they made the day of this miracle, the nineteenth day of the month of Iyar, an annual festival. They called it the "Purim of Ibrahim Pasha" or the "Purim of Hebron" and celebrated it for several generations.

On the side of the lintel, over the entrance to the Synagogue of Abraham, there was fixed a marble tablet on which were inscribed the various miracles that took place in Hebron, with their Hebrew dates. Among them was found the nineteenth day of Iyar. The tablet disappeared with the destruction of the ghetto in 1929.[36]

10 / THE OAK OF ABRAHAM

Near Hebron there stands a very old oak tree of the kind commonly found in the old forests of the Holy Land. Its Latin name is *Quercus pseudococcifera* (figs. 19 and 20). According to tradition, this is one of the oaks of Mamre, under whose shade Abraham pitched his tent: "And the Lord appeared unto him by the terebinths of Mamre, as he sat in the tent door in the heat of the day; and he lifted up his eyes and looked, and, lo, three men stood over against him. . . . And he took curd, and milk, and the calf which he had dressed, and set it before them; and he stood by them under the tree."

In the first century Josephus wrote: "There is also there [in Hebron] shown at the distance of six furlongs from the city a very large turpentine tree, and report goes that this tree has continued ever since the creation of the world."

Since it was under the Oak of Hebron that Abraham the patriarch received his guests with such generosity, it has become the symbol of hospitality. Saint Jerome, the Latin translator of the Bible who lived in Bethlehem in the fourth century, told of a woman who opened a hostelry in Italy and adorned it with a branch of Abraham's tree from Hebron, as a symbol of hospitality.

FIG. 19. OAK OF ABRAHAM THE PATRIARCH IN HEBRON
(c. 1860)

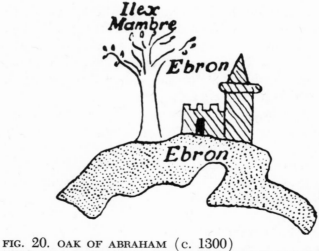

FIG. 20. OAK OF ABRAHAM (c. 1300)
Detail from ancient map of Holy Land, written in Latin. Fortified
castle indicates Hebron—"Ebron." Next to it is tree marked Oak
of Mamre—"Ilex Mambre."

FIG. 21. DRY TREE OF HEBRON AS DESCRIBED BY SIR JOHN
MANDEVILLE
Cotton Manuscript, preserved in British Museum in London.

Arculfus, who visited the Holy Land in 670, related
about the oak which existed from the beginning of the
world: "A spurious trunk still remained rooted in the
ground which has been cut on all sides by axes. Small chips
are carried to different parts of the world on account of
the veneration in which it is held, since according to
tradition it was underneath this tree that Abraham received the three angels. . . . It is said that the Oak of
Abraham grew up from the staff which one of these angels
put into the earth."

Sir John Mandeville wrote in 1322: "A little way from
Hebron . . . there is an oak tree which the Saracens [Arabs]
call Dirpe, which is of Abraham's time and the people
call it the dry tree [fig. 21]. They say that it has been there

since the beginning of the world and that it was once green and bore leaves, till the time that our Lord died on the cross, and then it dried, and so did all the trees that were then in the world. And there is a prophecy that a lord, a prince of the west side of the world, shall win the land of promise, that is, the Holy Land, with the help of the Christians, and he shall cause a mass to be performed under that dry tree, and then the tree shall become green and bear both fruit and leaves. And through that miracle many Saracens and Jews shall be converted to the Christian faith, and therefore they do great worship thereto, and guard it very sedulously. And although it be dry, still it has great virtue: for certainly he that hath a little thereof upon him, it heals him of the falling evil, and his horse shall not be afoundered, and many other virtues it hath, on account of which it is highly esteemed."*[37]

11 / THE TENT OF ABRAHAM

Next to Hebron, near the highway to Jerusalem, is a ruined building made of huge well-cut stones; it is known by the Arabic name *Ramat el-Khalil*—Height of Abraham. The Jews call it *Ohel Avraham*—Tent of Abraham. They hold that here Abraham pitched his tent and tarried awhile, and therefore the place is holy to the inhabitants of the land. Because Abraham lived here with his wife, Sarah, it was named after her too: *Ohel Sarah*—Tent of Sarah.

In the vicinity there is a well also named after Sarah. The learned traveler Rabbi Petahia visited Hebron in 1187. From his testimony it appears that "the waters of this well are sweet and pure. And next to the well is the Tent of Sarah . . . and he [Rabbi Petahia] was shown a rock

---

* The Jews call the Oak of Abraham *Eshel Avraham*—Tamarisk Tree of Abraham. This name is derived from the words of Genesis: "And Abraham planted a tamarisk tree [grove] in Beersheba, and called there on the name of the Lord, the Everlasting God."

twenty-eight ells long, on which Abraham the patriarch was circumcised. And an old man was there, whose hour would soon strike and who would not utter falsehoods, and he told him under oath that once on the Day of Atonement while praying at the Well of Sarah, he saw an angel of light riding a horse of fire standing by the well."[38]

12 / THE VINEYARD OF NOAH

After Noah the just and his sons left the ark, "Noah the husbandman began, and planted a vineyard. And he drank of the wine, and was drunken."

Legend holds that Noah planted his vineyard on Mount Hebron. A Christian pilgrim of about 1555 who passed this way tells us that Adam was made of the earth of this field: "And it is now covered with a vineyard and its earth is not as usual here but common earth . . . and the length of the vineyard stretches very far . . . and one can see the place where Noah planted the first vine. And to this day a vine has remained of these times; and it is higher than man can reach and it climbs on an olive tree. Pilgrims take small pieces of it for amulets. The inside of the tree is dark red. Today the vineyard stretches in the Valley of Hebron."

Arab tradition shows the tomb of Noah (in Arabic, *en-Nebi Nuh*) in the large Moslem village of Dura, the biblical Adoraim, in the vicinity of Hebron, on a high summit. The tomb is within the main mosque of the village.[39]

13 / THE PLACE OF THE CERTAIN TRUTH

In the mountain of Hebron there is a holy place called in Arabic *en-Nebi Yakin*—the Prophet of Truth. It is situated about 3,000 feet above sea level and about 4,400 feet above the Dead Sea, which can be discerned within a deep chasm in the distance. A mosque is built on the sacred site (fig. 22).

FIG. 22. EN-NEBI YAKIN—PROPHET OF TRUTH (1973)
Heap of stones to right encircles impression shown in figure 23.

Legend holds that from this spot Abraham saw the over-turning of the evil cities of the Plain: "And Abraham got up early in the morning to the place where he had stood before the Lord. And he looked out toward Sodom and Gomorrah, and toward all the land of the Plain, and beheld, and lo, the smoke of the land went up as the smoke of a furnace."

The Arabs relate that when Abraham saw this destruction, he exclaimed: "Verily, I now bear witness, for the word of the Lord is truth" (in Arabic, *yakin*), and therefore this place was called *el-Masjed el-Yakin*—the Mosque of the Truth.

Within the mosque a rock is shown encircled with an iron frame. It carried the impressions of two feet and two knees. These are said to be the signs left by Abraham kneeling in prayer (fig. 23).

A Moslem geographer from Jerusalem narrated in the tenth century: "In this mosque is seen the bedstead of Abraham, which is now sunk about an ell into the earth. It is told that when Abraham first saw from here, as in the

FIG. 23. IMPRESSION OF FEET OF ABRAHAM (1973)

air, the cities of Lot, he lay down, saying: 'Verily, I now bear witness for the word of the Lord is certain [*yakin*].' "

An Arab traveler who visited this place in 1693 stated that the same angel who announced to Abraham the birth of his son Isaac appeared to him at this spot and revealed to him the sad fate of Lot and his crowd. And when Abraham lifted his eyes he saw in front of him the cities of Lot's people sent flying into the air and overturning, as it is written in the Koran: "The upper became the lower." From afar he heard the screams of their evil inhabitants. At this sight Abraham prostrated himself on the rock, which has since kept on it his imprint, and he called out in a loud voice: "I bear witness that truth [*el-yakin*] shall last forever."[40]

14 / BOR SIRAH—THE CRUSE AND THE THORNY BURNET

Bor Sirah was a place in the environs of Hebron. It appears only once in the Bible, in the story of the death of Abner, the captain of King Saul's hosts, at the hand of Joab, the commander of King David's army: "And when

Joab was come out from David, he sent messengers after Abner, and they brought him back from Bor Sirah. . . . And when Abner was returned to Hebron, Joab took him into the midst of the gate . . . and smote him there in the groin, that he died. . . . And they buried Abner in Hebron."

The tomb of Abner son of Ner is shown to this day in Hebron, where it is venerated by Jews and Arabs alike.

What is the origin of the name Bor Sirah? *Bor* is Hebrew for well; *sirah* is the name of a common bush, the thorny burnet—in botany, *Poterium spinosum* (fig. 24). The Talmud says: "*Bor* and *sirah* were the cause of Abner's death," and it explains that when King Saul was pursuing David to kill him, the latter proved in two instances his true devotion to the king. In one case "David took . . . the cruse of water from Saul's head" while he slept. Another time "David arose, and cut off the skirt of Saul's robe privily."

FIG. 24. THORNY BURNET—SIRAH IN HEBREW (POTERIUM SPINOSUM)

Thus King Saul was twice at David's mercy to do with him as he wished and both times the young man's faithfulness to his master prevailed. Though Abner was well aware of the facts, he endeavored to deny David's loyalty. In the first case he intimated that the cruse (*bor*) had been taken by a soldier of Saul's own army. The second time he suggested that the thorn (*sirah*) in the fields had torn Saul's robe. For this reason David held a grudge against Abner and eventually had him slain. Thus it can be said that *bor* and *sirah* were the cause of Abner's death.[41]

FIG. 25. BUNDLES OF THORNY BURNET BEING CARRIED TO ARAB OVENS

V
THE WILDERNESS
OF JUDAH

1 / DAVID THE SHEPHERD IN THE WILDERNESS

The Wilderness of Judah stretches from Jerusalem and Bethlehem eastward to the banks of the Jordan and the shores of the Dead Sea. In ancient times it was in the inheritance of the tribe of Judah. The Wilderness of Judah is mountainous country with deep ravines bordered by massive rocky cliffs (fig. 26).

David the king was born in Bethlehem, on the border of the Wilderness of Judah. In his youth he tended to his flocks and rambled with his sheep and goats over this desolate expanse. And while his flocks grazed, he sang to the Lord: "O God, Thou art my God, earnestly will I seek Thee,/My soul thirsteth for Thee, my flesh longeth for Thee,/In a dry and weary land, where no water is."

David was an excellent shepherd, for he used to graze his flock according to their age. In the early morning he would set the young kids out to pasture so that they could eat the tender tops of the grass, then he took the goats to feed on the blades, and last the rams, who were strong and able to feed on the stalks of the grass. Then the Lord

FIG. 26. WILDERNESS OF JUDAH (1972)

saw that David was a good shepherd and said: "The one who knows how to tend his flocks and satisfy each one according to his demands, him shall I make the pastor of My flock, the people of Israel."[42]

2 / THE ROCK OF DISPUTE

In the Wilderness of Judea there stood a rock known in Hebrew as *Sela-hammahlekoth*. In this vicinity King David chased after the young David and his men. "So Saul returned from pursuing after David, and went against the Philistines; therefore they called that place Sela-hammahlekoth."

Legend suggests calling this rock *Sela-hammahloket*, meaning "Rock of Dispute," for on this spot Saul's heart was rent between his wish to chase David and the necessity to repulse the Philistines. It adds that "war to save Israel is preferable to the pursuit of the son of Ishai, who can be found whenever looked for."

In modern Hebrew *Sela-hammahloket* is a usual idiom for designating the cause of a controversy.[43]

3 / DAVID THE SHEPHERD AND THE WILD OX

While David was tending his flocks in the Wilderness of Judah he came across the wild ox who was asleep in the desert. He thought it was a mountain and grazed his sheep on its reclining body.

The wild ox woke and arose, and David was caught between his horns and lifted up as high as the skies. He then exclaimed: "Lord of the universe, if Thou wilt take me down from this wild ox, I shall build Thee a sanctuary one hundred ells high as the horns of this wild ox." What did the Almighty do? He sent a lion. When the wild ox saw the lion, he was filled with dread and crawled in front of the wild beast, the king of the animals. David, too, was frightened of the lion and dared not descend. Then the Lord sent a deer. The lion jumped after it, and David came down from the wild ox and went on his way—as it says in the psalms: "Save me from the lion's mouth;/Yea, from the horns of the wild oxen do Thou answer me."

And where is the proof that David fulfilled his vow?

FIG. 27. SHEPHERD IN WILDERNESS BETWEEN JERUSALEM AND JORDAN

Because it is said in the psalms: "And he built His sanctuary like the heights [*ramin*]/Like the earth which He hath founded for ever." *Ramin*—the Hebrew for heights—is given in the legend as *reemim*—wild oxen.

The sages of Israel relate in the third century that in the time of Rabbi Hiyya Raba son of Aba, the calf of a wild ox came to Eretz Israel. And he uprooted every tree and caused great damage. The people declared fasts, and Rabbi Hiyya prayed. Then the mother of this calf bleated from the desert. And when the calf heard his mother, he left the land and returned to his abode.[44]

4 / THE WILDERNESS IN THE MESSIAH'S TIME

In the end of time all the people of Israel shall gather in the Wilderness of Judah and proceed from there to Jerusalem, led by the Messiah, son of David the king, and by Elijah the prophet.

In a prayer attributed to Rabbi Shimon son of Yohai, a vision of the great redemption is pictured: "And all Israel shall hear the call of the trumpet [shofar] and shall know that Israel is delivered. . . . And forthwith the awe of God shall fall on all the people and on all the nations of the earth."

"And Israel shall return with the Messiah to the Wilderness of Judah; and there they shall reveal themselves to each other and then proceed together to Jerusalem. And they shall climb the ascents of King David, which have remained from the destruction of the Temple. And there the Messiah shall sit."

Many signs will announce to the world the advent of the Messiah: "The eighth sign—the archangel Michael shall arise and blow the trumpet three times.

"At the first blow, the Messiah, son of David, and Elijah the prophet shall appear to the pure and righteous men of Israel who fled to the Wilderness of Judah.

"At the end of forty-five days they shall take heart; their weak hands shall be strengthened and their trembling knees fortified. . . .

"And the Messiah, son of David, and Elijah the prophet shall come with the righteous who returned from the Wilderness of Judah and with the gathered people of Israel, and all together they shall go to Jerusalem."

The *Book of Zerubbabel* tells about the days of the Messiah: "And a great and terrible famine shall spread over all the land . . . and all Israel shall go out to the Wilderness of Judah and to the river Ha-Shittim and they shall pluck saltwort with wormwood and the roots of the broom plants for their food."[45]

5 / THE ASCENT OF ADUMMIM

The road from Jerusalem to Jericho and the Dead Sea passes through the Wilderness of Judah. It climbs the slope of a mount called in Hebrew *Maaleh Adummim*—Ascent of the Reds. Here ran the boundary between the inheritance of the tribe of Judah in the south and the tribe of Benjamin in the north, as it is told in the Bible: "And the border went up . . . over against the Ascent of Adummim." In the Ascent of Adummim stands the Inn of the Good Samaritan of Christian tradition.

The name Adummim, the Reds, is due to the red tints of its soil. Where does this color come from? Tradition holds that the earth is tarnished by the blood of the many pilgrims and wayfarers who were slain by robbers on their way from Jerusalem to Jericho, the Jordan, and the Dead Sea. Saint Jerome told that legend in the fourth century.

The Arabs call this mountain *Talaat ed-Damm*—Ascent of Blood. On the top of the Ascent of Adummim there are still remnants of a medieval fortress of the crusaders which they called *Castellum Rouge*—Red Castle—or *Turris Rubea*—Red Tower. Some pilgrims mention nearby a cistern called (French) *Rouge Cisterne* or (Latin) *Rubea Cisterna*—Red Cistern.[46]

6 / FROM THE ASCENT OF ADUMMIM

From the top of the Ascent of Adummim a beautiful landscape unrolls before the eye, and in the distant east the heights across the Jordan stand out sharply against the bright horizon.

In ancient times the first day of the month was determined by the appearance of the new moon. Those who witnessed this used to come and report to the assembly of sages of Israel in Jerusalem. A great feast was prepared for these witnesses, and each man was called and asked the following questions: "How did you see the moon?" "Was it before sunset or after?" "To the north of the sun or to the south?" "How high was it?" And the first day of the month was fixed according to the evidence of these witnesses, who usually came from the high places in the land, from which wider horizons could be scanned.

A certain man was paid two hundred pieces of silver to deceive the sages of Israel. He came to them and said: "As I was climbing the Ascent of Adummim, I saw the moon crouching between two rocks. Her head was like unto a calf, her ears like a kid, and her horns like a gazelle, while she appeared as if she had a tail between her legs. I peeped at her, and was so terrified that I fell backwards. Maybe you do not believe me. But what is that to me? Have I not received two hundred pieces of silver for telling you this?"[47]

7 / THE ROCK OF THE BACKS

By the side of the highway linking Jerusalem to the Jordan River, between the village of el-Azariya, the Bethany of the Christians, and the Ascent of Adummim, the Arabs of the vicinity used to show a rock called *Hajjar*

FIG. 28. ROCK OF BACKS BESIDE JERUSALEM–JERICHO
HIGHWAY

Abu ed-Duhur—Rock of the Father of the Backs (fig. 28).
They attributed miraculous curing powers to that stone.

An American tourist who passed along that way in 1921
recalled: "Shortly after I left Bethany I saw a curious
sight by the roadside. This was a man leaning backward
over a great gray boulder and rubbing himself violently
upon it. There were some stones on top of the rock, and
I observed that the man added another stone to the pile
and that he kissed the rock as he left. I asked my guide
the secret of his actions. He replied: 'That stone is called
the Father of Rocks, and it is said to be a sure cure for
backaches. The people here think that anyone so afflicted
will be cured if he can rub his sore back against it.' "[48]

8 / ELIJAH IN THE BROOK OF CHERITH

On the side of the road descending from the heights
of Jerusalem to the Valley of Jericho, there winds a deep
ravine enclosed between steep slopes and high rocks. The

ravine runs through the Wilderness of Judah, then across the Valley of Jericho, and falls into the Jordan River. The Arabs call it *Wadi Kelt*—Brook of Kelt. The monks who live in this wilderness believe that *Wadi Kelt* is the Brook of Cherith mentioned in the Bible. Here the prophet Elijah hid from the king of Israel. The First Book of Kings says that Elijah "went and dwelt by the brook Cherith, that is before the Jordan. And the ravens brought him bread and flesh in the morning, and . . . in the evening; and he drank of the brook" (fig. 29).

Legend holds that the ravens of this story (in Hebrew, *orbim*) were not birds, but inhabitants of a place called Orabo. Orabo would have been a town in the surroundings of Beth Shean, in the Jordan Valley.[49]

FIG. 29. PROPHET ELIJAH AND RAVENS
"*P[ro]ph[et]a Helias: Esca[m] quaq[ue] die; fert co[m]pare corvuus Helie.*" Old painting on pillar in Church of Nativity in Bethlehem.

9 / THE BUBBLING FOUNT

In the bed of the rocky Brook of Kelt, east of Jerusalem by the Jericho road, there is a fountain called by the Arabs *Ein Fawar*—the Bubbling Fount (fig. 30). Its water are fresh and pleasant and have a remarkable quality. They do not flow steadily and continuously; at times they disappear into the bowels of the earth and are completely lost to sight. If you stand and watch these waters in surprise, as well you may, the Arab will tell you the following story.

When Allah created heaven and earth, He created the demons and spirits according to their various kinds and, gathering them all together, He appointed them to their

FIG. 30. BUBBLING FOUNT IN WILDERNESS OF JUDAH (1930)

respective positions and spheres of work upon earth.

Now when Allah had ended, there came two spirits who had been far away. One was black and evil in deed; his name was Abed—Slave. The other was pure, white, and goodhearted; he was named Hur—Free. When they came to Allah to be given their positions, there was only one place left: the fountain of *Ein Fawar.* So Allah said: "Since you are late and there is only one vacant fountain left, let it belong to him who first reaches it. Hurry thither!"

So they hastened and, reaching the fountain, leapt into it and dwelt there together. Since they are entirely different in character, however, they cannot dwell in peace, and there is eternal warfare between them. When the good white demon Free prevails, he sends the fountain out into the open, so that men can assuage their thirst with the sweet waters. When the black evil demon Slave prevails, the waters stop and he hides them underground, so that men can receive no use or pleasure from them.

This battle of the demons will not cease so long as good and evil, day and night, strive with each other upon earth, and so the constantly recurring changes in the flow of water will go on forever.[50]

10 / THE HAUNTED FOUNTAIN

*"Even the demons and spirits need
the support of human beings."*

The Jewish legend too tells of demons and spirits who dwell in springs and fountains, like the Arab fable above.

Rabbi Berechia of the second century told the following story. "The fountain of our city was haunted by a spirit. One day another spirit came and tried to drive it away. In our city dwelt a pious man whose name was Rabbi

Yossi of Zaitor. The spirit of the fountain came to him and said: 'I have dwelt many years in this fountain, and neither by night nor by day have I harmed anyone. Now a strange spirit seeks to drive me forth and he will do evil unto you!' 'What is to be done?' asked Rabbi Yossi. The spirit answered: 'Take your sticks and your sickles and go forth in the daytime to the spring and shout: "Ours have conquered! Ours have conquered!"—and he will run away!' They did this and the evil spirit fled. It is said that the people did not leave the spring till a clot of blood appeared upon the surface of the waters."

Legend tells that in the waters of rivers and lakes there dwells a devil called Shaberiri whose danger is great. Man shall not drink water either from rivers or from lakes at night. If he does drink he shall be responsible for his own death. And if he is thirsty, what is he to do? He shall exclaim: "Mother said to me: 'Beware of Shaberiri-beriri-riri-iri-ri.'" The devil shall then flee in bewilderment and he can drink in peace.[51]

11 / THE CAVE OF THE SHEPHERD

In the Wilderness of Judah there is a cave, called in Arabic *Magharat er-Rai*—Cave of the Shepherd. The bedouins tell of a certain shepherd who had a sister named Wadada. Once he went out with his flock. As he sat in the cave at noon drowsing and content, 250 brigands with guns fell upon him. They seized him, bound him tight, and cast him into the depths of the cave. Then they slew a ram and some goats, kindled a fire, and prepared a meal.

The shepherd called to them: "I am in your hands; loosen me, I pray you, and I will pipe pleasing songs for you!"

So they freed his hands and let him pipe, saying: "How can one man harm us?" And the shepherd piped his song:

"O sister Wadada, they have slain my flock's ram and have burnt my sheep pen."

His sister heard the song and understood that her brother was in distress. And she said to her father: "Enemies are fallen upon my brother and have slain the ram of the flocks and have burnt the pens. Gather the men together and go forth to the foe!"

The father gathered his men and they went forth to the cave. There they fell upon the robbers slew many of them and delivered the shepherd. And since then it is known as the Cave of the Shepherd.[52]

VI

THE SCAPEGOAT IN THE WILDERNESS

1 / THE CLIFF OF THE SCAPEGOAT

In the Wilderness of Judah there are many barren hills with very steep slopes. One of these was called in Hebrew *Azazel* and its craggy summit was named *Ha-Zuk*—the Cliff. Every Day of Atonement the scapegoat sent to *Azazel* was brought thither and cast down, as it is written in the Torah: "But the goat, on which the lot fell for Azazel [to be the scapegoat], shall be set alive before the Lord, to make atonement over him, to send him away for Azazel [a scapegoat] into the wilderness . . . And Aaron shall lay both his hands upon the head of the live goat, and confess over him all the iniquities of the children of Israel, and all their transgressions, even all their sins; and he shall put them upon the head of the goat, and shall send him away by the hand of an appointed man into the wilderness. And the goat shall bear upon him all their iniquities unto a land which is cut off; and he shall let go the goat in the wilderness" (fig. 31).

The legend finds in the name *Azazel* two Hebrew words: *ez*—goat—and *azel*—to be gone.[55]

FIG. 31. SCAPEGOAT IN WILDERNESS (1855)
A painting by English artist W. Holman-Hunt.

2 / HOW WAS THE SCAPEGOAT CHOSEN?

The Bible instructed the high priest of Israel thus: "And he [the high priest] shall take of the congregation of the children of Israel two he-goats for a sin-offering, and one ram for a burnt-offering. And Aaron shall present the bullock of the sin-offering, which is for himself, and make atonement for himself, and for his house. And he shall take the two goats, and set them before the Lord at the door of the tent of meeting. And Aaron shall cast lots upon the two goats: one lot for the Lord, and the other lot for Azazel [the scapegoat]. And Aaron shall present the goat upon which the lot fell for the Lord, and offer him for a sin-offering. But the goat, on which the lot fell for Azazel [to be the scapegoat], shall be set alive before the Lord."

In modern Hebrew the word *azazel* means the abode of demons and devils and is the equivalent of the English word hell. A Hebrew-speaking person may be heard saying in anger: "*La Azazel*—to Azazel!"[54]

3 / THE FATE OF THE SCAPEGOAT

On the Day of Atonement the high priest led the goat to the courtyard of the Temple, and he lay both his hands and confessed and said: "I pray thee God! Israel, Thy people has faulted, sinned, and erred! I entreat Thee, O God Almighty, forgive the sins and the guilt and iniquity!"

When the priests and people standing in the Temple courtyard heard the name of God uttered by the lips of the high priest, they kneeled down and prostrated themselves and said: "Blessed be the Lord, may His kingdom last forever and ever!"

There were ten booths between Jerusalem and the cliff. When the scapegoat was conducted into the wilderness, the elders of Jerusalem escorted him to the first booth. At each stage they said to the scapegoat: "Here is food and water!" and accompanied it to the next booth, and so from stage to stage till they reached the last.

What did he who sat in the last booth do? He divided a scarlet strip into two parts; one piece he fastened to the rock and the other he twisted around the horns of the goat and then pushed the goat backwards. The goat rolled down and was shattered to pieces before it had got halfway down the precipice.

How did the inhabitants of Jerusalem know that the goat had reached the wilderness? Signal posts were set up on the wayside. When the goat reached the wilderness each one waved his cloak to the other till the signal reached Jerusalem.

There was also another sign. A scarlet strip was tied to the entrance of the Temple, and when the goat reached the wilderness, this strip turned white.[55]

4 / THE SCAPEGOAT IN THE TIME OF SHIMON THE JUST

During the life of Shimon the high priest, when the

scapegoat rolled down half the mountain he completely disintegrated.

After the death of Shimon the scapegoat fled to the desert and the Saracens (the nomads of the desert) devoured him.

If the gentiles beheld the scapegoat falling from the steep cliff and escaping death they took it as a sign that God was angry at His world.

With the destruction of the Temple the custom of sending the goat to the wilderness was suspended. In later days a similar practice came into use: the custom of kapparoth —expiatory sacrifices. On the eve of the Day of Atonement (Yom Kippur) the pious Jew takes hold of a cock which plays the part of the goat and whirls it above his head, an allusion to the leading of the goat to the wilderness, then throws it to the ground, a reminder of the goat's rolling down from the cliff to the slopes of the mount below.[56]

5 / MIRD—THE CITY OF NIMROD

In the Wilderness of Judah near Azazel, south of the Jerusalem–Jericho road, rises a high summit commanding the entire area. Upon it is a ruin called in Arabic *Mird*. This name is reminiscent of Mered, of the tribe of Judah, mentioned in the Book of Chronicles. The Arab legend tells us that on the summit of the mountain Mird was the well-fortified city of Nimrod (in Arabic, *Medinat Nimrud*), whose remnants have remained to the present day.

Nimrod denied the existence of God and in this city erected a statue to himself and forced the inhabitants to worship him. God sent to him a mosquito which went up his nose and preyed on him, until he met his death. It is said that he was buried here, though no one knows precisely where.[57]

VII
THE INHERITANCE
OF BENJAMIN

1 / THE LAND OF BENJAMIN

The land of Benjamin stretched from Jerusalem northward along the heights of the mountains, then descended eastward to the Valley of Jericho and the bank of the Jordan, as told in the Book of Joshua: "And the lot of the tribe of the children of Benjamin came up according to their families; and the border of their lot went out between the children of Judah and the children of Joseph. And their border on the north side was from the Jordan; and the border went up to the side of Jericho on the north, and went up through the hill country westward."

When the patriarch Jacob gave his blessing to his sons, he said to his lastborn: "Benjamin is a wolf that raveneth;/ In the morning he devoureth the prey,/And at even he divideth the spoil."

Therefore the standard of Benjamin displayed a wolf and in the breastplate worn by the high priest Benjamin was represented by a jasper. It was said that "Benjamin was jasper and the color of his flag was a combination of all twelve colors; embroidered thereon was a wolf in allusion to the text."

The Benjaminites settled both on high sites—like Bethel and its surroundings, about twenty-seven hundred feet above sea level—and on the lowest places of the country —like Jericho and its surroundings, about thirteen hundred feet below sea level.

This wide range of altitude within a small area has given rise to a picturesque explanation of Jacob's blessing: Benjamin, it is said, is a wolf, for as a wolf is swift to catch its prey, so is his land quick to yield its produce; this is Jericho, where the great heat causes the fruit to ripen earlier than in any other part of the country.

And why Benjamin "at even divideth the spoil?" Because on its high mountains, in the vicinity of Bethel the crop comes late as a result of the cool weather.[58]

2 / THE DIVINE PRESENCE IN BENJAMIN

The Shechinah—the divine Presence—favors Benjamin over all the other tribes and incessantly hovers over his inheritance. This is the meaning of Moses' blessing of Benjamin: "The beloved of the Lord shall dwell in safety by Him./He covereth him all the day,/And He dwelleth between his shoulders."

And these are the places of Benjamin where the divine Presence rested:

Nob (Nov)—a "city of priests" situated north of Jerusalem whose site is unknown today. It probably stood on the site of the village of Shuafat, which strides a height dominating the northern approaches of the Holy City.

Gibeon—a city north of Jerusalem where King Solomon offered a special thanksgiving prayer to the Almighty before he started to erect the Temple of the Lord: "And the king went to Gibeon. . . . In Gibeon the Lord appeared to Solomon."

Today the Arab village of Jib, an obvious alteration of the biblical name, stands over the ancient remains of Gibeon.

Beit Olamim—Eternal House, one of the many names of the Holy Temple in Jerusalem.

Why does the Almighty, blessed be He, show such preference to Benjamin? Because of all Jacob's sons he was the only one born in the promised land.*⁵⁹

3 / WHERE ARE THE THOUSAND BENJAMINITES?

In the time of the Judges, "when there was no king in Israel," war broke out between the Benjaminites and the other tribes of Israel. The Benjaminites assembled in the city of Gibeah, north of Jerusalem, many thousands strong: "And the children of Benjamin numbered on that day out of the cities twenty and six thousand men that drew sword, besides the inhabitants of Gibeah, who numbered seven hundred chosen men."

At the third encounter the Israelites overcame the Benjaminites and slew very large numbers of them: "And the children of Israel destroyed of Benjamin that day twenty and five thousand and a hundred men: all these drew the sword. . . . But six hundred men turned and fled toward the wilderness unto the rock of Rimmon."

In all likelihood the Rock of Rimmon (Pomegranate) stood at the site of the Arab village Rammun, on the border of the Wilderness of Judah.

According to the above texts one thousand Benjaminites are not accounted for. Legend tells us that they escaped to Romania. Undoubtedly the similarity of the two names Rimmon and Romania gave rise to this tale, which first appears in the medieval Hebrew literature.⁶⁰

* See *Legends of Jerusalem*, p. 74.

FIG. 32. RUIN IN BETHEL (1970)

4 / JACOB'S VISION AT BETHEL

"And Jacob went out from Beersheba, and went toward Haran. And he lighted upon the place, and tarried there all night, because the sun was set; and he took one of the stones of the place, and put it under his head, and lay down in that place to sleep. And he dreamed, and behold a ladder set up on the earth, and the top of it reached to heaven; and behold the angels of God ascending and descending on it. And, behold the Lord stood beside him and said: 'I am the Lord, the God of Abraham thy father, and the God of Isaac. The land whereon thou liest, to thee will I give it, and to thy seed. . . .'

"And Jacob awaked out of his sleep, and he said: 'Surely the Lord is in this place; and I knew it not.' And he was afraid and said: 'How full of awe is this place! This is none other than the house of God, and this is the gate of heaven.'

And Jacob rose up early in the morning, and took the stone that he had put under his head, and set it up for a pillar, and poured oil upon the top of it. And he called the name of that place Bethel [House of God]."

Why is it said that when Jacob went to sleep "he took one of the *stones*," in the plural, and when he awoke in the morning he "took the *stone*," in the singular?

The sages explain that when Jacob put his head on the stones they quarreled among themselves, for each wanted the holy man to lay his head on it. Then a voice was heard saying: "Oh, you stones, unite together and then all of you shall be equally honored." The stones harkened to the divine counsel and thus when Jacob arose in the morning he found one large stone for his pillow.[61]

5 / JACOB'S PILLOW IN WESTMINSTER ABBEY

In Westminster Abbey in London stands the coronation chair of the kings of England. Under the seat of the chair lies a large stone which is called Jacob's Pillow.

According to the English tradition it was brought from Bethel and it is the same rock on which Jacob the patriarch rested his head. It is said that members of the ten tribes carried it with them when they wandered from Eretz Israel to the British Isles in very ancient times.

This stone was for many centuries in the possession of Scotland, and it was held in reverence by the Scots from the earliest times. The Scottish kings were crowned while seated on it at the town of Scone, which is now near Perth, Scotland, and therefore it is also called the Stone of Scone.

King Edward I of England removed the stone from Scotland about 1269 and carried it with him to London. In 1300 the throne which encloses this stone was made, and since that time it has been the coronation chair of the kings of Great Britain.[62]

FIG. 33. CORONATION CHAIR IN WESTMINSTER ABBEY IN LONDON
Under seat is set stone allegedly from Bethel, called Jacob's Pillow or Stone of Scone.

6 / BETHEL IS JERUSALEM

According to legend the Bethel of Jacob the patriarch has no connection with the village of that name which lies north of Jerusalem. The Bethel (House of God) of Jacob is none other than Jerusalem and its sacred mount, Mount Moriah.

On the words of the Torah, "Surely the Lord is in this

place," the ancients expounded: This is Mount Moriah where the Divine Providence rests ever.

Rashi says that Bethel is Jerusalem, and as the House of God was destined to stand there, it was called Bethel and that is Mount Moriah.

Legend adds that in the same night when Jacob the patriarch slept in Bethel he saw in his dream "Jerusalem built on earth and Jerusalem built in heaven."[63]

7 / BETHEL WAS FIRST CALLED LUZ

After God revealed himself to Jacob the patriarch, he called the place Bethel—House of God: "And he called the name of that place Bethel, but the name of the city was Luz at the first."

The sages of Israel say of Luz that it is the same Luz which Sennacherib, king of Assyria, invested but could not subdue, and which Nebuchadnezzar, king of Babylon, besieged but did not destroy. It is the same Luz where the angel of death never held sway. What was the fate of the old men of the town? When they had attained a very great age, they were taken outside the walls and only then did they die.

And why was the city called Luz—Almond Tree? Because the good deeds of its inhabitants flourished like the blossoms of the almond tree. And as the green coat of the almond fruit is smooth and presents no sign of an opening, so was the town of Luz so tightly enclosed that one could not find its entrance.

Rabbi Shimon said that an almond tree stood at the entrance to a cavern, and its trunk was hollow, and through the hollow one entered the cavern and through the cavern, into the town.[64]

8 / THE ASCENT OF BETH HORON

The border of Benjamin went north of Jerusalem by "the

FIG. 34. ALMOND FLOWERS AND FRUITS (LUZ OR SHAKED)

mountain that lieth before Beth Horon." There was lower
Beth Horon, today the Arab village Beit Ur et-Tahta and
above it upper Beth Horon—Beit Ur el-Foka.

The ascent from the lower to the upper village is very
steep. It forms part of the high road from Ramallah, an
Arab village in the mountains of Jerusalem, to Latrun,
which is on the flanks of the coastal plain. This road is
built along the ancient main highway linking the mountains and the sea plain. On the ascent of Beth Horon many
decisive battles took place, from the first days of Joshua's
conquest through the wars of the Maccabees, the Crusaders'
campaigns, the British thrust to Jerusalem in the First
World War, and the Israeli victory in the Six-Day War of
1967.

In the Book of Joshua we read: "And the Lord discom-
fited them [the kings of Canaan] before Israel, and slew
them with a great slaughter at Gibeon; and they chased
them by way of the ascent of Beth Horon, and smote

them. . . . And it came to pass, as they fled from before Israel, while they were at the descent of Beth Horon, that the Lord cast down great stones from heaven upon them. . . . They were more who died with the hailstones than they whom the children of Israel slew with the sword."

The sages of Israel say that anyone who witnesses hailstones upon the ascent of Beth Horon should give praise and glory to the Creator.[65]

9 / THE MIRACLES IN THE ASCENT OF BETH HORON

It is said that if two camels go up the ascent of Beth Horon side by side, they will fall; but if one follows the other, they can ascend in safety. The story is told of a certain rock standing upon the ascent of Beth Horon, which was supposed to be a place of impurity but which could not be investigated because of the steepness of the place. An old man said to the people: "Bring me a sheet of linen." They brought one and he dipped it in water and spread it over the rock. The sheet remained moist in parts, thus proving that parts of the rock were permanently damp, which according to tradition was a sign of impurity. Thereupon they made further investigation and found beneath the rock a pit full of bones of the dead. This explained why the rock had been regarded as a place of impurity.[66]

10 / JOSHUA'S VICTORY IN THE VALLEY OF AYALON

"The face of Moses is like unto the sun;
The face of Joshua is like unto the moon."

The Valley of Ayalon (Aijalon) spreads in the coastal plain at the foot of the mountains of Benjamin. The highway from Jerusalem to Ramla passes along its side. The valley stretches eastwards between the hills toward Beth Horon and Gibeon in the mountains of Jerusalem. Joshua fought one of his biggest battles in the valley. It is written:

"Then spoke Joshua to the Lord in the day when the Lord delivered up the Amorites before the children of Israel; and he said in the sight of Israel: 'Sun, stand thou still upon Gibeon;/And thou, Moon, in the valley of Aijalon.'/And the sun stood still, and the moon stayed,/ Until the nation had avenged themselves of their enemies./ Is not this written in the book of Jashar? And the sun stayed in the midst of heaven, and hasted not to go down about a whole day. And there was no day like that before it or after it, that the Lord hearkened unto the voice of a man; for the Lord fought for Israel."

The legend relates: "From the time that the sun rises over the horizon till the time it sets in the sea, it says the praises of the Almighty God. Wherefore when Joshua stood in Gibeon and wished to check the sun, he did not stay: 'Sun stand thou!' But he said: 'Sun, stand thou still.' . . . Then the sun said unto Joshua: 'Thou telleth me to stand still. Should a smaller one order a bigger one than himself to stand still? I was made on the fourth day of creation and thou on the sixth. And thou presumeth to order me to stand still!'

"Said Joshua: 'Doth not a young freeman rebuke his old slave and tell him: "Be silent!" Hast thou not bowed down like a slave to Joseph, as it is written in the Holy Book: "Behold the sun and the moon and eleven stars bowed down to me." '

"Answered the Sun: 'Thou ordered me to stand still. Who then will say the praise of God?' Said Joshua: 'Stand thou still; I shall say the praise of God.' "

The halting of the sun and the moon is one of the seven great wonders which took place in this world. The sixth miracle is "Sun, stand thou still upon Gibeon." While Joshua waged war for Israel, the Sabbath drew near. He feared lest Israel desecrate the holy day. What did he do? He stretched his hand toward the sun and the moon and

FIG. 35. JOSHUA SON OF NUN BETWEEN SUN AND MOON
A third-century painting found in synagogue of Dura-Europos.

mentioned the ineffable Name; both then stood still in
their places for thixty-six hours until the Sabbath was over.

When King David saw the Temple that his son Solomon
built, he prayed to the Almighty and said: "Blessed be
Thou, O Lord, the God of Israel, our Father forever and
ever. Thine, O Lord, is the greatness and the power and
the glory, and the victory and the majesty."

The sages of Israel say: " 'And the glory'—that is the
sun and the moon which stopped in their course at the
request of Joshua son of Nun."

And after his death Joshua was buried in his town of
Timnath Heres (in Hebrew, *heres* is another word for
sun). Legend relates that the sun was pictured on his tomb,
and when they passed this way, people sighed: "Here lies
the man who stopped the sun. Alas, that one who did
such a powerful deed should be lying dead!"

In the Diaspora it was commonly believed by Jewish
children that whoever stares at the full moon beholds the
countenance of a man; it is the face of Joshua son of Nun.[67]

FIG. 36. JOSHUA SON OF NUN POINTING TO SUN
Hebrew inscription reads: "Sun, stand thou still in Gibeon." Thin
crescent of moon is underneath. This picture illustrates 1816
Hebrew map of Holy Land.

FIG. 37. JOSHUA'S VICTORY IN VALLEY OF AYALON
To left is city of Gibeon. This drawing is from Joshua's Roll, in
Vatican Library.

FIG. 38. PRECIPITOUS GORGE IN MOUNTAINS OF JERUSALEM

11 / THE CAVE OF THE GORGE

In the eastern part of the mountains of Jerusalem, in the land of Benjamin, there is a cave named in Arabic *Megharat-ej-Jai*—Cave of the Gorge.

It opens on the side of a steep and rocky height which rises over a deep winding defile named after the nearby village of Michmash, mentioned in the Bible.

The Cave of the Gorge is the shelter of wandering shepherds who collect their flocks here at night and on rainy days. In the course of the centuries the cave's floor was covered with many layers of goats' dung.

Legend tells us that from time to time some of the dung disappears, taken away by some mysterious hand.

It is told that the same devils who heat the Springs of Tiberias also carry away the dung to warm up the hot baths.[68]

VIII
JERICHO AND ITS SURROUNDINGS

1 / JERICHO—THE TOWN OF THE MOON

Jericho (Yeriho in Hebrew) is among the most ancient towns in the world. Its name is derived from the Hebrew *yareiah*—moon—for its first inhabitants worshiped the moon. The Holy Law prohibited moon worship to Israel: "... lest thou lift up thine eyes unto heaven, and when thou seest ... the moon ... and worship."[69]

2 / JERICHO—THE TOWN OF PERFUME

In ancient times the many gardens of balsam plants which grew in the Valley of Jericho made the air around heavy with their perfume, just as today the air of Jaffa is filled with the sweet scent of the orange blossoms.

Because of these sweet-smelling plants, it is said, the city received the name of Jericho, which is derived from the Hebrew *reah*, meaning "scent, perfume."

The sages of Israel say that Jericho was pervaded not only by the perfume of its own gardens, but by that of the incense from the Temple at Jerusalem, and it is said that the goats of Jericho used to sneeze from the smell of this incense!

FIG. 39. JERICHO—CITY OF PALMS (c. 1900)
Engraved on a brass plate affixed to "chair of Elijah" preserved in
Jewish Museum, New York.

There was no need for the women of Jericho to use
perfume because of the incense burnt at the Temple,
neither was it necessary for a bride to use scent, for the
same reason.[70]

3 / THE HOUSE OF RAHAB IN JERICHO

The spies dispatched by Joshua found shelter in the
house of Rahab: "And they went, and came into the house
of a harlot whose name was Rahab, and lay there."

The Hebrew for harlot is *zona*. Legend, wishing to favor
Rahab, finds in this word the root *zon*, meaning "to feed."
Thus Rahab truly was no harlot but an innkeeper.

In 1333 an anonymous pilgrim, the first Christian
traveler to leave an account of his journey, described
Jericho and the spring that emerged in the town and
added: "Above this spring stands the house of Rahab, the
innkeeper, to whom the spies came and she hid them and
therefore she was saved when Jericho was destroyed."

Tradition holds that great men came out of Rahab's
lineage, among them the prophetess Hulda as well as
Jeremiah and Ezekiel.[71]

ירחו עיר התמרים

FIG. 40. JERICHO—CITY OF PALMS (c. 1900)

4 / THE SPIES IN THE STREETS OF JERICHO

Joshua son of Nun sent spies to Jericho, a well-fortified town on the threshold of the land of Canaan. And he ordered them to "go view the land, and Jericho."

The sages ask why Joshua emphasized Jericho and weighed it against all the rest of the land. Because it was more difficult to conquer Jericho than all the other towns of the land put together.

"And Joshua the son of Nun sent out . . . two spies secretly" (in Hebrew, *heresh*). The legend finds in *heresh* the word *heres*—pottery—and it tells us that when the spies went to Jericho, they took along with them pottery and sold it to the inhabitants of the town, shouting their wares aloud like any street vendor. And so they kept their purpose secret.[72]

5 / WHY HAS THE BULL NO HAIR ON HIS NOSE?

Nebuchadnezzar, king of Babylonia, asked Rabbi Ben-Sira: "Why has the bull no hair on his nose?" Rabbi Ben-Sira said: "When the Israelites were circling Jericho to fell its walls, at their head went powerful and stout Joshua son of Nun. They brought him a horse and an ass and a mule to ride. But they all broke down under his weight. Then they brought him a bull, and it bore him. When he saw this, Joshua rejoiced in his heart and kissed the bull on his nose; therefore it grows no hair on its nose to this day."

The sages say that to Joshua was given the strength of a bull. The legend pictures Joshua, the conqueror of the land, with a bullock on one side and a wild ox on the other. This is a concrete representation of the blessing of Moses to the tribe of Joseph to which Joshua belonged: "His firstling bullock, majesty is his;/And his horns were the horns of the wild ox."[73]

6 / "WHOEVER SEES THE WALL OF JERICHO . . ."

Our forefathers instruct: "Whoever sees . . . the wall of Jericho which sank in the earth . . . should thank and praise the Lord Almighty." Another version says "the walls of Jericho" in the plural.

Jericho was protected against the Israelites by seven walls. Each one was built by one of the seven people who gathered in the town to repulse Israel. Their names are mentioned in the Book of Joshua: "And ye [Joshua] went over the Jordan, and came unto Jericho; and the men of Jericho fought against you, the Amorite, and the Perizzite, and the Canaanite, and the Hittite, and the Girgashite, the Hivite, and the Jebusite; and I delivered them into your hand."

Therefore Jericho at the time of the Israelite conquest is always represented as surrounded by seven circular walls (fig. 42).[74]

7 / SEVEN TIMES AROUND THE ALTAR

When the Temple stood on Mount Moriah it was the Israelite custom to encompass the altar, as it is said: "Every day they [the worshipers] used to march around the altar

FIG. 41. CONQUEST OF JERICHO BY TRIBES OF ISRAEL
This mosaic of about 435 is set in wall of Church of Santa Maria
Maggiore in Rome. In center is Jericho, surrounded by fortified wall
with towers. Rahab, the harlot, stands above, only inhabitant
who was saved with "her father's household, and all that she had
. . . because she hid the messengers, whom Joshua sent to spy out
Jericho" (Joshua 6:25). One of walls is about to fall. Israelites,
carrying shields and spears, surround city.

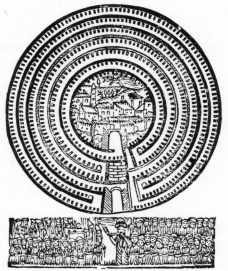

FIG. 42. JERICHO IS SURROUNDED BY SEVEN WALLS (1743)
Below are seen Israelites, fully armed, led by commander blowing
horn.

FIG. 43. ISRAELITES' WAR IN JERICHO AND ITS SURROUNDINGS
(1629)
Left: Israelites encompass town of Jericho, standing on bank of
Jordan River. Right: Israelites defeat Amorites. Top: victory in
town of Gibeon and Valley of Ayalon (Aijalon), with sun motionless
in sky in obedience to Joshua's behest: "Sun, stand thou still in
Gibeon;/And thou, Moon, in the Valley of Aijalon" (Joshua 10:12).

FIG. 44. PRIESTS ENCIRCLE WALLS OF JERICHO (1743)

in procession and say aloud 'O God! we beseech Thee, save us! O God! We beseech Thee, make us prosper!' On the seventh day they encircled the altar seven times and that is in memory of Jericho."

After the Temple was destroyed it became customary instead to make circuits in the synagogue on the last day of the Feast of the Tabernacles, called Hoshana Raba—the Great Salvation (fig. 44).[75]

8 / THE FATE OF HIEL, WHO BUILT JERICHO

After Joshua son of Nun conquered Jericho, he decreed: "Cursed be the man before the Lord, that riseth up and buildeth this city, even Jericho; with the loss of his first-born shall he lay the foundation thereof, and with the loss of his youngest son shall he set up the gates of it."

In the time of Ahab, king of Israel, who erected altars to pagan gods, Jericho was rebuilt. The First Book of Kings relates: "In his days did Hiel the Bethelite build Jericho; with Abiram his first-born he laid the foundation thereof, and with his youngest son Segub he set up the gates thereof; according to the word of the Lord, which He spoke by the hand of Joshua the son of Nun."

The legend narrates that Hiel was reluctant at first to build Jericho, but Ahab said to him; "Thou poor fool! The words of the Almighty God Himself were not fulfilled in regard to me. Although He warned me: 'Take heed to yourselves, lest your heart be deceived . . . and the anger of the Lord be kindled against you and He shut up the heaven, so that there shall be no rain, and the ground shall not yield her fruit. . . . !'

"And," added Ahab, "it is years that I worship idols and the heaven has not shut up, and the ground yields her fruit. The words of the Master were not fulfilled; all the more so will the words of His pupil Joshua remain unaccomplished."

Forthwith Hiel proceeded to build Jericho.

When Elijah the prophet heard the words of King Ahab to Hiel, his heart was filled with wrath, and he said to the king: "O fool, thou dost ignore the Creator of the whole world!"

And Elijah took "the key of rain" and shut the heaven, and a great hunger spread over all the world, until the Lord, blessed be He, relented and said to Elijah: "Go and give rain upon the earth!"[76]

9 / "GO TO JERICHO!"—"STAY IN JERICHO!"

In English literature the name of Jericho is proverbially a place of waiting or obscurity, or of a distant or out-of-the-way place.

The expression "from Jericho to June" means a prodigious distance. "Gone to Jericho" means gone to no one knows where. "Go to Jericho," means begone! "Stay in Jericho" means wait until you have grown older and wiser. To wish one in Jericho is to wish one far away.

Expressions containing the name of Jericho are thought to have arisen from the words of King David, who said to his servants: "Tarry at Jericho until your beards be grown, and then return."[77]

10 / JERUSALEM VOICES IN JERICHO

Jericho is situated about thirty miles east of, and lies about thirty-six hundred feet lower than, Jerusalem. Legend relates that noises in Jerusalem carried great distances and reached faraway Jericho. Even the voices of various instruments which the Levites played as part of the liturgy were heard, such as the shovel, an instrument pierced with one hundred holes, each of which, according to the legend, produced one hundred or one thousand different tunes.

In Jericho were heard, too, the sounds of the flute, the

cymbals, the shofar, and the singing of the Levites. In Jericho there also reached the voice of Gavinni the herald, who walked in the courtyard of the Temple and intoned: "Arise, priests, to your services; Levites, to your pulpits and Israel, to your stands."

It is told of King Agrippa that once on the way to Jerusalem he heard Gavinni the herald from a distance of three parasangs, and he was well pleased; and when he came home he sent him presents.

And these were the words of the ancients:

"From Jericho they could hear the noise of the opening of the great gate.

"From Jericho they could hear the sound of the shovel.

"From Jericho they could hear the noise of the wooden device which Ben-Katin made for the laver.

"From Jericho they could hear the voice of Gavinni the herald.

"From Jericho they could hear the sound of the flute.

"From Jericho they could hear the sound of the cymbal.

"From Jericho they could hear the sound of the singing.

"From Jericho they could hear the sound of the horn [shofar].

"And some say even the voice of the high priest when he pronounced the Name on the Day of Atonement.

"From Jericho they could smell the scent at the compounding of the incense."[78]

11 / THE SPRING OF THE PROPHET ELISHA

Near the city of Jericho flows a spring, which is called by the Arabs *Ein es-Sultan*—Fountain of the Sultan. It is the spring made famous by the prophet Elisha.

Once Elisha came to the city of Jericho. "And the men of the city said unto Elisha: 'Behold, we pray thee, the situation of this city is pleasant, as my lord seeth; but the water is bad, and the land miscarrieth.'

"And he said: 'Bring me a new cruse, and put salt therein.' And they brought it to him.

"And he went forth unto the spring of the waters, and cast salt therein, said: 'Thus saith the Lord; I have healed these waters; there shall not be thenceforth any more death or miscarrying.' So the waters were healed unto this day, according to the word of Elisha which he spoke."

On that account the Jew asks in his prayer: "As Thou hast turned . . . the water of Jericho from bitter to sweet through Thy servant Elisha, pray turn all my bad dreams and all the dreams that others have dreamt about me to advantage, to blessing, to healing, to long life, to happiness, to joy and to peace."

The pilgrim from Bordeaux who visited Palestine in the year 333 C. E. wrote of the fountain of Elisha: "Formerly if any woman drank of it, she did not bear children. Beside it lies an earthenware vessel; Elisha threw salt into it . . . And if any woman drinks of this fountain, she shall bear children."[79]

12 / THE MOURNING PLACE OF JACOB

The Torah relates how the children of Jacob who came from Egypt brought the bones of their father to bury in Canaan.

"And there went up with him both chariots and horsemen; and it was a very great company. And they came to the threshing floor of Atad, which is beyond the Jordan, and there they wailed with a very great and sore wailing; and he made a mourning for his father seven days. And when the inhabitants of the land, the Canaanites, saw the mourning in the floor or Atad, they said: 'This is a grievous mourning to the Egyptians.' Wherefore the name of it was called Abel Mizraim [the Mourning of Egypt], which is beyond the Jordan."

The atad is a thorny common shrub in Palestine. The

Arabs take its thorny branches and use them to encircle the heaps of wheat in the threshing floor to guard them from thieves and beasts.

The sages of Israel ask: "Does Atad have a threshing floor?" And they say: "The Canaanites out of respect to Jacob took off their crowns and encircled with them the coffin of Jacob like they encircle with atad their threshing floor. Thirty-six crowns were set round Jacob."

An old tradition holds that the threshing floor of Atad was on the site of Beit Hoglah, near Jericho on the way to the Dead Sea, where a Greek monastery stands today.

The Medaba map of the sixth century indicates in Greek the name "Threshing Floor of Atad, now Bethagla."

An Italian pilgrim who visited Beit Hoglah in 1347 mentions the mourning of Jacob which took place there.[80]

13 / GOG IN THE VALLEY OF JERICHO

Over the Valley of Jericho rises Mount Nebo, where Moses, the man of God, stood before his death. From this height he gazed searchingly upon the promised land which he was not to enter.

Moses saw from the distance the Valley of Jericho and visualized the death of Gog in the days to come within the confines of this valley.

The sages of Israel ask: "And where do we know that He showed him Gog and all his multitude? It is said, 'The Valley of Jericho.'"

"And we have learned that Gog and his multitude are destined to come up and fall in the Valley of Jericho."[81]

14 / THE SNAKES OF JERICHO

In the Valley of Jericho a certain poisonous snake was very common, and in medieval times a medicine prepared from its secretion was known by its Greek name *theriake* (theriaca).

Theriaca snakes are often described by pilgrims of the Middle Ages. A Christian traveler who went to Palestine in 587 mentioned them. Several centuries later a Jerusalem-born Arab writer told about a Moslem family in Jerusalem who dealt with the extraction and production of theriaca and therefore was named el-Theriaki.

The theriaca snake apparently had a great appeal to popular imagination, and many were the tales woven around it. Some of the more fanciful were repeated by the French pilgrim Ernoul (1231): "Near this city [Jericho] is a field which is full of serpents. There they catch the serpents of which the ointment is made, and I will tell you how they catch them. The man who catches them makes a ring around the field and goes saying his charm, singing around the ring. All the serpents who have heard him come to him, and he catches them as easily as he would a lamb, and takes them to sell in the cities to those who make the ointment. Now there are some wise ones among these serpents who, when they hear him begin his song, stop one of their ears against the ground and stop the other with the tail, so that they may not hear, and thus they escape. By that ointment which they make of these serpents all kind of poison is cured."

In 1350 the German Ludolphus of Suchem offered a much more fiery picture of the animal: "In this country the serpent called tyrus is found and taken, whence what is called tyriac [treacle or theriaca] gets its name, for it is chiefly made thereof.

"This is a serpent not half an ell long, as thick as a man's finger, of a yellow color mixed with red, and it is blind. No cure for its poison is known except cutting off the bitten limb. When it is angry it puts out its tongue like a flame of fire, and one would think that it was fire indeed, save that it does not burn the creature; it sets up the hair on its face like an angry boar, and its head at such time grows bigger. Were it not blind I believe that no man could escape from it, for I have heard from those whose trade it is to catch these serpents, that if they bit a man's horse, they would kill the rider."

A later German visitor (1496) claims a personal encounter with the redoubtable snake: "Beside the Dead Sea one finds poisonous snakes called tyrus, from which tyriack is made, of which I have seen many. They are reddish-white in color, half an ell long, as thick as a finger, and the skin is horny with bristles on it, like the tail of a ray, and it is stone blind, as I have often seen. When a heathen strikes at it, it becomes angry and thrusts its tongue, which is split like an arrow, far out of its mouth, which has the appearance of being fiery. At the same time its head swelled out and shot forward rapidly, like an arrow from a crossbow against the heathen who was by a rock, so that we saw pieces of it break off. But we were standing on a high rock, and the heathen told us that the tyrus is said to throw itself through a board three fingers thick when it is angry." The author showed in his book a legendary picture of the snake (fig. 45).[82]

15 / THE ROSE OF JERICHO

The rose of Jericho is a plant which, after it has produced seeds, rolls itself up into a dry ball. When this ball is plunged into water it opens and spreads out into the shape

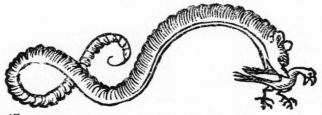

FIG. 45. THERIACA SNAKE OF JERICHO (1496)

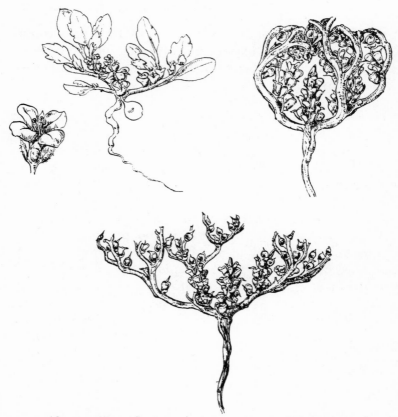

FIG. 46. ROSE OF JERICHO (ANASTATICA HIEROCHUNTICA)
Top left: young plant with minute white flowers. Top right: plant
with seeds, dry and closed. Bottom: plant with seeds moistened
and open.

of a rose; therefore it has become the symbol of resurrection (figs. 46 and 47).

For Christians it was the emblem of Jesus resurrected;
the pilgrims used to buy the rose of Jericho in the markets
of Jerusalem and carry it back to their homelands as a
memento of their visit to the Holy Land.

The rose of Jericho also became a symbol of the Jewish
national revival in the land of the forefathers.

Rosa Hierichuntica Rosen von Jericho.

18

FIG. 47. ROSE OF JERICHO (1675)

Here it is labeled "Rosa Hierichuntica—Rosen von Jericho."

In 1862 Moshe Hess, a Zionist precursor, told the following story. Once upon a time there was a powerful knight
who went east to take part in the siege of Jerusalem. He
had a Jewish friend, a famous rabbi who, faithful to his
people and his God, dedicated all his strength to the study
of the Torah.

When the knight returned from the wars he went to visit
his Jewish neighbor and found him engrossed in the holy
books. "God is with you, my friend," he said. "I come from
the Holy Land, and here is a precious gift as a token of our

devotion to each other. I live by my sword and you dedicate yourself to the teachings of the living God." And he extended to the rabbi a dry rose of Jericho. Deeply moved, the rabbi took it into his hands; his hot tears fell onto the dry leaves, and lo and behold, a miracle happened: the hard ball opened up and flourished like a rose. "Do not wonder, my friend," said the rabbi, "that the withered rose should flower again. This rose, when it is touched by the breath of love, warms up and then revives and blooms, even though it has been uprooted from the soil for a long time. Thus will the people of Israel bloom and flourish again, and the holy spark which has nigh been extinguished under the ash will be rekindled and burn like a fiery torch."[83]

IX
THE JORDAN OF JERICHO
1 / JACOB THE PATRIARCH ON THE JORDAN

When Jacob came to the land of Canaan from the East, he crossed the Jordan, north of Jericho. "And Jacob said: 'O God of my father Abraham, and God of my father Isaac, O Lord, who saidst unto me: Return unto thy country, and to thy kindred, and I will do thee good; I am not worthy of all the mercies, and of all the truth, which Thou hast shown unto Thy servant; for with my staff I passed over this Jordan.'"

The legend relates that when Jacob reached the Jordan, he knew not how to cross. He put up his eyes to God the Almighty and said: "My Lord, Thou knowest I have naught but this staff."

Said the Lord to him: "Strike the waters with thy staff and cross!" And He said: "Let this be a sign unto thy seed; as the Jordan opens before thee, so will it open before thy children."

The sages conclude that it is clear that the children of Israel crossed the Jordan only through the merits of Jacob our father.[84]

2 / THE JORDAN OF JERICHO

"When Israel came forth out of Egypt . . .
The Jordan turned backward."

When the tribes of Israel, led by Joshua son of Nun, came to the Land, they crossed the Jordan opposite Jericho. In the Book of Joshua it is told: "And it came to pass, when the people removed from their tents, to pass over Jordan, the priests that bore the ark of the covenant being before the people; and when they that bore the ark were come unto the Jordan, and the feet of the priests that bore the ark were dipped in the brink of the water—for Jordan overfloweth all its banks all the time of harvest—that the waters which came down from above stood, and rose up in one heap . . . and those that went down toward the sea of the Arabah, even the Salt Sea, were wholly cut off; and the people passed over right against Jericho. And the priest that bore the ark of the convenant of the Lord stood firm on dry ground . . . until all the nation were passed clean over the Jordan."

The sages of Israel add that on the tenth day of the month of Nisan the children of Israel crossed over the Jordan. On every other occasion in its journeyings the ark was carried by two standard-bearers, but on the day of crossing the Jordan it took the lead itself. On all other occasions the Levites went with the ark, but on that occasion the priests went with it.

The water of the Jordan formed itself into arches more than three hundred miles in height, which were seen by all the kings of the East and the West.

According to tradition the Israelites crossed the Jordan opposite the site of today's monastery of Saint John the Baptist; hence it is called by the Arabs *Kaser el-Yehud*— Fortress of the Jews.[85]

FIG. 48. JORDAN RIVER (1972)

3 / THE STONES ON THE BANK OF THE JORDAN

Before the tribes of Israel crossed the Jordan, Joshua son of Nun said: "Pass on before the ark of the Lord your God into the midst of the Jordan, and take you up every man of you a stone upon his shoulder, according unto the number of the tribes of the children of Israel; that this may be a sign among you, that when your children ask in the time to come, saying: What mean ye by these stones? then ye shall say unto them: Because the waters of the Jordan were cut off . . . and these stones shall be for a memorial unto the children of Israel for ever . . . and they are there unto this day."

Some sages of Israel from about the third century relate that they saw these stones on the bank of the Jordan and estimated each one to weigh forty *sah.*

FIG. 49. GILGAL IN MEDABA MAP OF SIXTH CENTURY
On side of church twelve stones are depicted. Above: in Greek,
"Galgala, also the twelve stones." Lower righthand corner: the name
Jericho next to palm tree.

In the Medaba map of the sixth century a church is
indicated with the twelve stones at its side (fig. 49).

These stones were still seen by a few early pilgrims. The
Italian Antoninus Martyr was the first to mention them,
in about 570: "The stones which the children of Israel
took from the Jordan are placed in a church not far from
the city [Jericho] behind the altar." A more pictorial description was taken from the mouth of the French bishop
Arculfus, who passed this way about a hundred years later:
"And he [Arculfus] saw a large church in Gilgal built on
the spot where the children of Israel encamped for the
first time in the land of Canaan. In this church too the
sainted Arculfus noted the twelve stones . . . six of them
lying on the pavement on the right side of the church and
an equal number on the north side, all of them polished and
common; each of them is so large that . . . two strong men
of this time can scarcely raise it from the earth; while one
had by some unknown accident been broken in two parts
and has been artificially joined again by an iron clamp."

Apparently the last pilgrim to leave a record of these
stones was the Englishman Willibald, the first traveler
from the British Isles to undertake the holy journey. He
came about 180 years after Arculfus, in 754. He too saw

the stones, "in the church, which is of wood, and not large."[86]

4 / THE HOLY FIELD OF GILGAL

When Jesus came up from the Jordan Valley on his last journey to Jerusalem, "he entered Jericho and was passing through."

This short mention inflamed Christian imagination, which in time originated a story that Jesus had plowed with his own hands a field in Gilgal, near Jericho.

Theodosius recorded the tale in 530: "There [in Gilgal] is the Field of the Lord, *Ager Domini*, where the Lord Jesus Christ plowed one furrow with his own hand and sowed it. And there is a monastery, and in the monastery three hundred monks who own the field. . . . The Field of the Lord in Gilgal is watered from the Fountain of Elisha; it produces six bushels more or less. . . . There too is the vine that the Lord planted, which vine bears fruit at Pentecost; from this the oblation [of wine] is taken. And so from the field as from the vine the produce is transmitted at the proper season to Constantinople" (this city was the capital of the Byzantines, who ruled the Holy Land at the time).

About forty years later Antoninus Martyr mentioned the church in Gilgal (Galgala), where he saw "the holy Field of the Lord, in which the Lord sowed with His hand, casting in seed . . . which is still reaped twice in the year."[87]

5 / THE PRAYER ON THE JORDAN

The sages of Israel say that whoever sees the fords of the Jordan should give praise and glory to his Creator.

In the Middle Ages, Jewish pilgrims came to the fords of the Jordan, recalled the wonderful events in the life of their ancestors which took place here, and said a special prayer of thankfulness: "On the banks of the Jordan./I bless, praise, and glorify Thy name!/For the sake of Thy chosen people/Thou hast divided the waters of the Jordan like those of the Red Sea/O God, reveal Thy holy arm, Thou, the Sanctity of Israel!/And rescue a feeble people!/ And may Thy goodwill save Zion!"[88]

6 / ADAM IN THE WATERS OF THE JORDAN

After Adam was expelled from the Garden of Eden, he came to the Jordan. The legend narrates that Adam ordained forty days of fasting for himself while he stood in the Jordan River. After he had mounted the stone in the middle of the Jordan and stood on it, with the waters surging up to his neck, he said: "I adjure thee, O thou water of the Jordan! Afflict thyself with me and gather unto me all swimming creatures that live in thee. Let them surround me and sorrow with me, and let them not beat their own breasts with grief, but let them beat me. Not they have sinned, only I alone!"

Very soon they all came, the dwellers of the Jordan, and they encompassed him, and from that moment the water of the Jordan stood still and ceased flowing.[89]

7 / ELIJAH AND ELISHA ON THE JORDAN

Once Elijah the prophet and Elisha his disciple came to the Jordan. "And fifty men of the sons of the prophets went, and stood over against them afar off; and they two stood by the Jordan. And Elijah took his mantle, and wrapped it together, and smote the waters, and they were divided hither and thither; so that they two went over on dry ground. . . .

"And it came to pass, as they still went on, and talked, that, behold, there appeared a chariot of fire, and horses of fire which parted them both asunder; and Elijah went up by a whirlwind into heaven.

"And Elisha saw it, and he cried: 'My father, my father, the chariots of Israel and the horsemen thereof!'

"And he saw him no more; and he took hold of his own clothes and rent them in two pieces. He took up also the mantle of Elijah that fell from him, and went back and stood by the bank of the Jordan."

On the bank of the Jordan, Elisha performed a miracle for his disciples: "And when they came to the Jordan, they cut down wood. But as one was felling a beam, the ax head fell into the water, and he cried and said: 'Alas, my master, for it was borrowed.'

"And the man of God said: 'Where fell it?'

"And he showed him the place. And Elisha cut down a stick and cast it in thither and made the iron to swim.

"And he said, 'Take it up to thee.'

"So he put out his hand and took it."[90]

8 / JEREMIAH ON THE BANKS OF THE JORDAN

Over the Valley of Jericho, the Dead Sea, and the banks of the Jordan rises Mount Nebo. Moses ben Amram is buried in one of its deep ravines, but from the most ancient times his grave has been unknown; as it is written: "And no man knoweth of his sepulcher unto this day."

After the destruction of Jerusalem, the prophet Jeremiah went to the Jordan to bewail his misfortunes in front of Moses, the man of God: "Jeremiah stood on the banks of the Jordan, lifted up his voice and called: 'Son of Amram! Son of Amram! Stand up! The time has come when thou art wanted in front of God the Almighty!'

"Said Moses: 'In what doth today differ from yesterday that I should be wanted in front of the Almighty, blessed be His name?'

"Said Jeremiah: 'I know not.'

"Moses, the man of God, went to the angels and asked them: 'Servants of the Above! Perchance you know why I am wanted in front of the Almighty?'

"They told him: 'Son of Amram! Dost thou not know that the Temple of Jerusalem is destroyed?'

"At these words, Moses rent the mantle of honor, which he had received from the Almighty Lord, held his head between both his hands in great pain, and cried and mourned aloud, until he came to the patriarchs of the world (who are buried in Hebron).

"They asked him: 'Moses, shepherd of Israel, in what doth today differ from yesterday?'

"He told them: 'Have you not heard that the Temple of Jerusalem lies destroyed?'

"Forthwith they rent their garments, put their hands up to their heads as in agony, and cried and mourned until they reached the gates of the Temple. And lamenting, they went from gate to gate with the sorrow of men who see their most cherished ones lie dead in front of them."[91]

9 / "LET THE JORDAN BE THY BORDER"

The rugged banks of the meandering Jordan were a shelter for various beasts of prey who hid in the depths of its thickets of wild bushes and shrubs. The fearsome lion, too, was found hidden in these thickets.

The prophet Jeremiah describes the enemy: "Behold, he shall come up like a lion from the thickets of the Jordan."

Zechariah prophesies the destruction of the country: "Hark! The roaring of young lions,/For the thickets of the Jordan are spoiled."

Jeremiah says: "And though in a land of peace thou art secure,/Yet how wilt thou do in the thickets of the Jordan?"

The thickets of the Jordan sheltered not only wild beasts, but also men who fled from the authorities. Therefore when a man had to escape and hide himself he was told: "Let the Jordan be thy border."[92]

10 / TWO FISHERMEN IN THE JORDAN

In the second century Rabbi Yehuda Hanassi related that once while two men were casting nets in the Jordan one of them entered a subterranean pond crowded with fish. He swam around for a while; meanwhile, the sun set and he could not find the way out. His companion, after waiting for him a long time, gave him up for lost and reported the accident to his household.

When the sun rose on the following day, the man discovered the entrance to the cave. On returning to his house, he found his family in deep mourning.[93]

11 / FISH FROM THE JORDAN AND THE MEDITERRANEAN

The saltwater fish of the Great Sea (Mediterranean) is tastier than the sweetwater fish of the Jordan. Accordingly, sages of Israel made a parallel between these two kinds of fish and two types of scholars.

Rabbi Gamaliel said that a fish from the Jordan is like a scholar who studies the Holy Scriptures, Mishnah, Midrash, the laws and the legends, who has erudition but not the wisdom to apply his knowledge.

A fish from the Great Sea is like a scholar who has studied all the above literature and has acquired erudition, but whose mind, besides, has come out from the depths of knowledge enlarged in vision and in thought, and bears the beautiful fruit of human wisdom.[94]

12 / THE JORDAN AND THE MEDITERRANEAN SEA

The Jordan streams into the Dead Sea, which is also called the Sea of Sodom. This large body of water lies in the deepest depression on the surface of the globe. It is surrounded by high mountains and has no outlet.

Some of the sages of Israel held the belief that the Dead Sea ran into the Great Sea, the Mediterranean.

The disappearance of the Jordan into the Dead Sea, which has no exit to any other sea, was a wonder to some travelers. The English traveler Timberlake wrote in 1601: "The river Jordan runs into this lake [Dead Sea], and there dies, which is one of the greatest secrets (in my mind) in the world, that a fresh water should run continually into this said Lake . . . [which] has no further issue that has been seen by any man."

The French traveler Florent Goujon, who visited Palestine in 1669, wrote about "this beautiful Jordan, which becomes lost in the Dead Sea and after passing underground flows out into the Red Sea and thence into the Great Sea. This was proved by an incident which happened to a pilgrim who dropped a curiously wrought wooden cup into the Jordan River. He arrived at Messina [in Sicily], having completely forgotten the cup, and discovered it in the hands of those who had found it on the seashore. He did not hesitate to buy it at once, and without bargaining very much either."[95]

13 / THE LION ON THE BANKS OF THE JORDAN

A German pilgrim, Ludolphus of Suchem, who was in the Holy Land in 1350, described the monasteries on the banks of the Jordan, near the site of Jesus' baptism, and went on: "Every evening on the banks of this same river one may see countless wild beasts, both great and small, drinking, especially lions, foxes, roes, stags, lores, wild boars, and the like, which walk among men like tame beasts.

"In my time there always used to be a lion at one particular place, on the farther bank of the Jordan, who would watch people passing by, wagging his tail like a dog, and did not run away, neither did he hurt anyone by day or by night.

"At last one of our archers, wishing to frighten and anger him, shot an arrow at him. The lion did not stir, but seemed to pray toward the arrow, but when the man shot another, the lion reared up at it, as though he would catch it with his mouth and paws. After this the lion was seen no more in this place, but did much hurt both to men and beasts of burden."[96]

14 / THE JORDAN FLOWS INTO THE BEHEMOTH

It is said that at the end of the Jordan River there is a big animal called behemoth which swallows its waters.

In the Book of Job that legendary beast is described: "Behold now behemoth, which I made with thee;/He eateth grass as an ox. . . ./He straineth his tail like a cedar; . . ./His gristles are like bars of iron. . . ./Surely the mountains bring him forth food, . . ./He lieth under the lotus-trees,/In the covert of the reed, and fens./The lotus-trees cover him with their shadow;/The willows of the brook compass him about./Behold, if a river overflow, he trembleth not;/He is confident, though the Jordan rush forth to his mouth."

The sages of Israel add the following: "The Jordan flows into the Sea of Tiberias. From here the water winds and falls into the Dead Sea and then winds and descends until it arrives at the mouth of the behemoth."

The Almighty, blessed be He, said to His righteous men: "I created one creature for your food in the coming world, that is the behemoth, and she crunches one thousand mountains, and a thousand mountains prepare for her various grasses and vegetables for food.

"And from whence does she drink? Her head lies opposite the Jordan and her mouth is open and the waters of the Jordan pour into it and so she drinks.

"All the waters that the Jordan receives for six months, the behemoth swallows in one sip."[97]

X

THE DEAD SEA AND ITS SHORES

1 / "NO MAN EVER DROWNED IN THE DEAD SEA"

The waters of the Dead Sea are so rich in minerals and so heavy that it is difficult to sink in them. It needs very little knowledge of swimming and very little effort to float on their surface. Hence the ancients said: "No man ever drowned in the Dead Sea!"

It is held that after Vespasian, the commander of the Roman army, had conquered Jerusalem, he came to the Dead Sea. Curious to investigate its special features, he ordered the many captives he had taken to be thrown into the water with their hands tied behind their backs. But they all remained floating on the surface of the water.

About 1250 the Englishman Bartholomeus Anglicus wrote: "There is a lake . . . called the Dead Sea . . . Whensoever thou wouldst have drowned therein anything that hath life with any craft or gin, then anon it plungeth and cometh again up; through it be strongly thrust downward, it is anon smitten upward. . . . All things that hath no life sinketh down to the ground. . . . And a lantern without its light sinketh therein, as it telleth, and a lantern with light floateth above."[98]

2 / "TAKE IT TO THE DEAD SEA!"

In the olden days, when there were no roads and little security, the Dead Sea appeared remote and difficult of access. Hence "take to the Dead Sea"—in Hebrew, *leholich el Yam Hamelah*—was an ancient expression meaning "send to perdition."

The rabbis ruled: "If a man found objects on which there was a figure of the sun, a figure of the moon, or a figure of a dragon, he must throw them into the Dead Sea. If a man set apart money for a sin offering, and the money was lost, and he offered another sin offering in its stead, and the money was then found, the money must be thrown into the Dead Sea."

Today a vast potash factory has been built near the Dead Sea, beautiful hotels and baths line its shores, and excellent roads bring many visitors to its banks.[99]

3 / THE DEAD SEA IN THE END OF TIME

The legend tells that in the end of time the waters of life will gush forth from the sanctuary of Jerusalem, and stream both to the Dead Sea to the east and to the Great Sea to the west.

The prophet Zechariah foretold: "For I will gather all nations against Jerusalem to battle; . . ./And it shall come to pass in that day,/That living waters shall go out from Jerusalem/Half of them toward the eastern sea,/And half of them toward the western sea;/In summer and in winter shall it be./And the Lord shall be King over all the earth."

Elaborating on the same theme, Ezekiel adds: "These waters issue forth toward the eastern region, and shall go down into the Arabah; and when they shall enter into the sea, into the sea of the putrid waters, the waters shall be healed . . . and there shall be a very great multitude of fish; for these waters are come thither, that all things be healed and may live withersoever the river cometh."

"And it shall come to pass, that fishers shall stand by it from Ein Gedi even unto Ein Eglaim; there shall be a place for the spreading of nets; their fish shall be after their kinds, as the fish of the Great Sea, exceeding many. But the miry places thereof, and the marshes thereof, shall not be healed; they shall be given for salt. And by the river upon the bank thereof, on this side and on that side, shall grow every tree for food, whose leaf shall not wither, neither shall the fruit thereof fail; it shall bring forth new fruit every month, because the waters thereof issue out of the sanctuary; and the fruit thereof shall be for food, and the leaf thereof for healing."

The sages of Israel explain the words of Ezekiel:

" 'Toward the eastern region'—that is the Sea of Sumchu [the Sea of Hulah today].

" 'Shall go down into the Arabah'—that is the Sea of Tiberias.

" 'Shall enter into the sea'—that is the Salt Sea, the Dead Sea.

" 'Into the sea of the putrid waters'—that is the Great Sea [the Mediterranean]."[100]

4 / THE MIRACLE OF THE ARNON RIVER

From the lofty heights of Moab, the Arnon flows down into the Dead Sea through a narrow and winding gorge between two steep and impressive walls of rock (fig. 51).

Because the waters of the river murmur along their course, some derive the name Arnon from the Hebrew *ranen,* to sing.

The Arnon is well known from the wars that the Israelites waged in the mountains of Moab on their way to the promised land.

The Torah relates that the tribes of Israel pitched their tents on the other side of the Arnon, which is in the wilder-

FIG. 50. OUTLET OF ARNON RIVER INTO DEAD SEA (1932)

ness. Hence it is said in the book of "The Wars of the Lord": "And the Valley of Arnon, and the slope of the riverbeds."

Legend narrates the war between Israel and its foes in the Arnon River: "And the Almighty, blessed be He, gave them proof and wrought them miracles in the riverbeds of the Arnon, of the kind He had performed for them in the Red Sea. And what were the miracles? One stands on the top of the bank of the river on this side and converses with another who stands on the top of the opposite bank, although one would have to walk seven miles down one slope and up the other to reach his companion.

FIG. 51. DEEP GORGE OF ARNON RIVER (1932)

"And across the river lay the path of Israel; so all its foes gathered there, multitudes without an end. Some remained in the bed of the river. And the others hid in the numerous caves which are hewn in the rocky banks. And opposite the caverns, from each slope [in Hebrew, *eshed*], rocks project like breasts [in Hebrew, in the singular, *shad*] as it is written: 'And the slope [*eshed*] of the riverbeds.'

"The multitudes entered the caves and said: 'When the children of Israel descend into the riverbed . . . we shall kill them all.' But when the Israelites came to that same place, they did not have to climb down into the narrow gorge; for the Almighty, blessed be He, intimated to the mountains, and the breastlike rocks on one side penetrated into the cavities on the other side . . . and the mountains embraced, and over them, the path lay unbroken. And it was not known which mountain leaned upon which . . . and when the rocks entered into the caves into which they fitted exactly . . . they crushed all the fighters [of the enemy].

"And the well [of Miriam] went down into the river and swelled its waters and washed away all the crowds in the same way that the sea [the Red Sea] had done . . . and Israel crossed these mountains with no knowledge of all these miracles.

"The Almighty, blessed be He, said, 'I shall inform My children and let them know of all the people that I have destroyed for their sake.' The well [of Miriam] streamed into the caves and flowed out carrying skulls, arms, and legs without number. . . . And Israel retraced its steps to look for the well, and they saw it running out of the river-bed bearing limbs endlessly. . . . And Israel stood on the banks and called out to her: 'Spring up, O well! Spring up, O well!' "[101]

5 / THE TWO LEPERS IN THE BATTLE OF THE ARNON

The Torah reports the victory in Moab on the banks of the Arnon and ends with these words: "Wherefore it is said in the Book of the Wars of the Lord: 'Vaheb in Suphah, and the valleys of Arnon.' "

What is the meaning of "Vaheb in Suphah" (in Hebrew, "*Et vaheb Be-Suphah*")? The legend relates that Et and Heb were the names of two lepers who followed the Israelites. Because they were afflicted, they walked in the rear (in Hebrew, *soph*) of the hosts of Israel. Accordingly, the above quotation reads: "Et and Heb in the rear."

And the following tale is told. When the Israelites crossed the heights of the Arnon, the two banks of the

river joined together and crushed between them all the
enemies who hid in the caves below to ambush them.
After the sons of Israel had passed, the banks of the Arnon
separated again and returned to their place, and from
their midst poured streams of blood and heaps of bones
fell out.

Only the two lepers who walked behind the army saw
the fate of the enemy. They brought these tidings to the
Israelites. And therefore they were privileged to be mentioned by name in the Book of the Wars of the Lord.[102]

6 / THE BATTLE OF THE ARNON—A "MIGHTY DEED"

The sages of Israel expound: "God the Almighty did
all His miracles and mighty deeds on the [Red] Sea, on
the Jordan, and in the valleys of the Arnon, to sanctify
and extol His name in the world."

The legend finds a reference to these mighty deeds of
the Almighty in the words of Moses: "O Lord God, Thou
hast begun to show . . . Thy greatness, and Thy strong
hand; for what god is there in heaven or on earth, that
can do according to Thy words, and according to Thy
mighty acts?"

" 'Thy greatness'—in the [Red] Sea.

" 'Thy strong hand'—in the valleys of the Arnon.

" 'Thy works'—in the [Red] Sea.

" 'Thy mighty acts'—in the valleys of the Arnon."

The prayer of King David, as well, alludes to the wonderful deeds of God: "God of Israel our father for ever
and ever. Thine, O Lord, is the greatness, and the power,
and the glory, and the victory, and the majesty."

" 'The majesty'—that is the battle in the valleys of the
Arnon."

The sages ordain that "whoever sees . . . the fords of
Arnon . . . should give praise and glory to his Creator."[103]

7 / THE POOL OF ABRAHAM THE PATRIARCH

Near Ein Gedi (Spring of the Kid), close to the Dead Sea, on the way to the fortress Masada, there is a small pool which is called in Arabic *Birkat el-Khalil*—Pool of Abraham.

One day Abraham the patriarch rode on his donkey from Hebron to the Dead Sea. Abraham saw a pool and noted that people from Hebron were collecting salt from it. He approached them and asked for a little salt for his meal.

The laborers rudely answered that they had no salt, although a large quantity was lying about. Irritated at their insolence, Abraham replied: "Henceforth in this place ye shall have neither salt nor a road to Hebron."

In an instant the salt, although retaining its original appearance, turned into gravel, and the road to Hebron became practically impassable.

Since that time the people have called this pool the Pool of Abraham, and the name remains to this very day.[104]

8 / THE FATE OF LOT'S WIFE

"And the two angels came to Sodom. . . . And the men said unto Lot: . . . 'Whomsoever thou hast in the city, bring them out of this place; for we will destroy this place, because the cry of them is waxed great before the Lord; and the Lord hath sent us to destroy it.' And Lot went out, and spoke unto his sons-in-law, who married his daughters, and said: 'Up, get you out of this place; for the Lord will destroy the city.' But he seemed unto his sons-in-law as one that jested. And when the morning arose, then the angels hastened Lot, saying: 'Arise, take thy wife, and thy two daughters that are here; lest thou be swept away in the iniquity of the city. . . . Escape for thy life; look not behind thee, neither stay thou in all the Plain; escape to

FIG. 52. LOT'S WIFE (WESTERN SHORE OF DEAD SEA)

FIG. 53. LOT'S WIFE (EASTERN SHORE OF DEAD SEA)

FIG. 54. DOG OF LOT'S WIFE

the mountain, lest thou be swept away.' . . .

"But his wife looked back from behind him, and she became a pillar of salt."

Why was Lot's wife turned into a pillar of salt and not

FIG. 55. LOT'S WIFE (1800)
The eastern shore of Dead Sea, opposite mountains of Moab.

FIG. 56. LOT'S WIFE AS PILLAR OF SALT AND OVERTURNING
OF SODOM

one made of any other mineral, ask the sages of Israel.
Because salt was the cause of her sin.

On the night that the angels came to Lot, his wife, wishing to show her neighbors how hospitable she was, went
to them and shouted: "Send me some salt, I have visitors."
And so the people knew that visitors were at the house of
Lot, and they came to attack them. For that reason Lot's
wife was turned into a pillar of salt.

In the Book of Wisdom, it is written: "A standing pillar
of salt is a monument of an unbelieving soul."[105]

9 / LOT'S WIFE—PILLAR OF SALT

From the most ancient times a projecting rock on the
shore of the Dead Sea was related to Lot's wife.

The sages of Israel advise the Israelites that "whoever
sees . . . Lot's wife should give praise and glory to his
Creator."

The historian Flavius Josephus, in the year 80, told
about the rock of Lot's Wife: "And I saw it, and it remains
till today."

The Jewish traveler Benjamin of Tudela, who visited Palestine about 1173, wrote: "Two parasangs from the Dead Sea stands the salt pillar into which Lot's wife was changed: and although the sheep continually lick it, the pillar grows again and retains its original size."[106]

10 / EIN GEDI—A VINEYARD IN CYPRUS

Ein Gedi is a beautiful oasis which blossoms on the western shore of the Dead Sea, at the foot of the barren rocky hills of the Wilderness of Judah. The name is biblical and means "Spring of the Kid," for it was a main source of fresh water for the shepherds tending their flocks in this vicinity.

Ein Gedi was named for its fruitful vineyards and for its plantations of camphire, whose fragrant flowers, tinged a pale yellow, grew in clusters. From the camphire (in Arabic, *henna*) Arabic women obtain a dye. The leaves are dried and crushed, then mixed with water and made into a paste. With this mixture the women paint their nails and the palms of their hands a vivid yellow or orange, and also brighten their dark hair with warm copper tones. The henna is not only a beautifier but also a shield against the evil eye.

"My beloved is unto me as a cluster of henna [in Hebrew, *copher*] in the vineyards of Ein Gedi," exclaims the Song of Songs.

The Latin translation of the Bible (the Vulgate) rendered "cluster of henna" as *"botris Cypri."* Confusion grew out of this name, and in the Middle Ages the vineyards of Ein Gedi were shown on the island of Cyprus, one in the vicinity of the town Paphos, the legendary birthplace of Aphrodite (Venus) and another "small Ein Gedi" next to Limassol. In 1340 a German traveler who passed through Cyprus on his way to the Holy Land mentions both plantations, and of the largest he says that "the like of it is not in the world. This vineyard stands upon an exceedingly lofty mountain two miles long. A tall cliff girds it on every side, like a wall."[107]

11 / ZOAR AND ITS SPRING

At the south end of the Dead Sea there was in ancient days the town of Zoar, which is mentioned in the Torah: "The king of Bela—the same is Zoar." The legend derives the name Bela from the Hebrew *bala*, to swallow, because the inhabitants of Zoar were swallowed up by the earth when Sodom and Gomorrah were overthrown. Lot escaped to Zoar from the burning Sodom.

When Moses, the man of God, stood on the height of Mount Nebo above the shore of the Dead Sea, he saw into the distance "as far as Zoar." The legend adds that God showed him the place where hell is, nearby.

In medieval times Zoar was an important town, with a Jewish community from which interesting remains have been found. The palms of Zoar were famous.

Legend tells us that Zoar was named after Lot's daughter; because of its hot weather, the Arabs nicknamed her Sakar—the Fire of Hell.

The Moslem geographer al-Mukaddasi, a Jerusalemite, related in the tenth century that a native from Jerusalem stayed in Zoar and wrote a letter to his family, saying: ". . . from the lower Sakar to the upper Paradise." And al-Mukaddasi continues: "Verily, this is a country that is deadly to the stranger, for its water is execrable, and he who should find that the angel of death delays for him, let him come here."

In Zoar there was a spring, and it used to be said that when it dried up, the Antichrist, who is called in Arabic Massih ed-Dajjal (the false Messiah) would appear and fight his last fight.[108]

XI
SODOM AND GOMORRAH

1 / THE OVERTHROW OF SODOM AND GOMORRAH

"And the Lord said: 'Verily, the cry of Sodom and Gomorrah is great, and, verily, their sin is exceeding grievous. I will go down now, and see whether they have done altogether according to the cry of it, which is come unto Me.' . . . And Abraham drew near, and said: 'Wilt Thou indeed sweep away the righteous with the wicked? Peradventure there are fifty righteous within the city; wilt Thou indeed sweep away and not forgive the place for the fifty righteous that are therein?' . . . And the Lord said: 'If I find in Sodom fifty righteous within the city, then I will forgive all the place for their sake. . . . I will not destroy it for ten's sake.' And the Lord went His way, as soon as He had left off speaking with Abraham; and Abraham returned unto his place.

"Then the Lord caused to rain upon Sodom and upon Gomorrah brimstone and fire from the Lord out of heaven; and He overthrew those cities, and all the Plain, and all the inhabitants of the cities, and that which grew upon the ground. . . . And Abraham got up early in the morning to the place where he stood before the Lord. And he looked out toward Sodom and Gomorrah, and toward all the land of the Plain and beheld, and, lo, the smoke of the land went up as the smoke of a furnace."

The overthrow of Sodom and Gomorrah—in Hebrew, *mahapechat Sedom ve'Amorah*—with their evil inhabitants, became proverbial in Hebrew literature. When the prophets of Israel wanted to foretell the bitter end of important cities of their time, they threatened them with the fate of Sodom and Gomorrah.

Amos called to Israel: "I have overthrown some of you/ As God overthrew Sodom and Gomorrah."

In the Book of Lamentations, the author expressed his great sorrow for Zion: "For the iniquity of the daughter of my people is greater/Than the sin of Sodom,/That was overthrown as in a moment,/And no hands fell upon her."

The expression Sodom and Gomorrah was known by the ancient Romans and is mentioned in an old inscription that was discovered in the ruins of Pompeii, Italy.

The European languages use the name Sodom for an extremely wicked or corrupt place. Sodomy designates unnatural sexual relations, as between persons of the same sex or with an animal. A Sodomite is one who is guilty of sodomy or practices gross wickedness.[109]

2 / THE FATE OF THE CITIES OF THE PLAIN

In the surroundings of Sodom and Gomorrah were three other cities: Admah, Zeboiim, and Zoar, which shared their fate.

They are the "cities of the Plain" of the Torah, and the Greek *Pentapolis*—the Five Cities.

When these sinful cities were overthrown, the Dead Sea appeared in their place (fig. 58). Therefore in the talmudic literature the sea is called *Yama shel Sedom*— the Sea of Sodom. Likewise, in the Moslem medieval lit-

FIG. 57. SODOM (1278)
From Hebrew manuscript in British Museum. Below is written:
"This is Sodom when the angels overturned it."

erature, it is called *Beheirat Sadum wa-Ghamur*—the Sea
of Sodom and Gomorrah—or *el-Maklub*—the Overturned.
Ando the sunken cities are named *el-Mutafikah*, an alteration of the Hebrew *mahapecha*—overthrown.[110]

3 / THE KINGS OF SODOM AND GOMORRAH

The Torah tells of Abraham the patriarch and his men
that "they made war with Bera king of Sodom, and with
Birsha king of Gomorrah; Shinab king of Admah, and
Shemeber king of Zeboiim, and the king of Bela—the same
is Zoar. All these came as allies unto the vale of Siddim—
the same is the Salt Sea."

The sages of Israel comment on the names of the kings
thus:

" 'Bera'—from the Hebrew *ben ra*—son of evil.

" 'Birsha'—from *ben rasha*—son of the wicked.

" 'Shinab'—from *shoeb mamon*—money-extorter. [An-
other version makes it *sonehab*—father-hater.]

" 'Shemeber'—from *sam eber*—stretches his wings [that is, hovers like a bird of prey]."[111]

4 / JUDGES IN SODOM AND ITS NEIGHBORHOOD

The sages of Israel give the names of the judges who sat in the courts of the sinful cities:

Sharek in Sodom
Sharkar in Gomorrah
Zabnek in Admah
Manon in Zeboiim.

Eliezer, the bondsman of Abraham our father, made slight changes in the names of these judges in accordance with the nature of their cities, and named them thus:

Sharek, Shakkaria—Liar
Sharkar, Shekrura—Arch Deceiver
Zabnek, Kazban—Falsifier
Manon, Mazle Din—Preceptor of Judgment.[112]

5 / THE RULING OF SODOM'S JUDGES

The judges of Sodom issued rules to oppress the poor.

The owner of one ox was obliged to render one day's shepherd service, but he who had no ox had to give two days' service.

Whoever was wounded was ordered to pay his aggressor a fee for effecting upon him the operation of bleeding.

For the use of the bridge a traveler had to pay four zuzim, but if he waded through the water he had to pay eight zuzim. Once a laundryman waded through the river. He was told: "Give four zuzim." He protested: "I passed in the water!" They answered: "If so, pay eight zuzim." When he refused, they beat and injured him. He was then hauled before the judge, who said: "Pay the fee for drawing your blood and eight zuzim for crossing in the water!"

In the neighborhood of Sodom there was a place by the name of Galahi, whose judges were renowned for their

FIG. 58. MAP OF DEAD SEA (1650)

Three Latin names of sea are inscribed: *Mare Mortuum, Mare Salsum, Lacus Asphaltitis*. Within sea four destroyed cities are pictured plunging down in flames: Zeboi[i]m, Sodom, Gomorrah, Admah.

systematic miscarriage of justice. And when the sages of Israel want to express their contempt of a worthless judgment, they say: "This ruling is a bad ruling and so would it have been settled in Galahi!"[113]

6 / THE EVIL ANGELS DWELL IN SODOM

The sages of Israel reject with distaste various false faiths and practices of black magic, which were common among the folk in the olden days.

To cure boils and burns the superstitious used to invoke in Aramaic: *"Baz-Bazia, Mas-Masia, Kas-Kasia/Sharlai and Amarlai*—Black angels come from the land of Sodom/ To cure boils and burns."[114]

7 / THE ARROGANT INHABITANTS OF SODOM

The Book of Job says: "The stones thereof are the place of sapphires/And it hath dust of gold. . . ./The proud beasts have not trodden it,/Nor hath the lion passed thereby."

The sages of Israel believe that these words of Job refer to Sodom. The legend relates that the people of Sodom said: "We do not need any man to come to us. Behold, food is taken from us, and silver and gold and precious stones and pearls are taken away from us. Let traveling among us be forgotten."

Said to them the Holy One, blessed be He: "Fools that you are! You act so proudly with the good things which I lavished upon you and you say: 'Let us cause traveling among us to be forgotten.' I, too, will cause you to be forgotten from the world, for it says: 'They are forgotten of the foot that passeth by./They hang afar from men,/They swing to and fro.'"[115]

8 / THE PEOPLE OF SODOM WERE EVIL SINNERS

Our ancestors foresaw that "the people of Sodom will have no part in the next world. As it is said [in the Torah], the people of Sodom are bad and sin against the Lord.

" 'Bad'—in this world.

" '. . . and sin'—in the next world."

The commentators of the Talmud explain:

Bad (i. e., rotten)—in their bodies. Sinners—in their money affairs.

"Whereas the people of Sodom hated each other, the

Almighty, blessed be He, wasted them in this world and forfeited them from the next world."

There is no town more wicked than Sodom. Hence anyone who is bad is called Sodomite. "Whoever says—which is mine is mine only—/And which is thine is thine only—/That is the feature of Sodom."[116]

9 / WOE TO THE GUEST IN SODOM

Every visitor who came to Sodom was thrown onto a bed. If he was tall, they put him in a small bed and hacked away his protruding feet. If he was short, they put him in a big bed and stretched his limbs out from head to feet until the dismembered body filled it up.

Once Eliezer, the bondsman of Abraham the patriarch, came to Sodom. They told him: "Climb into bed!"

He answered: "On the day of my mother's death, I swore solemnly never again to lie in a bed."

Another version relates that he answered: "Let me be, as I am under oath never to sleep in a bed until I am deemed worthy to see the face of the Almighty."[117]

10 / THE TREATMENT OF A GUEST IN SODOM

A man entered Sodom riding on an ass, and as he had no lodging he was received by a resident named Hedor.

On preparing to depart he missed his colored blanket and the cord by which it had been tied to his animal's back.

When he asked his host about the matter, he received the answer that he had only dreamed of a cover, but that the vision was a good omen, since the cover meant that he would possess large vineyards, and the cord indicated that his life would be prolonged.

Hedor insisted upon being paid for having interpreted his dream to him. His usual price was four silver pieces, but as the man was Hedor's guest, Hedor would content himself with three pieces of silver.

The stranger protested, but he was dragged before the tribunal and sentenced to pay for the interpretation of his dream.[118]

11 / AT A WEDDING IN SODOM

It was a custom in Sodom that anyone who invited a stranger to a wedding forfeited his coat.

Once Eliezer, the bondsman of Abraham, came to Sodom. Being very hungry he entered a house where a wedding was being celebrated, but could get nothing to eat. He then sat down next to one of the wedding guests. On being asked by his neighbor who had invited him, he replied: "You did." The neighbor, fearing to lose his coat, left the house precipitately.

Eliezer then sat near another, on whom he played the same trick, with the same result, until at last he had succeeded in driving all the guests out of the house.

He then secured the meal for himself.[119]

12 / THE GOOD MAID OF SODOM

In the Torah it is related: "And the Lord said: 'Verily, the cry of Sodom and Gomorrah is great [in Hebrew, rabah], and, verily, their sin is exceedingly grievous. I will go down now, and see whether they have done altogether according to the cry of it, which is come unto Me."

The legend says that the Hebrew word rabah, which is rendered "great," is in truth the word rivah—maid. And on this interpretation, the legend builds the following tale.

There was a maid in Sodom who brought bread to a beggar in her pitcher. When three days passed and the beggar did not die, the matter was disclosed.

The Sodomites smeared the maid with honey, exposed her on the wall of the city, and the bees stung her to death.[120]

13 / THE FATE OF A BEGGAR IN SODOM

And what were the deeds of the people of Sodom?

When a beggar happened to come to Sodom he was not given a piece of bread, but everyone presented him with a coin (dinar) inscribed with the name of the donor. And when the poor man died of hunger each one came and retrieved his dinar.

It was decreed and proclaimed in Sodom that anyone who offered a piece of bread to the poor, the stranger, the needy would be burnt alive.

Our fathers said: "Although the people of Sodom were guilty of all the sins, their fate was sealed against them only because they refused to give alms."[121]

14 / THE PIOUS DAUGHTER OF LOT IN SODOM

The legend relates that Paltit, the daughter of Lot, was married to a Sodom notable. Once she saw a wretched beggar in the streets of the town, and she was moved with pity for him. What did she do? When she went to draw water from the well, she took her water pitcher filled with food from her house and provided the poor man.

The people of Sodom wondered: "From what does this beggar live?" Then the matter was revealed to them, and they burned her upon a pyre.

She cried out: "O God, Lord of the universe, hear my cause and pass thy sentence upon me and check the people of Sodom." And her bitter plea went up unto the throne of the Almighty.

And the Almighty, blessed be He, said: "I will go down and see whether they have done altogether according to the cry of it which is come unto Me, and if they have done according to the cry of this young woman, I shall overturn Sodom, foundations up and face down."[122]

15 / THE FRUITFUL TREES OF ANCIENT SODOM

In fruitful Sodom grew many trees bearing the most succulent fruit. Their branches interlaced and, falling to the ground, formed natural tabernacles. Under their shade the roads and paths met, then ramified.

The psalmist sang: "God spoke in His holiness; that I would exult/ . . . and mete out the valley of Sukkoth." The name *Sukkoth* in Hebrew means Tabernacles. The sages of Israel say that *sukkoth* in this case refers to the natural tabernacles of Sodom.

The legend relates that in Sodom seven kinds of trees interlaced and grew one on top of the other: vine trees and fig trees and pomegranate and peach and almond trees and nut trees and date trees on top of them.

With the destruction of Sodom, its numerous trees were also laid waste, and the land turned into a salty desolation. In the days to come Sodom will be rebuilt and its trees restored to her in their full glory.

As our elders said: "Whoever celebrates the Feast of Tabernacles [Sukkoth] and erects a booth [*sukkah*] and spends in it the holidays, the Almighty, blessed be He, will give him a place in the days to come in the fruitful booths of Sodom redeemed."[123]

16 / THE EAST WIND IN SODOM

The east wind, the dreaded *hamsin* (sirocco), blows intermittently from the desert and covers the land with the stifling, depressing heat. Under its burning breath plants wither, beasts pine away, and man is helpless.

Sodom also received the visitation of this destructive force. The legend expounds: "And you also find that God punished the people of Sodom, only by means of the east wind, as it is said [in the Book of Job]: 'By the breath of God they perish./And by the blast of His anger are they consumed.' "[124]

17 / AN ANGEL OVERTHROWS SODOM AND ITS SISTER CITIES

The Torah relates: "And the two angels came to Sodom at even; and Lot sat in the gate of Sodom."

The legend comments: "Gabriel was sent to overthrow and Raphael, to save Lot."

The sages add: "These five cities [Sodom, Gomorrah, Admah, Zeboiim, and Zoar] were built on the same rock. The angel stretched his hand and overthrew them."

To this action Job refers: "He putteth forth his hand upon the flinty rock:/He overturneth the mountains by the roots."

A Moslem legend describes the destruction of Sodom and its sister cities: "Gabriel thrust his wing under them and lifted them up so high that the inhabitants of the lower heaven heard the barking of the dogs and the crowing of the cocks, and then, inverting them, threw them down to the earth."[125]

18 / THE ANGEL STRUCK AT DAWN

The inhabitants of the cities of the Plain worshiped the sun and the moon. If destruction had come upon them by day, they would say that the moon would have helped them; if by night, they would declare that the sun would have been their aid; wherefore they were destroyed in the morning twilight—when both the sun and the moon were shining.[126]

19 / THE STONES WHICH FELL ON SODOM

According to the biblical tradition, when God overthrew the sinful cities, "then the Lord caused to rain upon Sodom and upon Gomorrah brimstone and fire from the Lord out of heaven."

The Koran, too, tells about the overthrowing of Sodom and Gomorrah: "And when our command came, we turned those cities upside down, and we rained upon them stones

of baked clay, one following another, and being marked
from the Lord."

The Moslem commentator continues: "The common
opinion is that each stone had the name of the person who
was to be killed by it written thereon."[127]

20 / THE CURSED PLANTS OF SODOM

Not only were the inhabitants of the sinful cities cursed
and smitten, but also all the plants: "And He overthrew
those cities . . . and that which grew upon the ground."

"Of Sodom" became proverbial to denote a plant bearing bad and rotten fruits.

Moses, the man of God, sang thus: "For their vine is of
the vine of Sodom,/And of the fields of Gomorrah;/Their
grapes are grapes of gall./Their clusters are bitter."

Besides men, beasts, and plants, the very air of Sodom
was poisoned to such an extent that the sages warn: "If
a man would water his field with rain collected at Sodom,
its plants would not grow."[128]

21 / SODOM REDEEMED

Ezekiel prophesies the redemption of Jerusalem and of
Samaria in the end of time: "And I will turn their captivity,
the captivity of Sodom and her daughters . . . in that thou
art a comfort unto them. And thy sisters, Sodom and her
daughters, shall return to their former estate."

The restoration of Sodom and Gomorrah will be one
of the forerunning signs of the redemption of the whole
world; and the rabbis of the Middle Ages describe it at
length.

Today, with the return of Israel to its land, even remote
and burnt-out Sodom is waking to life again. And at the
foot of the mountain called Sodom, a big potash factory
and its hosts of Jewish workers are bringing to these forsaken surroundings the dawn of a new day, the token of
redemption.[129]

XII
BETWEEN JERUSALEM
AND RAMLA

1 / WHERE DID THE NAME MOZAH COME FROM?
Modern Mozah is a small Jewish settlement located
near Jerusalem, next to the site of ancient biblical Mozah,
a town in the territory of Benjamin. The name means
"Spring."

The sages relate: "There was a place below Jerusalem
called Mozah. Thither they went and cut themselves wil-
low branches. They came and set these up at the sides of
the altar so that their tops were bent over the altar."

Next to ancient Mozah the Romans founded a settlement, Colonia, for their veteran soldiers.

The sages of Israel expound: "What was ancient Mozah?
. . . The Colonia of today. Whereas it was a colony of
soldiers, they were exempted from paying taxes to the
government treasury. Why is the same [place] called
Mozah? . . . Because it is exempted and released [in Hebrew, *muza*] from the king's taxes."[130]

2 / WHERE DID GOLIATH FALL?
The Valley of Elah, where the crucial encounter be-

tween David the shepherd and Goliath the Philistine took place, is situated in a remote place among the mountains of Judea. But in the Middle Ages, probably to spare both the pilgrim and his guide, it was said to have taken place at a much more accessible spot: in the valley stretching at the foot of Mozah, around the bridge which carries the main Jerusalem–Tel Aviv highway. The credulous travelers collected pebbles from the riverbed and carried them back to their homes as precious amulets.

Rabbi Meshullam from Volterra, Italy, who crossed this valley in 1481, wrote: "Go down into the valley where there is a large stone bridge, in which place David the shepherd slew the Philistine."

A Christian pilgrim who passed along the same site in 1586 left an illustration of the place (fig. 59) and called it *Vallis Therebenti*, after the terebinth tree (in Hebrew, *elah*), reminiscent of David's battlefield, and added: "*Hic occisus fuit Goliad*—Here Goliath was slain."[131]

3 / THE STONES OF BEIT HAKEREM

The Torah dictated: "And if thou [Israel] make Me an altar of stone, thou shalt not build it of hewn stones; for if thou lift up thy tool upon it, thou hast profaned it."

The sages report that the stones for the altar of the Temple of Jerusalem were brought from the vicinity of ancient Beit Hakerem (House of the Vineyard) named today Ein Kerem—Fount of the Vineyard, a suburb of modern Jerusalem: "The stones of the ramp and the stones of the altar were alike taken from the Valley of Beit Hakerem, where they were quarried from below virgin soil and brought from thence as whole stones upon which no [tool of] iron had been lifted up. For iron renders [the stones] invalid [for the altar]; even by a touch and by a blemish [it renders them invalid] in every respect. . . . They did not plaster them with an iron trowel lest it touch

FIG. 59. BATTLEFIELD OF DAVID AND GOLIATH IN VALLEY
NEAR JERUSALEM (1586)
This valley (called in Latin *Vallis Therebenti*), mistaken for biblical
Valley of Elah by pilgrims of Middle Ages, stretches west of Jeru-
salem. Flanking it today are villages of Mozah and Mevasseret
Yerushalaim. Above valley, on height, is Colonia, an Arab village.
Under hill is written, in Latin: *"Hic occisus fuit Goliad*—Here
Goliath was slain."

[the stones] and render them invalid; for iron was created
to shorten man's days, while the altar was created to
lengthen man's days: what shortens may not rightly be
lifted up against what lengthens."[132]

4 / THE MIRACULOUS STONE OF EIN KAREM

Ein Karem, today a suburb of Jerusalem, spreads in a
narrow picturesque vale ensconced between the mountains rising west of the city. It is one of the holiest sites
of Christian tradition.

Here two important events took place: the birth of Saint

FIG. 60. STONE WHICH CONCEALED INFANT JOHN

This stone is preserved in alcove in Church of the Visitation in Ein Karem. Around alcove is Latin inscription: "*In hac petra Elisabeth Johannem abscondisse traditur*—In this stone Elizabeth hid John."

John the Baptist and Saint Mary's visit to his mother, Elizabeth, sometime before Jesus' birth.

Two large Franciscan churches indicate these spots: Saint John's birthplace among the houses of the little town and the Church of the Visitation about a mile away, on the slope of the mountain. In a grilled alcove of the Church of the Visitation there is shown a much-venerated rock, the same rock which swallowed the child Saint John to save him from the Roman murderers; when they left, the stone brought him forth safe and whole (fig. 60).

A French pilgrim who was in Jerusalem in 1432 mentioned this miraculous stone, but according to his story it was kept at the time at the birthplace of Saint John: "At the birthplace of Saint John the Baptist a rock is shown, which during the time of Herod's persecution of the innocents opened itself miraculously in two, when Saint Elizabeth having therein hid her son, it closed again of itself, and the child remained shut up, as it is said, two whole days."[133]

5 / MONTJOIE—THE MOUNT OF JOY

The tomb of the prophet Samuel—*en-Nebi Samuil* to the Arabs—is set within a turreted edifice that stands out conspicuously on a high mountaintop rising north of Jerusalem. From this spot a wide view unfolds over the Holy City and its surroundings.

The ancient highway from the coastal plain to the capital passed over this height. Along this road the Maccabees climbed the hills to deliver Jerusalem from the Greek yoke. The Romans in their turn advanced through this same vicinity to suppress the Jewish revolt. During World War I the British broke through the Turkish lines at this very spot in their successful thrust toward Jerusalem. Again in 1967 a column of Israeli tanks proceeded along this same ridge to participate in the deliverance of eastern Jerusalem.

The name Montjoie was given to this height by the Crusaders, for a tremor of joy passed through their ranks when from its summit they had their first glimpse of the Holy City, the sacred goal of their long campaign. Carried on a great wave of jubilance they assaulted the Moslems and wrested the city from their hands.

The English writer John Mandeville related, in about 1322: "Also from Jerusalem two miles is the Mount Joy, a fair place and delicious, and there is Samuel the prophet in a fair tomb, and men call it Mount Joy, for it gives joy to pilgrims' hearts, because there men see first Jerusalem."

Eighty-eight years after the Crusaders' conquest Jeru-

salem again fell to the Moslems, led by Saladin, and the
Holy City remained for the Christian knights an unful-
filled aspiration.

In 1191 Richard the Lion-Hearted (Coeur de Lion),
at the head of his troops, reached Beit Nuba at the foot of
the mountains of Jerusalem. Followed by a small retinue
he climbed and reportedly reached Montjoie. According
to Joinville, the French chronicler of the Crusades, one
of the king's knights cried out: " 'Sire, sire, come so far
hither, and I will show you Jerusalem!' and when the king
heard this he threw his coat of armor before his eyes, all
in tears, and said to our Savior: 'Fair Lord God, I pray
thee suffer me not to see thy Holy City since I cannot
deliver it from the hands of thine enemies.' "[134]

6 / THE PROPHET JEREMIAH IN ABU GHOSH

Abu Ghosh is an Arab village set west of Jerusalem, by
the side of the highway leading to the coastal plain (fig.
61). It is named after a Moslem family that settled here
many generations ago and held sway over the whole countryside.

Although the village is located on the site of biblical
Kiryat Yearim, pilgrims in the Middle Ages fancied that
this was Anatot, the hometown of the prophet Jeremiah,
and therefore they called this place Saint Hieremia. An
English traveler in 1819 even called the valley leading up
to it the Valley of Jeremiah.

Indeed, Anatot was located east of Jerusalem, on the
site of the Arab village of Anata, a very obvious variation
of the old biblical name.[135]

7 / KIRYAT YEARIM—ABODE OF THE ARK OF THE LORD

Kiryat Yearim, a name which means City of Forests,
was a biblical town in the inheritance of Judah: "And the
border was drawn to . . . Kiryat Yearim . . . and passed
along unto the side of mount Yearim."

FIG. 61. ABU GHOSH—S[AINT] HIEREMIA
This is Arab village on highway between Jerusalem and Jaffa.

After the Philistines returned the ark of the Lord, which
they had captured from the Israelites, "the men of Kiryat
Yearim came, and fetched up the ark of the Lord, and
brought it into the house of Abinadab in the hill, and sanctified Eleazar his son to keep the ark of the Lord."

Twenty years later King David carried it to Jerusalem
amid songs and great rejoicing. Praising the deeds of the
great king, the psalmist sings: "We found it [the ark] in
the field of the wood"—*sedeh year*, a clear allusion to the
City of Forests.

Ancient Kiryat Yearim was on top of a hill overlooking
Abu Ghosh. On this site today stands the Catholic monastery of Notre Dame de l'Arche d'Alliance, whose monks
hold that here Eleazar guarded the ark of the Lord. The

Arabs still call this hill *Tel el-Azhar*, presumably a reminiscence of the ancient story.[136]

8 / THE HOLY UZEIR IN ABU GHOSH

In medieval Arab literature Abu Ghosh is called Karyat el-Anab—Village of the Grapes—from which the neighboring Jewish village takes its name: Kiryat Anavim.

In abbreviated form the Arab village was called Karya, and the local legend attributes to this place the following tale from the Koran: ". . . or like him who passed by a town [Karya], and it had fallen in upon its roofs. He said: When will Allah give it life after its death? So Allah caused him to die for a hundred years, then raised him. He said: How long hast thou tarried? He said: I have tarried a day, or part of a day. He said: Nay, thou hast tarried a hundred years; but look at thy food and drink, years have not passed over it! And look at thy ass! And that we may make thee a sign of men. And look at the bones, how we set them together, then clothed them with flesh. So when it became clear to him, he said: I know that Allah is possessor of power over all things."

The mosque of Abu Ghosh is named for Uzeir, and the local Arabs believe that this is the same Uzeir who is mentioned in the Koran and of whom it is said: "And the Jews say: Uzeir is the son of Allah."

It is most likely that Uzeir is a corruption of the name of the biblical Eleazar, who was appointed to guard the holy ark when it stood in Kiryat Yearim after the Philistines returned it to the Israelites.[137]

9 / IMAM ALI AND THE PLATE OF CREAM

Coming down from Jerusalem the highway winds over the mountaintops and then slowly descends into a narrow gorge whose sides are covered with young pine forests. Before the end of the pass, on the left side of the road, a

FIG. 62. SITE CALLED IMAM ALI (1970)
On Jerusalem–Ramla highway.

small edifice stands almost completely concealed amid
ancient oak trees. This was a place of prayer named after
Imam Ali, a popular saint of the Moslem tradition (fig.
62).

When caravans plodded along their route to and from
Jerusalem the camel drivers snatched a moment's rest
under the shade of the venerable trees, murmuring a
prayer toward the revered santon, that he might protect
them on their journey over the dangerous roads. Two
more shrines are dedicated to Imam Ali, one in the surroundings of Jaffa and the other in the Jordan Valley.
Why are there several places in his name?

Imam Ali was a holy man, and the Arabs of the country
venerated him greatly. Once he met a little girl crying
bitterly. He asked her: "Why dost thou cry, my child?"
And she answered: "Mother sent me to bring cream
[*samneh*] in this plate, and I have spilled it on the ground,
and now I dare not go back home and face my mother's

anger—for we are poor, and there is no money at home."

Imam Ali's heart filled with pity for the child's plight; he grasped in his hands the cream-soaked earth and squeezed it, strong and long, between the palms of his hands—and lo, white and pure cream fell drop by drop onto the plate, to the great joy of the little girl.

Under the powerful pressure of Imam Ali's hands, the earth squirmed with pain and said significantly: "Imam Ali! Imam Ali! Remember well, a day will come and I shall avenge myself upon thee, and I shall squeeze thy body, so that thou shalt find no peace for thy bones!"

When Imam Ali died they placed his body on the hump of his camel and carried it to be buried. But when they laid him in the grave, the earth contracted itself and squeezed his body out of the ground. They put him back on the camel and led him to another place, and the same thing happened again. The earth did not want to receive his body.

And the poor camel roamed all over the country, looking for a resting place for his master, but to no avail. The earth did not want to accept him. And every place where the camel kneeled down, where they unloaded the body of Imam Ali and tried to bury him, is called after him to this very day.[138]

10 / LATRUN—THE HOME OF THE GOOD THIEF

On the side of the highway running from Jerusalem to Ramla and Tel Aviv lie the ruins of Latrun, on top of a hill which commands a large view over the Valley of Ayalon, the famous battlefield of Joshua son of Nun.

At the foot of Latrun a Christian monastery of the Trappist fathers has been built to consecrate the holy memory of these surroundings. The Christian legend relates that the village which preceded Latrun on this site was the home of the same good thief who was crucified by

FIG. 63. LATRUN—DOMUS BONI LATRONIS (1586)
Latrun is built on top of hill (A). Its Latin name, *Domus Boni
Latronis*—Home of Good Thief—appears on top. Below village
(B) Arabs gallop on horseback. At small widening of road stands
well (C) named after Job. Left of village is fort (D). Travelers
are climbing on horseback to Jerusalem (E). At bottom left is
building with cupola (F), believed to contain tombs of Maccabees.

the side of Jesus and was promised a share in the next
world.

Therefore Christian pilgrims in the Middle Ages called
this place in Latin *Domus Boni Latronis*—Home of the
Good Thief (fig. 63). From the corruption of the Latin
Latronis arose the modern name Latrun.[139]

11 / RABBI YOHANAN AND THE JEWISH MAIDEN

On the side of the Jerusalem–Ramla–Tel Aviv highway, near Latrun, is the site of ancient Emmaus, the
battlefield of the Maccabees against the Greeks. About two
hundred years later, after the Romans quelled the Jewish
rebellion, there was in Emmaus a big military camp where

mercenaries of various nations were stationed—among them, Arab horsemen.

Rabbi Yohanan ben Zakkai lived in Jerusalem at the time of its destruction and participated in all the sufferings of its inhabitants. "Once Rabbi Yohanan ben Zakkai was going up to Emmaus in Judea, and he saw a girl picking barleycorns out of the excrement of a horse.

"Said Rabbi Yohanan ben Zakkai to his disciples: 'What is this girl?' They said to him: 'She is a Jewish girl.' 'And to whom does this horse belong?' 'To an Arab horseman,' the disciples answered him.

"Then Rabbi Yohanan said to his disciples: 'All my life I have been reading this verse [of the Song of Songs], and I have not realized its full meaning: "O, thou fairest among women/Go thy way forth by the footsteps of the flock."'

" 'You were unwilling to be subject to God; behold, now you are subjected to the most inferior of the nations, the Arabs.

" 'You were unwilling to pay the head tax to God; now you are paying a head tax under a government of your enemies.

" 'You were unwilling to repair the roads and streets leading up to the Temple; now you have to keep in repair the posts and stations on the road to the royal [Roman] cities. . . .

" 'Because thou didst not serve the Lord thy God with love, therefore, shalt thou serve thine enemy with hatred.

" 'Because thou didst not serve the Lord thy God when thou hadst plenty, therefore thou shalt serve thine enemy in hunger and thirst.' "[140]

12 / KING SOLOMON AND THE VILLAGERS OF KEBAB

On the road from Jerusalem to Tel Aviv, at some distance from Latrun, is the settlement of Mishmar Ayalon on the site of the former Arab village of Kebab. It is said that this site was already settled in biblical days.

King Solomon was displeased with the people who dwelt in Kebab, because notwithstanding the great numbers of their flocks and herds, they refused for several years to pay the tax which the king had imposed on each owner of thirty oxen and forty sheep or goats. These sons of evil made a secret compact to elude the law by dividing their herds among themselves and passing off the women, servants, and children as owners; so that no one appeared to possess more than twenty-nine oxen and thirty-nine sheep or goats. Solomon detected this trick and was very angry; but before punishing these rude peasants, he determined to send a prophet to endeavor to move them to repentance. A holy man accordingly visited the village, but his words were scorned and he was mocked, beaten, and driven away with stones.

The wise king then determined to punish them. By his orders a number of wolves surrounded the village and, by casting forth devouring flames from their jaws, burned it together with the surrounding fields, full of rich crops ripe for the harvest.

The ashes of the inhabitants and their flocks formed the hill on which Kebab stood, an eternal monument of the vengeance of God wrought by the hand of Solomon, to whom may He be merciful.[141]

13 / THE ROOFLESS CAVE OF GEZER

Near the ruined biblical city of Gezer, on the flank of a rocky mountain, there is a big cave, part of whose roof has collapsed. Here and there fragments can still be seen. In very early times, before the flood, Noah and his family lived in Gezer. Noah would go forth from there, wander through the earth, and call the dwellers thereon to go upright in the ways of the Lord, lest there come a great flood and sweep the earth clear of all who dwelt upon her.

But the wicked men would not hearken to him, and grew very wroth because he disturbed their ways.

Once when they grew very angry indeed, they gathered together and went up against Gezer and laid siege to the city. And they wished to storm the city and be avenged on Noah, who walked upon the walls laughing at them. One day when the chiefs of the besiegers came together they entered the cave to take counsel; and a miracle occurred, for the roof of the cave fell upon them and slew them.[142]

14 / THE OVEN OF MOTHER EVE

Among the ruins of the hill where the city of Gezer stood a tunnel 130 feet long is hewn out (fig. 64). This tunnel is like an oven; and they say that this was the oven of Eve and here she baked her loaves. This oven had been handed down through the ages from one patriarch's wife to another until the time of Noah.

When the foundations of the deep burst forth and the earth was flooded in the days of Noah the righteous, a stream of water flowed from Eve's oven as well, flooding all the land of Judah.[143]

15 / THE ORIGIN OF THE NAME ABU SHUSHA

On the western slope of the hill of ancient Gezer to the west stood an Arab village named Abu Shusha. The Arabic word *shusha* refers to the tuft of hair which every Moslem grows faithfully on the top of his head, and which he never clips short. They believe that on the Day of Resurrection, the angel Gabriel will pull the dead by this lock on the head and so wake them up to eternal life. Woe to the man whose head does not carry this convenient tuft of hair on the Great Day!

And why is the village called Abu Shusha—Father of the Tuft of Hair? Because once upon a time there lived a saintly dervish who grew on his head an unusually luxuri-

FIG. 64. TUNNEL OF GEZER—OVEN OF MOTHER EVE

ant crop of hair and so was nicknamed Abu Shusha.

Once in a drought year his numerous followers came to him and entreated him to conduct prayers to Allah and beseech Him to send rains. The dervish prayed, but to no avail. His disciples were very angered. He then faced Allah again and said: "O Allah, the Compassionate and the Merciful! I consent to drown in water for the glory of Thy name, but let the water be from the rain that Thou shalt precipitate from the skies presently!"

He had but uttered these words when the skies covered with dark, heavy clouds, and strong rain poured on the ground. The waters accumulated in one place and the dervish began to sink in them rapidly, while his hair kept floating on the surface of the water, and the whole crowd shouted: "O Abu Shusha! O Abu Shusha! Thanks to thee, we have received this blessed rain! Thanks to thee we shall have a year of abundance!"

Many generations later Arabs came from the south and built a village on this site. They did not know what to name it until some old man acquainted them with the story of Abu Shusha. They decided to call their village after him, and so it was for many years.[144]

16 / THE HEROIC BROTHERS OF KEFAR HARRUBA

East of Gezer there stood a small Arab village: Harruba. It was named after the carob trees—*harub* in Hebrew and Arabic—which grow commonly in the country. This is likely the site of Kefar Harruba, the birthplace of two valorous brothers who joined the Jewish rebellion of Bar-Kokhba and earned glory in the fight against the Romans under the reign of Hadrian in 132 C.E.

On their way out to war a venerable old man of their village called out to them: "May your Creator strengthen your arms!"

And when they were killed on the battlefield, a lamentation was said over them: "O God, Thou hast cast us off,/ Thou hast broken us down." And the famous words of Moses were repeated: "How should one chase a thousand,/ And two put ten thousand to flight,/Except their Rock [the Lord] had given them over/And the Lord had delivered them up?"

When the death of the two heroes was reported to Hadrian, he sent a man to bring them back to him. They were found with a big poisonous snake coiled around their necks.

Said Hadrian: "If their God had not cut off their lives with His own hand, none could have slain them."[145]

XIII
RAMLA
AND LOD

Ramla and Lod (Lydda) are twin cities, located next to one another in the coastal plain, but each has a distinctive history and folklore.

Ramla was established by the Arabs in the wake of their conquest, about twelve hundred years ago, and built on sands; hence its name, which derives from the Arabic *raml*, meaning "sand."

Lod, known from biblical times, is mentioned only once in the Old Testament, and the origin of its name is obscure.

Ramla still holds monuments from the time of the Moslem rule, around which popular tales have been woven.

Lod is linked up with memories and associations from ancient Jewish literature.

1 / THE PROPHET SALEH OF RAMLA

Who was the prophet en-Nebi Saleh who is buried in Ramla and is sacred to all Moslem inhabitants of the land? Before the appearance of Mohammed in Arabia, en-Nebi

Saleh came to the Arabs and proclaimed: "There is no God save the one Allah!" And he battled with idolaters and star-worshipers.

It is told that this Saleh was Methuselah of Genesis; and he was the fifth of the great prophets who have arisen since Adam.

Once Saleh came to a certain tribe and said: "O men! Serve Allah, for ye have none other!" And they answered: "If you are indeed a messenger from on high, show us a wonder; change this boulder into a camel. Do this and we shall believe you and follow your ways." And Saleh showed them this wonder and said: "Take heed and do not harm the camel or her young, lest a great punishment befall you!" And the camel and her young wandered over all the feeding places and grazed across the wastes of Arabia, all the way to Damascus. And grievous peril faced the stock of the Arabs, for no grass was left them.

And a certain rich woman, possessed of great herds, said: "I shall give the hand of my beautiful daughter in marriage to any man who slays this she-camel." And a certain youth rose and slew the camel and pursued her young, but it fled and disappeared within the same boulder from which its mother had come.

After this ill deed Saleh cursed the infidels and caused the hue of their flesh to change in many different ways. And the earth trembled and overturned their dwellings and they were all slain. The land which en-Nebi Saleh treated thus became known as *madina Saleh*—the country of Saleh—and it is so called to this day. It lies southeast of the land of Israel.

When en-Nebi Saleh's time drew near to die, Allah said to him: "Ascend to the Holy Land, where you will be buried; for it is the resting place of prophets and saints." And en-Nebi Saleh went up to the Land and was buried in the city of Ramla.

His grave, close to the tower of the old mosque, is sacred to the Moslems, who yearly celebrated a popular festival there.[146]

2 / THE OVERTURNED CISTERN

In the city of Ramla there is a pool named after Saint Helena (fig. 65). It is covered by a large roof supported by many pillars. Should you ask why this cistern is covered when pools are always open, the townsmen will tell you the tale of the wealthy princess who, in days gone by, did much charitable work in Ramla and spent a great deal of money beautifying the town. There was but one fault in this princess. She did not believe in God and,

FIG. 65. POOL IN RAMLA NAMED AFTER SAINT HELENA
(1681)

trusting to her wealth and wisdom, was very proud of herself.

Now, in Ramla there are no springs of fresh water issuing from the earth. The princess decided to remedy this situation, so she assembled a great number of slaves, whom she ordered to dig an aqueduct to carry water from the large spring at Yarda, near the ruined city of Gezer, to Ramla. And in Ramla itself she built a fine pool to hold this springwater. The labor was slow and she spent much money upon it.

When the pool was completed, the princess went to inspect it; she was proud of her work and was very much pleased with herself. Just then a saintly man passed by and greeted her, saying: "O princess, give praise to the Almighty God who aided you to bring your thought to fruition, and by whose might you have done all this." And he pointed to the big cistern.

The princess answered: "Nay, holy man, it is my money that did it." The words had scarcely passed her lips when the cistern was turned upside down and its bottom became its ceiling. Therefore it is sometimes called *Birkat el-Kufara*—Pool of the Unbelieving Woman.[147]

3 / RAMLA—A CHRISTIAN CITY

In about 1340, when the land was under Moslem rule, a German pilgrim who passed through Ramla reported that the town was solely inhabited by Christians, for "there is a belief that no Jew or Saracen [Moslem] can survive in this town over one year."

The assumption was that not long after coming to Ramla they would meet their death.

This superstition has not survived the test of history. Today Ramla is an entirely Jewish town with only a handful of Christians and Moslems.*[148]

* See legend II:2.

FIG. 66. TOWER OF RAMLA (1972)

4 / THE WISE MEN OF LOD

The lofty tower which rises above their houses has been
the pride and jewel of the Moslems of Ramla for many
years (fig. 66). It is known as the White Mosque and is

FIG. 67. TOWER OF RAMLA AND TOMB OF PROPHET SALEH
(c. 1880)

adjacent to the holy grave of the prophet Saleh, prayer and
peace be upon him! (fig. 67).

In the spring crowds used to gather from the whole
district to celebrate with great pomp the festival of en-
Nebi Saleh. The rejoicing in the city was great and the
faces of the dwellers there glowed, for its merchants and
shopkeepers profited well from it.

As the joy of the men of Ramla and their pride in the
grave and the mosque increased, so increased the envy of

the neighboring city of Lod, the people of which also came
to bow before en-Nebi Saleh. Their hearts seethed within
them when they perceived the honor and greatness of
Ramla. For Lod was of old a city and a mother in the land,
whose wares were known and whose merchants were
famed.

Year by year the envy of the men of Lod increased, till
they could no longer control their wrath and bitterness.
One year at the holy festival a quarrel broke out between
them and the men of Ramla. The dispute speedily developed into a tussle and the tussle into a battle royal, and
there was much noise and tumult that day, the voices of
the smiters mingling with the voices of the smitten. But
on this occasion fortune favored the Ramlans, who drove
their foes from the city with contumely.

So the Loddites went home mourning and, hanging their
heads, summoned an assembly to tell their fellow townsmen how the fair fame of their town had been cast to the
ground and trampled upon. In the marketplace, which is
the center of the town, the old sheiks stood in a ring, their
faces dark with anger, gazing at the ground; all around
stood the young men, their blood boiling.

One of the old men began: "In the name of the blessed
Allah and in the name of His holy prophet, I would have
you understand that the source of the whole mischief is
the tower with its grave, which the men of Ramla have
and which is their entire claim to distinction. As long as
those two things belong to the Ramlans they will be
mighty and we shall be naught. The only thing to do is
to steal the mosque and grave from Ramla and bring them
here."

But how could they steal the tower?

In those days there lived on Mount Ephraim an aged
and respected sheik whose wisdom was known throughout
the land. Men went up to him from the whole land for

counsel. So the assembly decided to send messengers with a gift to this old sheik, in order that he might advise them how to carry the tower of Ramla away to Lod.

The old sheik hearkened, thinking: "Truly envy doth twist the understanding of the upright and swallow the wisdom of the wise." So he decided to mock them and said: "I have in my possession magic ropes which I shall give you. Go to Ramla secretly at night, tie the ropes around the tower; then walk to Lod, pulling the ropes, and do not turn around. Thus shall you bring the tower to you."

So he gave them ropes of elastic—but they did not know. And they went home rejoicing.

On a chosen night all the men gathered together, and after prayers, the young men of the community set out for Ramla, their ropes in their hands. Stealthily they went to the tower, knotted their ropes securely around it, and began to drag at the ropes, their backs to the tower and their faces to Lod, as the old sheik had ordered. The elastic ropes stretched and the men strode on, dragging the ropes, till they reached Lod, and cried with joy: "It's coming! It's coming!" The Loddites rushed out to meet them and to gaze at the tower approaching the town.

But the tower wasn't there.

So now if anyone wants to mock and tease a Loddite, he says to him: "The tower of Ramla is coming."[149]

5 / THE GREAT RABBI ELIEZER IN LOD

After the destruction of Jerusalem, Lod became a great center of learning, the recognized heir of the Holy City.

When Zephaniah exclaims: "Hark! a cry from the fish gate,/And a wailing from the second quarter," the second quarter (*min hamisheneh*) "that is Lod, which is second to Jerusalem," say the sages.

Rabbi Eliezer son of Horcanus, better known as the Great Eliezer, was one of Lod's most famous sages.

FIG. 68. OLD CITY OF LOD (LYDDA) (1880)

"Our Rabbis taught: Justice, justice shall thou follow;
this means: Follow the scholars to their academies . . .
Rabbi Eliezer to Lod."

Rabbi Eliezer used to sit on a stone in the great academy
and teach the pupils. After his death, Rabbi Yehoshua
entered and kissed the stone and said: "This stone is like
Mount Sinai and the one who sat on it like the ark of the
covenant."

The famous Rabbi Akibah was one of Rabbi Eliezer's
most outstanding pupils.[150]

6 / RABBI AKIBAH ON A WELL IN LOD

In the surroundings of Lod there are some very ancient
wells (fig. 69). One recognizes their age by the upper
layer of stones which form the mouth of the well. The con-
stant drawing of the ropes attached to the buckets against
the stones have, down many generations, cut long crevices.
In the course of centuries the soft rope has worn out the
hard stones; the older the well, the deeper the crevices in
the mouth's stones.

Before Rabbi Akibah took to the learning in which he

FIG. 69. ANCIENT WELL IN JUDEA (1900)

was to achieve such fame, he was an obscure and illiterate shepherd tending his flocks. But though no longer young in years, the yearning to the Torah was strong within him. It is told that once when roaming in the neighborhood of Lod, he happened to sit on a well and noticed the crevices on the mouth of the well. He asked: "Who carved this stone?" He was told: "The rope." He asked again: "How can it?" He was told: "Because it rubs steadily and constantly against it." And they added: "Verily, why shouldst thou wonder: is it not said [in the Book of Job]: 'The waters wear the stones'?"

Rabbi Akibah wondered: "Can my heart be harder than stone? Let me go forthwith and learn, one by one, steadily, the chapters of the Torah."

He went to school with his small son and learned to read from a slate like a child. Then he learned the Bible, the oral traditions, the sayings of the fathers. He learned everything and became the outstanding scholar of his generation owing to his steadfastness.[151]

7 / THE MARTYRS OF LOD

It is told by the sages of Israel that a certain great lady,
a daughter of Caesar, was killed and it was not known who
killed her. The heathens said: "This can only have been
done by Israel; for the Jews are our foes." So they decreed
the slaughter of all Israel.

Now, there were two brothers in the city of Lod; and
when they knew of this, they, being zealous for the Lord,
denounced themselves for the sanctity of His holy name
and gave themselves up for execution. They went and said
to the heathens: "Why have ye decreed against Israel
thus? We alone killed her."

When they heard this they annulled the decree against
Israel and imprisoned these two brothers. What did they
do to them? They tortured them and each day they tore
some flesh from them, piece by piece, limb by limb, so
that they should die in agony and torture.

And because of their heroic deed in sacrificing themselves to save Israel, the sages say: "There is no creature
that can stand within the bounds of the martyrs of Lod."[152]

8 / LOD'S MARTYRS IN PARADISE

A late Hebrew legend describes the Messiah of Israel
as sitting in paradise in a luminous palace. And within it
is a holy curtain, and beyond it images of the martyrs of
Lod, who gave up their lives for the glory of God. And
these are the words of the legend:

"And within that same palace is an opening and farther
on is a holy curtain, and beyond it all the images of the
martyrs of Lod and the Ten Martyrs of the [Roman] Empire.

"The Messiah arises and enters, and sees those same
images, and he raises his voice and roars like a lion. And
all of paradise and all of the righteous tremble, and the

pillar in the middle of paradise rises and falls; and the firmament revolves, and the Voice is heard in the heavens, and the Holy One, blessed be He, sheds two tears.

"And the patriarchs enter all of them through the Eastern Gate of that palace, and there they see all the virtues of the righteous ones of Lod, who won their places next to the King of kings, the Holy One, blessed be He."[153]

9 / THE PIOUS WOMEN OF LOD

In ancient times Lod played an important part in the life of Israel. It was even said that she stood second only to Jerusalem. For thirty miles a road from Lod climbed up the hills to Jerusalem to a height of about one thousand feet. To reach the capital meant a long day of hard walking from the first glimpse of dawn till after sunset, about twelve to fourteen hours.

The women of Lod were pious and very devout. The legend relates that they used to knead their dough, ascend to Jerusalem, pray in the Temple, and manage to return home in time to bake bread thereof before it could turn sour.

The Roman legions subdued the Jewish revolt with great cruelty: "What was done to them [the women]?—Their hair was bound to the tails of their horses and they were made to run from Jerusalem to Lod. That is what is written [in the Book of Lamentations]—'The virgins of Jerusalem hang down/Their heads to the ground.' "[154]

10 / "WHICH WAY LEADS TO LOD?"

Lod was a very important Jewish town in the second century. It was a famous center of learning, and pupils from all over the country flocked to its houses of study.

There is a tale about Yossi the Galilean, who left his home and went to Lod to study the Law. On his way he met Berurya, the wife of Rabbi Meir. He asked her: "Which way leads to Lod?"

And she answered: "Thou, Galilean, doth thou not know that our sages have warned men: 'Do not converse at length with a woman?' Thou shouldst have said: 'Which to Lod?'"

The sages have said: "He that talks much with woman-folk brings evil upon himself and neglects the study of the Law—and at best will inherit Gehenna."[155]

11 / THE CAVE OF LOD

In the environs of Lod, at the foot of the mountains of Judah, there are a number of caves. In one of them which is "three miles from Lod" the following occurred.

Rabbi Joshua son of Levi stood with Elijah the prophet on Mount Carmel and said to him: "Peradventure you can show me the precious stones from which the Temple will be built at the end of time." And Elijah answered him: "I will show them to you," and he showed them to him by means of the following miracle.

A boat was sailing on the high seas when a whirlwind caught it up and it was in great danger. On the boat there was a Jewish lad to whom Elijah appeared and said: "If you will fulfill my task, I will save this boat for you." The lad agreed, whereupon Elijah said to him: "Go to Rabbi Joshua son of Levi, who lives in the great city of Lod, and show him these precious stones. But take heed that you show them to him not in the town, but in the cave outside the town."

The lad came to Lod and said to Rabbi Joshua son of Levi: "Follow me." When they reached the cave, he showed him the precious stones, and immediately the whole of Lod became illuminated from the brightness of these wondrous stones.[156]

12 / THE DISCOURSE IN LOD'S CAVE

A group of rabbis was walking along the way. Two of them parted from the rest and sought shelter from the heat of the day in the cave of Lod.

Said Rabbi Abba: "Let this hollow be filled with thoughts of the Torah and resound with its holy words."

While discoursing, they heard the voice of Rabbi Shimon approaching and went out to meet him. Said Rabbi Shimon: "From the aspect of the walls, I could perceive that the divine Presence is resting on this cave." And he asked: "What did you deal with?" Said Rabbi Abba: "With the ardent love of the House of Israel for the God Almighty."[157]

13 / SAINT GEORGE IN LOD

An ancient tradition places the birth of Saint George in the town of Lod; hence in the Middle Ages the Christians called it Georgeopolis. To this day, in the crypt of the Greek Orthodox church of the town there is shown a cenotaph that is connected with the Christian hero martyred in the fourth century.

The earliest comment which connects Saint George with Lod or Diospolis (as the Romans named it) probably occurs in the itinerary of Theodosius in 530: "Diospolis . . . where Saint George suffered martyrdom: there is his body, and there many wonders are worked."

A hundred years later another pilgrim, the bishop Arculfus, added new details: "In a house in the city of Diospolis there stands the marble column of George the Confessor, to which, during a time of persecution, he was bound while he was scourged and on which his likeness is impressed."

Arabic-speaking Christians used to hold a popular festival on this tomb in the first days of the month of November

FIG. 70. SAINT GEORGE KILLING DRAGON

and called it *Id Lidd*—the Holiday of Lod.

This pilgrimage was mainly celebrated by the peasants, and it marked the end of the olive-picking season and the beginning of plowing time; hence the saying: "*Id Lidd uhrut wa-jidd*—At the Feast of Lod plow and pick [the olives]."

It was also commonly repeated: "At the Feast of Lod pull, peasant, pull; you can't keep back the rains—*Fi id Lidd shidd ya, fellah, shid; ma biki lil shita didd!*"[158]

14 / WHERE DID SAINT GEORGE KILL THE DRAGON?

Saint George, the patron saint of England, is always depicted wearing full armor, riding a fiery steed, and piercing with his spear the frightful dragon crawling at his feet. This exploit is a well-known motif in Christian art and appears in various styles through the periods (fig. 70).

Legend holds that this famous encounter took place at the entrance to Lod, his native town.

Another tale, current among Middle Ages pilgrims, situated it in Beirut, on the Lebanese coast. After this brilliant success Saint George "converted the city and all the country to the Christian faith."

To this day the majority of the inhabitants are Christian, and Saint George is one of their major saints.[159]

FIG. 71. IRON CHAIN IN CHURCH OF SAINT GEORGE

15 / THE ANTICHRIST AT THE GATE OF LOD

The Arab legend holds that the Antichrist, ed-Dajjal, will appear in the end of time before the advent of the Redeemer of the world. Meanwhile, ed-Dajjal lives on a solitary land, far away in the heart of the seas. He will come to the land forty days before the Messiah. And at the gate of Lod a fight will break out between them, and the Messiah will have the upper hand and subdue the evil forces.

The renowned caliph Omar ibn Hattab went to Palestine at the time of the Arab conquest in the seventh century. The Moslem tradition says that before he conquered Jerusalem a Jew told him: "On, prince of the believers! Do not return to thy country until Allah delivers Jerusalem into thine hands."

When Jerusalem was conquered, Omar sent for the same Jew and asked about ed-Dajjal. The other said: "Why dost thou ask about him, O prince of the believers? Truly, you, the Arab people, you will be the ones to kill him about ten ells from the gate of Lod."[160]

16 / BETWEEN LOD AND KEFAR ONO

To the west of Lod, toward Tel Aviv, stretches the fertile plain of Ono, where ancient Kefar Ono prospered. In its vicinity a new Jewish settlement has been built which is called by this old biblical name. Kefar Ono was an important town in olden times. According to tradition, it was already surrounded by a wall at the time of Joshua son of Nun. It was inhabited by pious, learned Jews, some of whom became renowned sages. It is told of Rabbi Hiyya and Rabbi Yezekiah that as they sat learning the Torah under the shade of the trees out in the fields of Ono, Eliahu the holy prophet revealed himself to them.

The Valley of Ono was rich and very fruitful. Besides corn, it also grew excellent figs. Rabbi Yacob son of Dusstai related: "From Lod to Ono is three miles. Once I strolled there in the evening and walked ankle-deep in the figs' honey."[161]

17 / WHERE DID NAHUM OF GIMZO COME FROM?

In the vicinity of Lod there is a settlement called Gimzo; near it is Jimzu, an Arab ruin which has preserved the ancient name. Here, in biblical times, stood the city of Gimzo, mentioned only once in the Holy Scriptures. The origin of the name is obscure.

Gimzo was settled in postbiblical times too; one of its outstanding citizens was Rabbi Nahum, the man of Gimzo.

He was famed for his even temper and used to receive all afflictions with equanimity. His favorite saying was: "*Gam zu letova*—This too is for the good." Hence he was known not as the man of Gimzo, but as the man of Gam Zu.[162]

XIV
JAFFA
AND ITS SEA

1 / WHY IS IT CALLED JAFFA?

Jaffa is picturesquely built on a hill which commands a beautiful view of the open sea. It is said to have been called Jaffa—in Hebrew, Yaffo, from the word *yaffeh*, meaning "beautiful." Jaffa is one of the world's most ancient cities. The Roman historian Pliny wrote: "Jope, this is said to have existed before the flood."

According to tradition Jaffa was named after Japheth, the son of Noah the righteous, who founded the town when he left the ark after the waters had subsided.

In 1322 the English writer Sir John Mandeville repeated the same tale: "The town is called Jaffa, because one of the sons of Noah, named Japhet, founded it, and now it is called Joppa. And you shall understand that it is one of the oldest towns of the world, for it was founded before Noah's flood."

One legend narrates that after his death Noah the righteous was buried in one of the rocks which rise above the waters in front of the old harbor.[163]

2 / HOW JAFFA WAS CAPTURED

Many, many ages ago, before the people of Israel had yet entered the Land, there lived a mighty king in Egypt who on several occasions attempted to subdue Jaffa, which was a very important port in the ancient world. But his project never succeeded.

Once a certain officer approached the king and promised that Jaffa could be taken by him if the king would give him his scepter. The scepter was given to the officer, who concealed it amid his belongings. Then he got ready to visit the "accursed lord of Jaffa," and before he went he prepared five hundred great jars. He hid two hundred men-at-arms in a like number of jars and in the others he concealed ropes and yokes for warfare. And his men sealed the jars and bore them to the vicinity of Jaffa.

Then the officer, with a small retinue, appeared before the ruler of Jaffa, who received them very hospitably and prepared a fine feast for them. When the ruler had made himself drunk, the officer told him that he and his few companions were fleeing from the army of Egypt, having despoiled the land; and that they had hidden their booty in the great jars which were already near the town. Furthermore, he had succeeded in stealing the king's very scepter. When the governor saw the scepter he believed the officer, and therefore did not instruct his men to guard the city against the new arrivals. He also allowed the officer to bring his five hundred jars of booty into the town. While his men busied themselves with the jars, the officer rose and said to the governor: "Here is the scepter of the august lion-eyed king of Egypt, whose father Amon gave him might and power!" And raising it, he smote the governor on the temple, so that he fell and perished.

The officer went to his men at once and bade them open the jars. The two hundred men leaped forth, seized the guard of the city, and bound them with ropes and the yokes. And in this simple way the fort of Jaffa was taken.

Then the officer wrote to the king of Egypt: "Rejoice in your lot! Amon, your benevolent father, has given you Jaffa and the dwellers therein. Send men now and take them into captivity and fill the temple of Amon your father, king of the gods, with menservants and maidservants prostrating themselves at your feet forever!"*[164]

3 / AT JAFFA "THY PROUD WAVES BE STAYED"

Twice did the ocean rise and flood the world: first, in the time of Adam and Eve; second, when humanity divided into various nations.

How far did the flood reach the first time and how far did it reach the second time?

The first time the ocean rose up to the rocks of Barbary, one of which is the Rock of Gibraltar; the second time it penetrated as far as Acco (Acre) and Jaffa, where it remained forever.

A reference to the second deluge is found in the words of Job: ". . . and set bars and doors./And said: 'Thus far shalt thou come but no further./And here shall thy proud waves be stayed.' "

The sages of Israel expound:

" 'Thus far'—as far as Acco [Acre].

" 'And here'—at Jaffa."[165]

4 / KING SOLOMON'S WINEPRESS IN JAFFA

Zechariah the prophet pictures the expansion of Jerusalem in the end of time, and he says that she will spread "from the tower of Hananel unto the king's winepresses . . . Jerusalem shall dwell safely."

The sages of Israel explain that this is the winepress which King Solomon built in Jaffa.[166]

---

* This episode calls to mind the story of Ali Baba and the forty thieves in *The Thousand and One Nights*.

5 / THE MIRACLE AT JAFFA'S HARBOR

In Alexandria, Egypt, there lived a wealthy Jew named Nicanor. When he heard of the rebuilding of the Temple he prepared two magnificent doors for the entrance of the holy of holies. Each door was made of copper inset with panels of gold and silver, all of the finest craftsmanship. Their height was fifty cubits and their width was forty cubits, and so great was their weight that it took twenty men to carry one.

The doors were set on a ship to be taken to Jaffa, whence they would be borne to Jerusalem; and Nicanor himself accompanied his gift. While on the sea a great storm arose and the ship nearly foundered under its burden. In face of this peril, sailors threw one door overboard to lighten the boat. But the storm increased and they wished to cast the other overboard as well. Then Nicanor embraced the door and said in anguish: "Men! If you cast this door overboard, my life is no life! Cast me with it!" And at these words the storm subsided and the sea ceased raging.

The ship reached Jaffa at length, Nicanor weeping and lamenting the door which had sunk. But when they neared the port, a miracle happened. Something began to foam amid the waves and breakers, and the lost door suddenly emerged.

Both doors were joyfully borne up to Jerusalem, where they were set up in the gate of the Temple known to all as the Gate of Nicanor.[167]

6 / THE SEA OF JAFFA

The sages of Israel relate that the sea of Jaffa is set aside for the saints in days to come. How is this known? All the ships containing silver, gold, jewels and all fine things that are lost in the Great Sea will be projected by it into the sea of Jaffa and these treasures are set aside for the righteous of the future ages.

FIG. 72. PERSEUS DELIVERS ANDROMEDA
Exhibited at Museo Capitolino in Rome.

When the Messiah appears in the land of Israel, the
Lord God will give the righteous wealth untold. For in
whatever sea gold, silver, and jewels are sunk, that sea is
sworn to bring it all to the sea of Jaffa. Whatever was sunk
between the six days of the creation of the world and the
time of King Solomon was washed up at Jaffa for Solomon,
and it was in this manner that he gained his wealth.

From the death of Solomon until now and until the
ingathering of the exiles of Israel, all the treasures which
have been sunk will be brought to the sea of Jaffa, which
will project it forth upon the dry land. And the Messiah
will apportion it to each righteous man according to his
merits.[168]

7 / THE ROCK OF ANDROMEDA

In ancient times a fearsome monster lived in the sea of Jaffa and cast dread over all the sailors. He caused great storms, sank ships, and destroyed many lives. But if a human sacrifice of the most beautiful maiden in Jaffa was made to the monster he would, for a year, leash the tempests and protect the sailors that go down to the sea in ships.

Once beautiful Andromeda, the daughter of Cepheus, was taken to a certain rock and chained there as an offering to this dragon, lord of the sea. But when the monster approached to receive his gift, Perseus appeared, riding on a winged horse, and slew the monster. He snapped Andromeda's chains and delivered her (fig. 72).

For many years the relics of these chains were shown on a certain rock at Jaffa. The Roman historian Pliny reportedly saw them; he wrote: "It [Jaffa] is situated on a hill, and in front of it is a rock on which they point out marks made by the chains with which Andromeda was fettered" (figs. 73 and 74).

The second-century geographer Pausanias, who traveled in Palestine, wrote: "Red water, red as blood, may be seen in the land of the Hebrews, near the city of Jaffa. The water is hard by the sea, and the local legend runs that when Perseus had slain the sea beast, to which the daughter of Cepheus was exposed, he washed off the blood at this spring."

One of the monster's ribs was shown in Jaffa, said Mandeville in 1322, "a rib of whose side, which is forty feet long, is still shown." Others say that it was taken to Rome, "where it was greatly wondered at." Felix Fabri, the German pilgrim, added: "Saint Sylvester and the other saints who consecrated Rome to Christ, broke up those bones . . . lest pilgrims should come hither to see them

FIG. 73. JAFFA AND ITS PORT (1726)
Among rocks pictured in foreground is one to which legend says beautiful Andromeda was chained, offered as sacrifice to monster of sea.

. . . and waste hours which might be spent in prayer."

The Roman poet Ovid, in the beginning of the first century, related the story of Andromeda in his *Metamorphoses*, but made Ethiopia the scene of this legend: "As soon as Perseus saw her there bound by the arms to a rough cliff, save that her hair gently stirred in the breeze and the warm tears were trickling down her cheeks, he would have thought her a marble statue. . . . Smitten by the sight of her exquisite beauty, he almost forgot to move his wings in the air. Then when he alighted near the maiden, he said: 'Oh! Those are not the chains you deserve to wear, but rather those that link fond lovers together! Tell me, for I would know, your country's name and yours, and why you are chained here.' She was silent at first, for, being a maid, she did not dare address a man; she would have hidden her face modestly with her hands but that

FIG. 74. ROCK OF ANDROMEDA IN SEA OF JAFFA

her hands were bound. . . . So did Perseus plunging head-
long in a swift swoop through the empty air. . . . He
plunges his sword into the vitals of the monster. At this
the shores and the high seats of the gods reecho with mild
shouts of applause. The maiden also now comes forward,
freed from chains. . . . Forthwith the hero claims Andromeda as the prize of his great deed, seeking no further
dowry; Hymen and love shake the marriage torch."[169]

8 / THE ROCK OF ADAM

Near the coast of Jaffa, opposite the city of Bath Yam
—Daughter of the Sea—there projects from the waters a
rock which is like a tiny islet among the waves (fig. 75).
In the Middle Ages the Arabs called it the Rock of Adam.
A medieval legend holds that the fish used to swim to the
rock and kiss it.

And this is how an anonymous Christian traveler of the

FIG. 75. ROCK OF ADAM IN BATH YAM

twelfth century repeated the tale: "Among other wonders
we must not be silent about this, that at Jaffa, on the sea
beach, there is a Rock of Adam [in Latin, *Lapis quidam
Adam*], whereunto an exceeding great, nay, an infinite
multitude of the fishes called salmon resort in summertime, bearing long yellow lines upon their backs, and after
kissing the stone, as though it were a holy place, depart
swiftly.

"The fishermen of that land declare that when the Lord
bade Saint James go into Galilee, Saint James answered
'I will go if that rock will go with me.'

"The rock broke in two, and one half went into Galilee,
where it is visited by pilgrims at this day, and is called
Saint James's Pitcher, while the other half remained
here."[170]

9 / GOING TO JAFFA

In medieval times the voyage to the shores of Palestine
was dangerous indeed because of the pirates who attacked
the ships and robbed the travelers. In addition, the approach to the ports, and especially to Jaffa, was very

difficult because of the many boulders in the sea. From time to time ships would sink during storms, and their sailors and passengers would go to the bottom of the sea.

The expression "going to Jaffa" was current among the Dutch, who were noted medieval seafarers, to denote a long and hard voyage from which return was doubtful.[171]

10 / THE CURSE OF THE GOVERNOR

At the beginning of the nineteenth century, when Jaffa was an Arab city, Muhammad Abu Nabbut—Father of the Oak Club—was the Turkish governor of the town. He was known by that name because whenever he walked in the street he carried with him his staff of authority. He was a very good and just ruler who built many fine buildings, including the big mosque named after him: Muhammadiye. He always strove to improve the town and better its inhabitants, and his fame spread far and wide. Under his rule the population and prosperity of Jaffa increased greatly; and all men blessed Abu Nabbut.

In those days Jaffa was walled and fortified, its gates being shut every night at sundown. All who reached the town after sunset had to stay outside the wall, in the open, till dawn.

One day Governor Abu Nabbut went out of the town and walked a long distance amid the orchards. When he returned the sun had already set and the gates were closed. So Abu Nabbut knocked at the gate and called upon the guards to open; but none answered. He shouted in wrath: "I am Abu Nabbut, the governor; open the gates and let me in!" But the only answer was laughter behind the walls.

Abu Nabbut thought the watch did not believe him, so he entreated: "Send to my house and ask if the governor is at home; then you will know I speak the truth." But they took no heed. So he had to stay outside the town the whole night long.

FIG. 76. SEBIL ABU NABBUT AT ENTRANCE TO JAFFA (c. 1880)

When Abu Nabbut entered the town the next day he summoned all the inhabitants, told them his tale, and bitterly upbraided them for their boorish behavior.

In order to set in full view the ill heart and rudeness of all Jaffa men, he ordered his curse to be engraved on a stone on the main highway, so that all passersby might see it, and Jaffa and the dwellers therein might be eternally shamed.

At the exit from Jaffa on the way to Jerusalem they show a half-effaced inscription. It is on a three-domed edifice which is called in Arabic *Sebil Abu Nabbut*, a watering place for caravans in bygone days (fig. 76), and this is alleged to be the remains of the governor's curse: "Accursed is he and accursed is the father of whoever takes a friend among the people of Jaffa!"[172]

XV
𝒯𝓔𝓛 𝒜𝒱𝒥𝒱 𝒜𝒩𝒟
𝒥𝒯𝒮 𝒮𝒰𝑅𝑅𝒪𝒰𝒩𝒟𝒥𝒩𝒢𝒮

1 / "IF YOU WILL IT IS NOT A LEGEND"

When Eretz Israel was under Turkish rule, some of the Jewish inhabitants of Jaffa founded a new suburb on the barren sands stretching north of the town.

On a clear summer day during the Feast of the Tabernacles in 1909 a small group of pioneers were seen proceeding in the deep sand dunes toward a flattened hill. There they set the foundation stone of the new suburb which came to be called Tel Aviv—Hill of Spring, after the Hebrew title of Theodor Herzl's book *Altneuland*, a utopian description of the state of the Jews in the land of their forefathers.

Most people looked with commiseration at these impractical daydreamers, and few believed that they would be able to hold out in this remote desolation with no roads, no water, and no security.

But determined to bring their project to fruition, they clung to Herzl's famous slogan: "If you will it is not a legend," and they named their first street after the great Jewish missionary and prophet. From a small cluster of

FIG. 77. EMBLEM OF TEL AVIV FAIRS

houses there rapidly grew up a bustling, thriving city, the largest in Israel.

At first "Little Tel Aviv" was a daughter suburb of old Jaffa, the metropolis, the mother town.

But it soon outgrew its parent city and Jaffa in turn became the suburb of Tel Aviv; it was said that the daughter had become the mother and the mother, the daughter.[173]

2 / WHY IS A FLYING CAMEL THE EMBLEM OF
TEL AVIV'S FAIRS?

The emblem of all the fairs held in Tel Aviv is a flying camel (fig. 77). Why? The first fair in Tel Aviv was held in the time of the British Mandate in 1933. When it was still in its preparatory stages the mayor of Jaffa and his council were invited to participate. They objected violently, and in a flight of oriental rhetoric the Arab mayor exclaimed: "When the camel grows wings and flies, only then will there be a fair in Tel Aviv!" "Indeed," said the promoters, "let the flying camel be our emblem!" The fair was held at the proposed time and met with great success.[174]

3 / WHERE DID THE NAME NAHLAT BINYAMIN COME FROM?

Nahlat Binyamin—Inheritance of Benjamin—was one of the first streets carved out of the sands of Tel Aviv. Its first settlers were small artisans and shopkeepers of small means who wished to build for themselves a quiet residential quarter away from the din and bustle of Jaffa.

They applied for help both to the Zionist Organization and to the Rothschild family. They said: "If the Zionists come to our rescue we shall tell them we have named this street after Zev Benjamin Herzl; and if the Rothschilds, we shall declare that our intention was to honor Benjamin (Edmond) Rothschild, the head of the French branch of the family."

World War I broke out, help came from no one, and to this day it is not clear what Benjamin the street is named for.[175]

4 / KEREM HATEIMANIM—VINEYARD OF THE YEMENITES

Kerem Hateimanim is a suburb of Tel Aviv named after its founders and present inhabitants: the Yemenite Jews— Teimanim in Hebrew—who originate from Yemen in Arabia.

Large-scale Yemenite immigration started in 1882 or according to the Jewish calendar the year (5)642 from the creation of the world—in Hebrew characters, *tarmab*.

The Yemenite elders find a hint to this date in the following words of the Song of Songs: "I will climb up into the palm tree." "Into the palm tree" in Hebrew is *batamar*; it is composed of the same letters as *tarmab* and also equals (5)642. In the Book of Psalms the palm tree symbolizes the just man: "The righteous shall flourish like the palm tree." It is also an emblem of Israel and its land and is engraved on old Jewish coins.

The Yemenites newcomers were very poor in worldly goods but rich in spirit and well versed in Jewish law and traditions. And this is the story they tell. When God Almighty distributed the wealth of the world, every community came forth to receive its portion. They thronged together, jostling each other noisily. The Almighty said: Let all stand in line in alphabetical order, and so it was done.

First came the Ashkenazim, who received a goodly portion, then the Bavlim from Iraq, the Bukharim from the central Asia, the Georgians from Georgia in Russia, and so on.

The Teimanim came last, and by that time the hands of the Almighty were almost empty. Said He: "I have little material riches to give you; instead, since your name starts with a T, I bestow upon you the gift of learning Torah." From that time the Teimanim have excelled in the holy texts and in all branches of Jewish learning.[176]

5 / WHO WAS SHEIK SALAMEH?

One of Tel Aviv's suburbs is named Kefar Shalem. Its more ancient part is built on the site of an Arab village called Salameh, of which an old sprawling house remains and is today a youth center; within a locked room on the side the tomb of Sheik Salameh is preserved.

In former times war broke out in this neighborhood between the Moslems and the unbelievers (*kuffar*). The war was waged with ceaseless ferocity, and many fell on both sides. Victory was slow in coming, for the forces were very well balanced. At the head of the faithful was a certain holy dervish who fought with Allah's name on his lips. And when he saw that his forces could not subdue the foe, he grieved and fasted and prayed for many days.

One night an angel of God appeared to the dervish and said: "God has heard your prayer; go now to the village, where you will find an old woman who has an only son born in her old age. Take this lad, put the standard of the faithful in his hands, and set him on the field at the head of your men. And Allah shall be with him, and through him will you prevail. And you will smite your foes and root out their remnant from the land."

In the morning the dervish arose and hastened down to the village, where he sought the woman, and, coming to her, he said: "Give me your son to be our standard-bearer in the battle, for without him the faithful fail and fall." But the woman refused to give her son, saying: "Indeed, you must know that he is my only son and our souls are knit together; and should ill befall him in the battle, I shall go down in sorrow to the grave."

The dervish responded: "I swear by Allah that I shall bring the lad back as I take him; and you can demand him from me. But now do the will of Allah and do not fear that any evil can befall those who serve him." And he swore that he would bring the lad back whole. And the woman hearkened to him and kissed her son farewell and gave him to the dervish.

The next day battle was joined anew with yet more vigor, and the lad went before the army of the faithful with the standard. And there was a great onset, and the corpses on the battlefield far outnumbered those of previous battles; only at evening did the faithful drive the foes from the field and utterly destroy them.

At night the dervish saw that the lad had not returned;

and he trembled greatly and went forth to seek him amid the dead. For many hours the dervish searched through the darkness, and at dawn he found the lad lying on the ground, drenched in blood and expiring. And the dervish cried out bitterly, for he remembered the oath he had sworn to the lad's mother. And he kneeled and prayed with tearful eyes that God should not allow him to break the oath sworn by His sacred name. And Allah hearkened to the dervish's prayer, and the lad rose to his feet and came to life anew.

Then the dervish took the boy in his arms and hastened with him to the village, took him to his mother, and said: "Behold, I have brought your son. As God lives, I took him hale and have brought him hale." And the woman rejoiced and stretched out her arms to take the lad and clasp him to her bosom. And as she took the lad, he gave his soul back to God and died.

And the Arabs sanctified his name, so that he became a saint unto them. And they called him Sheik Salameh, meaning "Peace." He was the saint of the village Salameh which was called by his name.

At the place where he fell a large jujube tree was planted in his memory, and today, protected by an iron railing, it grows among the new houses of spreading Tel Aviv.[177]

6 / THE MOUNT OF NAPOLEON

Near the close of the eighteenth century Napoleon Bonaparte, at the head of his army, proceeded from Egypt along the coastal plain to the Holy Land. His main objective was to capture Acco (Acre) from the Turks and secure the Middle East for the French.

His way was barred by the city of Jaffa. He laid siege to it in 1799, and after a bitter fight it fell into his hands.

In the vicinity of Jaffa, between Tel Aviv and Ramat Gan, a hillock stands out in the flat countryside (fig. 78).

This is a clear indication of an ancient city still unidentified, probably one of the towns of the tribe of Dan, who inherited this area. But popular imagination has created another tale; it holds that this mound was raised overnight by the French army by order of the commander in chief, as a military position to stop all possible Turkish reinforcements from Acco or Shechem to the invested Jaffa. And therefore it is known as Mount Napoleon to this day.[178]

FIG. 78. MOUNT OF NAPOLEON (1920)
On hill appear letters C. I. H.: Central Indian Horse, the British-Indian brigade that camped on this site at end of First World War.

XVI
JN THE SURROUNDJNGS
OF TEL AVJV

1 / THE FERTILITY OF BNEI BERAK

Bnei Berak, a famous city in ancient times, stood near its namesake of today, in the vicinity of Tel Aviv. It was reputed for its academy of Jewish learning, from which many scholars and wise men came.

The surroundings of Bnei Berak were very fruitful; rich fields of corn, luscious vineyards, and luxuriant plantations covered the countryside.

Rabbi Rami, son of Ezekiel, who came to Bnei Berak, saw goats browsing under fig trees, and the honey that dripped from the figs mingled with the milk from the goats. Said Rami: "This is what is meant by a 'land flowing with milk and honey.' "[179]

2 / RABBI AKIBAH IN BNEI BERAK

Rabbi Akibah was one of the outstanding sages of Bnei Berak and the head of its academy in the beginning of the second century.

"Our Rabbis taught: Justice, justice shalt thou follow; this means: Follow the scholars to their academies, Rabbi Akibah to Bnei Berak."

FIG. 79. ASSEMBLY OF RABBIS IN BNEI BERAK (1712)
This assembly is discussing story of exodus from Egypt.

On the eve of Passover, the night of the Seder, it is customary to recollect the events and the miracles which happened to the children of Israel in Egypt, and anyone who enlarges on the narrative of the departure from Egypt is accounted praiseworthy.

The story is told of certain rabbis, Rabbi Akibah among them, who, being entertained on the eve of Passover at Bnei Berak, were discussing the story of the exodus and the wanderings of the tribes; they deliberated all through that night until their disciples came and said unto them: "Masters, the time has arrived to read the morning prayers!" (fig. 79).[180]

3 / THE VINEYARDS OF BNEI BERAK

Bnei Berak was surrounded by rich vineyards which

produced grapes in exceedingly large clusters.

It is told that Rabbi Yehuda Hanassi, of the second century, came to visit Bnei Berak and met Rabbi Pereda, an
inhabitant of the town. "Will you not show me the clusters
in your vineyards?" asked Rabbi Yehuda. "Certainly," said
Rabbi Pereda and went with him to the groves. When they
were still far off, Rabbi Yehuda cried out: "That looks like
a bull there! Will he not damage the vines?" "That is no
bull, that is a cluster of grapes," answered Rabbi Pereda.[181]

4 / THE FATE OF THE DESCENDANTS OF HAMAN

Haman was the main chamberlain of King Ahasuerus,
whose name is connected with the Purim festival. The king
loved Haman and "set his seat above all the princes that
were with him."

When Haman's plot to exterminate all the Jews was
foiled by Queen Esther, he and his sons were put to death.
But the rabbis tell a different story; they hold that his
repentant sons came to the land of Israel and they say:
"The descendants of Haman studied the Torah in Bnei
Berak. The Holy One, blessed be He, purposed to lead
the descendants of that wicked man too under the wings of
the divine Spirit [Shechinah]."[182]

5 / THE MEETING AT ANTIPATRIS

On the top of a small hill in the neighborhood of Petah
Tikvah there is an old ruined fortress (fig. 80). This is
the site of an earlier stronghold built by King Herod and
named after his father, Antipatris. It guarded an important crossroads where the Way of the Sea, the famous
Via Maris of the Romans, met the main ancient highway
from Jerusalem to Caesarea, the Roman capital of Palestine.

When Alexander the Great, king of Macedonia, approached the land of Israel, Shimon the Just, who was the

FIG. 80. FORTRESS CALLED ANTIPATRIS (1970)

FIG. 81. MEETING OF ALEXANDER AND HIGH PRIEST
A seventeenth-century gold medallion. Left: on top is imaginary picture of Jerusalem, through whose gate come notables of
town, headed by Shimon the Just, the high priest. Alexander the
Great kneels in front of them. Behind Alexander is his prancing
horse and his mounted soldiery. Right: on obverse side of medallion,
miter of high priest and below is word "Jehova" in Hebrew characters. Around edge is indication, in Latin, of sources recording this
encounter: Josephus' *Antiquities of the Jews* and biblical verses men-
tioning miter of high priest.

high priest, arrayed himself in his priestly robes and, accompanied by the nobles of Israel who carried torches in their hands, went out to meet the royal conqueror (fig. 81). Both parties traveled all night, Alexander from the north (Syria) and Shimon from the west (Jerusalem); they came in sight of each other at dawn. Alexander asked his attendants: "Who are these men?" He was told that they were the Jews.

As the sun rose both parties met in Antipatris. On seeing Shimon the just, Alexander alighted from his chariot and bowed before him. His courtiers expressed their astonishment that a great monarch like Alexander should bow to a Jew. He replied: "The image of this man was in front of me in all my victories."[183]

6 / WHY IS IT CALLED BEIT DAGON?

Beit Dagon, a new settlement in the vicinity of Tel Aviv, bears an ancient biblical name, which was preserved by the Arabs under the form Beit Dajan.

Beit Dagon was named for Dagon, the god of the Philistines. In their five main cities—Gaza, Ashdod, Gath, Ekron, and Ashkelon—temples were dedicated to him. It was to the house of Dagon in Ashdod that the Philistines brought the ark of the Lord after they captured it from the Israelites; and then woe befell the heathen god: "And when they arose early on the morrow morning, behold, Dagon was fallen upon his face to the ground before the ark of the Lord; and the head of Dagon and both the palms of his hands lay cut off upon the threshold; only the trunk of Dagon was left to him. Therefore neither the priests of Dagon, nor any that come into Dagon's house, tread on the threshold of Dagon in Ashdod unto this day."

It is generally accepted that the name Dagon is derived from the Hebrew *dagan*—corn—for Dagon was the god of the corn, but legend connects it to the Hebrew *dag*—

FIG. 82. THE GOD DAGON: MAN AND FISH (c. 870 B.C.E.)
Assyrian relief preserved in British Museum in London.

fish—and portrays Dagon as half man and half fish (fig. 82).[184]

7 / ZERIFIN'S OFFERING TO THE TEMPLE

In the vicinity of Ramla, in a fertile valley, there stood in ancient times the town of Zerifin—Cottages—also known as Gagot Zerifin—Roofs of Cottages.

In the olden days the corn of Gagot Zerifin was praised throughout the land, and it ripened earlier than the corn growing on the mountains of Jerusalem. It was the custom of Israel to bring the omer, a bundle of sheaves of the first corn, as an offering to the Temple, as the holy Law prescribed: "When ye are come into the land which I give you, and shall reap the harvest thereof, then ye shall bring the sheaf of the firstfruits of your harvest unto the priest. And he shall wave the sheaf before the Lord, to be accepted for you."

The sages of Israel say that the omer preferably was to be brought from the neighborhood of Jerusalem. When the corn around Jerusalem had not ripened, however, it was permitted to bring corn from other parts of the land.

Once the omer came from the village Gagot Zerifin and this is how it came about.

One year as the time for the offering of the omer approached and the corn of Jerusalem had not yet ripened, they did not know where to get the omer. The elders of the Temple, therefore, issued a proclamation: "The time of the omer is nigh; therefore let whatever place in Israel hath its corn ripe bring the omer to the Temple!"

A man who was dumb of speech came to the courtyard of the Temple and stood before the priests. He stretched forth one hand to the roofs (in Hebrew, *gagot*) and the other hand to some neighboring cottages (in Hebrew, *zerifin*).

The elders could not understand what the afflicted of God meant, until a servant of the Temple came forward and said: "Look where this dumb man points with his hands; he points to the roofs [*gagot*] and to the cottages [*zerifin*]. Is there a place in the land of Israel known as Gagot Zerifin or Zerifin Gagot?"

They searched and found that there was a place called Gagot Zerifin. Accordingly, in that year they went to this village and collected the omer for the Temple.*185

8 / HOW DID THEY BRING THE OMER?

"The land of Israel is holier than any other land; wherein lies its holiness?"—that from it they may bring the Omer.

"How was it made ready?—The messengers of the court used to go out on the eve of the festival day and tie the corn in bunches while it was yet unreaped to make it the easier to reap; and from the towns nearby all assembled there together that it might be reaped with much pomp.

"When it grew dark he called out:

"Is the sun set?—and they answered: Yea!

---

* See legend XXV:8.

"Is the sun set?—And they answered: Yea!

"Is this a sickle?—and they answered: Yea!

"Is this a sickle?—and they answered: Yea!

"Is this a basket?—and they answered: Yea!

"Is this a basket?—and they answered: Yea!

"On this Sabbath?—and they answered: Yea!

"On this Sabbath?—and they answered: Yea!

"Shall I reap?—and they answered: Reap!

"Shall I reap—and they answered: Reap! . . .

"They reaped it, put it into the baskets, and brought it to the Temple Court."

"The sheaves were winnowed, parched, and ground into coarse flour. It was then sifted and one-tenth was given to the priest who mixed it with oil and frankincense and waved it before the Lord. The ceremony was interpreted as a prayer to God to protect the harvest from injurious winds and other calamities.

"After the omer was offered the new corn was forthwith permitted."[186]

9 / THE LOT OF THE PEACHES OF DORON

In the beginning of the third century three Jewish scholars came to a place called Doron. They crossed an orchard and the land tenant offered them one big peach which filled up his hand. They ate from it, they gave some to their ass drivers, and still there was some left.

After awhile they happened that way again. And the same land tenant presented them again with peaches— two or three small ones in his outstretched palm. They told him: "We want peaches from the same tree from which you gave us once." He answered: "These are from the same tree!"

Then the scholars recalled the words of the psalmist: "A fruitful land into a salt waste,/For the wickedness of them that dwell therein."

According to one interpretation, Doron stood on the place of present-day Rehovot. This site was formerly called Deran by the Arabs, likely a corruption of the ancient name.[187]

10 / WHERE DID THE NAME ZARNUKA COME FROM?

Zarnuka is a suburb of Rehovot. On this site stood an ancient town mentioned once in the Talmud as the home of the learned Rabbi Hiyya bar Zarnuka.

Arab legend holds that previously this village had another name which no one now remembers. Once war broke out in the district between the Moslems and the unbelievers. One of the unbelievers slew the chief of the Moslems as he rode on a she-camel.

The camel which bore the body of the commander became frightened at the tumult of battle and fled wildly to the hills, so that none could catch it and take the body from its back.

At length the camel came to a certain village where it rested, and the inhabitants removed the body and buried it. Then the name of this village was changed and it was called Zarnuka, a contraction of the Arabic words *zur*—visit—and *naka*—she-camel. And the original name of the village has passed from the memory of men.[188]

XVII

IN THE LAND OF SAMSON

1 / THE INHERITANCE OF DAN

Dan, one of the smallest tribes of Israel, inherited part of the hilly country reaching down to the coastal plain in the surroundings of Jaffa and to the banks of the Yarkon River, which today streams through Tel Aviv: "The seventh lot came out for the tribe of the children of Dan according to their families." The Danites' border met the land of Judah at the foot of the mountains of Jerusalem.

When the patriarch Jacob bestowed his last blessing on his children, to Dan he said: "Dan shall judge his people,/ As one of the tribes of Israel./Dan shall be a serpent in the way,/A horned snake in the path." After that time the serpent was the emblem of Dan and the jacinth symbolized it on the breastplate of the high priest: "Dan was jacinth and the colour of his flag similar to sapphire, and embroidered on it was a serpent, in allusion to the text."

Jacob ended his blessing to Dan with the words: "I wait for Thy salvation, O Lord."

Why did Jacob expect Dan to bring salvation? Because the tribe of Dan was to give rise to Samson, who started to deliver Israel from Philistine bondage: "And he shall begin to save Israel out of the hand of the Philistines."[189]

2 / ZORAH—THE BIRTHPLACE OF SAMSON

Zorah, today a flourishing settlement at the foot of the Judean mountains, was one of the towns of Dan on the border of Judah. Here, in the time of the Judges, was born Samson, son of Manoah the Danite and Zelelponit, his Judean wife: "So Manoah took the kid with the meal-offering and offered it upon the rock unto the Lord, and [the angel] did wondrously, and Manoah and his wife looked on. For it came to pass, when the flame went up toward heaven from off the altar, that the angel of the Lord ascended in the flame of the altar; and Manoah and his wife looked on, and they fell on their faces to the ground. . . . And the woman bore a son, and called his name Samson."

The name Samson is clearly derived from the Hebrew *shemesh*—sun—and the sages say: "Samson is named after the Almighty, blessed be He, as it is said in the Book of Psalms: 'For the Lord God is a sun and a shield.'"

Near present-day Zorah, set in the valley on the slope of the mountain on which the biblical Zorah stood, a carved rock can be seen (fig. 83). In ancient times it served as an altar. The steps which led up to it are still visible, and on its leveled surface the marks of cups for the offerings are clearly noticeable. Today it is called *Mizbeah Manoah* —Altar of Manoah.[190]

3 / BETWEEN ZORAH AND ESHTAOL

About two miles from Zorah is the village of Eshtaol. The Book of Judges says of Samson: "And the spirit of the Lord began to move him . . . between Zorah and Eshtaol."

Legend adds: "When the divine Presence rested upon

FIG. 83. ALTAR OF MANOAH
This lies between villages of Zorah and Eshtaol.

Samson, each one of his steps covered the distance from
Zorah to Eshtaol, and his hair cracked with a loud sound
which was heard from one of these places to the other."

The Talmud expounds: "Zorah and Eshtaol were two
mountains and Samson uprooted them and ground them
one against the other."

South of Zorah and Eshtaol spreads the Valley of Sorek,
where Samson met Delilah, the Philistine: "And it came
to pass afterward, that he loved a woman in the valley of
Sorek, whose name was Delilah."

The sages derive the name Delilah from the Hebrew
daldel—to weaken—and they explain: "Delilah deserved
her name well. She reduced Samson's strength, enfeebled
his heart, and weakened his deeds."[191]

4 / SAMSON THE HERO IN RAMAT LEHI

The Book of Judges relates: "Then the Philistines went

up and pitched in Judah, and spread themselves against
Lehi. And the men of Judah said: 'Why are ye come up
against us?' And they said: 'To bind Samson are we come
up, to do him as he hath done to us.' . . .

"When he came unto Lehi, the Philistines shouted as
they met him, and the spirit of the Lord came mightily
upon him. . . . And he found a new jawbone of an ass, and
put forth his hand, and took it, and smote a thousand men
therewith. And Samson said: 'With the jawbone of an ass,
heaps upon heaps,/With the jawbone of an ass, have I
smitten a thousand men.' And it came to pass, when he
had made an end of speaking, that he cast away the jawbone out of his hand; and that place was called Ramat
Lehi—Height of the Jawbone."

In the days of King David, too, the Philistines invaded
Judah: "And the Philistines were gathered together into
a troop, where was a plot of ground full of lentils; and the
people fled from the Philistines."

But one of David's swordsmen smote them: "He stood
in the midst of the plot and defended it and slew the
Philistines; and the Lord wrought a great victory."

This story is repeated in the First Book of Chronicles:
"The Philistines were gathered together to battle, where
was a plot of ground full of barley," not lentils as written
in the Second Book of Samuel.

The legend explains this difference. The Philistines came
to the battle standing upright like the barley in the field
and went away depressed and low like the lentils on the
ground. Barley grows in height. Its stems stand straight
and its ears point up; while the lentil grows low, its stems
spread over the ground, and its fruit points down.

Such is the rule with men going to war. At first they
proceed erect, their heads held up proudly. But once
defeated on the battlefield, they escape full of shame, their
heads hanging down.[192]

FIG. 84. ROCK OF DESTRUCTION IN HILLS OF JUDEA

5 / SAMSON'S SPRING IN BEIT GUVRIN

When Samson armed with the jawbone of an ass had smitten the Philistines in Ramat Lehi: "And he was sore athirst, and called on the Lord and said: 'Thou hast given this great deliverance by the hand of Thy servant; and now shall I die for thirst, and fall into the hand of the uncircumcised?' But God cleaved the hollow place that is in Lehi, and there came water thereout."

In 570 Antoninus Martyr was reportedly shown the place of the water in Eleutheropolis (City of Freedom), the Roman name for ancient Jewish Beit Guvrin, at the foot of the mountains of Judea. "This spring," he wrote, "even up to the present day waters that region; for we went to the spot where it rises."[193]

6 / THE ROCK OF DESTRUCTION

On a stony height between Eshtaol and Zorah stands an upright rock which dominates the surroundings. It is known as the Rock of Destruction—*Sela-hahurban* (fig. 84). Why is it so named?

Legend has it that when the enemy went up to besiege Jerusalem, an order was sent by the leaders of the people to the men of Israel saying: "The hosts of our foes are around us; let every Jew and Jewess bring a large stone wherewith to fortify the city and the Temple, to make them impregnable."

In those days there lived in the village of Zorah a mighty man descended from Samson, and his spirit was wroth within him when he heard of the straits of his people and the city. He therefore tore a massive rock from the mountainside and, placing it upon his shoulder, turned his steps toward the Holy City. He was still on the mountain pathway when he beheld thick, heavy pillars of smoke rising above the hills in the east. Then he knew that the city had been taken and that the Temple of the Lord had been burned down. The spirit which had upheld him in his mighty strength forsook him, and bowing under the weight of his burden, he found his grave under it.

Since then the upright pillar has been called the Rock of Destruction, in memory of the destruction of Jerusalem and its Temple, may they be rebuilt soon, in our time.[194]

7 / THE ARK OF GOD IN BEIT SHEMESH

Beit Shemesh—House of the Sun—is a new town situated at the foot of the mountains of Jerusalem, next to the mound which covers the remains of biblical Beit Shemesh (Beth Shemesh). Here the Philistines sent back the ark of the Lord after it had wrought havoc in the temple of Dagon in Ashdod: "And the kine took the straight way by the way to Beth Shemesh; they went along the highway, lowing as they went, and turned not aside to the right hand or to the left; and the lords of the Philistines went after them unto the border of Beth Shemesh. . . . And the cart came into the field of Joshua the Beth-Shemite, and stood there, where there was a great stone; and they

FIG. 85. ARK OF GOD IN BEIT SHEMESH
Painting found on wall of third-century synagogue in Dura-
Europos, on Euphrates River, is now in archaeological museum in
Damascus, Syria.

cleaved the wood of the cart, and offered up the kine for
a burnt-offering unto the Lord. . . . And He smote the men
of Beth Shemesh, because they had gazed upon the ark
of the Lord, even He smote of the people seventy men,
and fifty thousand men; and the people mourned, because
the Lord had smitten the people with a great slaughter."
Why did the Lord smite the people of Beit Shemesh?
Because of the neglect they showed toward the ark. The
Almighty God said: If one of you had missed a hen, he
would have looked for it through many gates. And my
ark has been standing in the field of the Philistines these
seven months and you do not miss it. If you do not care
for it, I shall look after it.
The sages of Israel comment on the words of the Bible:

"And the kine took the straight way"—in Hebrew, *vayisharna*. They relate it to the word *shira*—song. One rabbi says: "The kine turned their heads to the ark and sang thus: 'Sing, O sing, acacia tree*/Ascend in all thy gracefulness/With golden weave they cover thee/The sanctuary-palace hears thy eulogy,/With diverse jewels art thou adorned.'"

Rabbi Shemuel son of Nahman expounded: "Moses, the man of God, had much labor, teaching the Levites the song of God, and you kine knew to sing it all by yourselves. May God sustain your strength!"†[195]

8 / THE BATTLEFIELD OF DAVID AND GOLIATH

The Vale of Elah stretches in the mountains of Judea between Beit Shemesh in the north and Beit Guvrin in the south. It is named after the numerous terebinth bushes, *elah* in Hebrew, which grow on the slopes of the mountains.

The valley starts from the heights of Bethlehem, the birthplace of King David, and winds downward between the hills through the land of the Philistines—Pleshet—to the Mediterranean Sea.

In the Vale of Elah, David the shepherd encountered Goliath the Philistine: "Now the Philistines gathered together their armies to battle.... And Saul and the men of Israel were gathered together, and pitched in the vale of Elah, and set the battle in array against the Philistines. And the Philistines stood on the mountain on the one side, and Israel stood on the mountain on the other side; and there was a valley between them."

David stepped out from the lines of the Israelites toward Goliath the giant:

* From the acacia tree (in Hebrew, *shitta*) which grows in the desert, the ark of the Lord was prepared, as told in the Book of Exodus: "And they [the Israelites] shall make an ark of acacia wood."

† See legend XVI:6.

FIG. 86. RUIN ON MOUND OF ANCIENT BEIT SHEMESH (1906)

"And he took his staff in his hand, and chose him five smooth stones out of the brook, and put them in the shepherd's bag which he had, even in his scrip; and his sling was in his hand; and he drew near to the Philistine. . . .

"And when the Philistine looked about, and saw David, he disdained him; for he was but a youth, and ruddy, and withal of a fair countenance. . . .

"And David put his hand in his bag, and took thence a stone, and slung it, and smote the Philistine in his forehead; and the stone sank into his forehead, and he fell upon his face to the earth."[196]

8 / GOLIATH'S BURIAL PLACE

Apparently the tomb of Goliath was at one time shown to the credulous pilgrims in the vicinity of his famous battlefield with David. Antoninus Martyr, the pious traveler of the year 570, is the only one to record this story.

According to his words, he saw this tomb in the mountains of Judea, on his way from Jerusalem to Eleutheropolis, the Beit Guvrin of today. "Goliath," he wrote, "lies there in the midst of the road, having above his head a great mass of wood, and upon it a heap of stones, insomuch that for twenty miles around you cannot find a stone which

זה גלית חפי.לשתי   ודוד הזורק לו
    וכלב ושליו סביבו '

FIG. 87. DAVID THE SHEPHERD AND GOLIATH THE PHILISTINE
Painting found in Hebrew manuscript from 1278. On left is written: "David throws a stone at him and his dog is near him." On
right: "That is Goliath the Philistine."

you can move: because this is the custom—everyone who
passes by there brings with him three stones and throws
them upon the tomb. So likewise did we."[197]

10 / THE CAVE OF ADULLAM—THE SHELTER OF DAVID

The Cave of Adullam is hidden among the mountains of
Judea, to the south of the Vale of Elah.* Within its depths

* Some of the medieval pilgrims called a large cave in the environs of
Bethlehem the Cave of Adullam and believed that David found refuge
there.

David sought shelter when he flew from the wrath of King Saul. "David therefore departed thence, and escaped to the cave of Adullam. . . . And every one that was in distress, and every one that was in debt, and every one that was discontented, gathered themselves unto him; and he became a captain over them; and there were with him about four hundred men."

In modern political history the expressions "the Cave of Adullam" (Cave, for short) and "Adullamites" were applied to any group of seceders from a party on some special subject; it was first used by John Bright in referring to seceders from the Liberal party in the U. S. in 1866.

The Book of Psalms reproduces the prayer which David entreatingly addressed to the Almighty while he was in the cave: "With my voice I cry unto the Lord;/ With my voice I make supplication unto the Lord."

And when he was saved, he exclaimed in thankfulness: "I will cry unto God, Most High;/Unto God that accomplisheth it for me."

The Aramaic translation adds: "I will pray to the God, most High, who ordered upon the spider to spin the web for me."[198]

11 / DAVID AND THE SPIDER'S WEB

When David was a young shepherd tending his flocks, he once watched a spider spinning its web, and he said: "Lord of the universe, what is the purpose of the things Thou hast created? What is the use of the spider which spins all the year round to no purpose or end?"

The Lord said: "David! You mock at My creatures now, but a time will come when you will have need of them and then you will see why they were created."

The time came when David fled before Saul and hid in a cave. The Lord then sent a spider, which spun a web across the entrance, closing it. When Saul saw the web

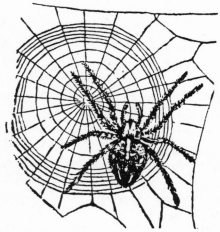

FIG. 88. SPIDER IN HIS WEB

he said: "He could not have gone in here, for he would have broken the web," and he passed by. When David came forth he kissed the spider, crying: "Blessed art thou and blessed is thy Maker! Thou alone hast saved my life."[199]

12 / THE CAVE OF THE MOTHER OF TWINS

In the Judean mountains, near Beit Shemesh, lies a large cavern hidden within a wild ravine. A small pool has been formed in its depths by the waters dripping from its roof and walls. The Arabs attribute many magic virtues to these waters, especially the ability to make a barren woman fecund.

It is told that a childless woman once bathed in these waters and brought forth twins; from that time on the cave was called the Cave of the Mother of Twins.

The Arabs believe that in this cave the evil spirits gather, and therefore no man dares to enter it after dark. Once the men of the neighboring village assembled in their guest house and bragged loudly of their brave deeds. One arose and asserted that only the man who dares enter the Cave of the Mother of Twins in the darkness of night deserves to be called brave.

At these words the young and adventurous Hamdan stood up, collected his strength, and declared: "Brothers, I shall enter the cave! But what shall be my reward?"

The chieftain of the village said: "My daughter I shall give thee for wife and no dowry shall I demand from thee. But what will be the proof that verily thou hast entered the cave to its very depths?"

A villager arose and suggested: "Here is a wedge. Let Hamdan strike this wedge into the cave. In the morning the elders of the village will enter it, and if they find the wedge inside the cave, they will know that Hamdan has been true to his word."

Hamdan took the wedge and turned his steps toward the Cave of the Mother of Twins. When he approached it, his heart beat fast in his breast, and the sound of the water dripping, the flutter of the wind, and the squeaking of the hovering bats seemed to him as many signs of the whirling and mischievous demons.

Controlling his fear, he strode forcibly forward into the cave and hastily struck the wedge into its floor.

But in his careless haste he did not notice that when he pushed the wedge home, he had caught in it the flap of his coat and stuck it fast to the ground. When he stood up to go, he found that he could not move—and immediately concluded that the devils had got hold of him and were dragging him to the abyss.

He fainted from fear and turned to stone on the spot.

If you enter the Cave of the Mother of Twins today you see in a dark, low corner a pillar in the shape of a man (fig. 89). It is said that this is Hamdan, who was turned into stone because he dared disturb the devils in their abode.*[200]

* When I neared the Cave of the Mother of Twins for the first time, an Arab shepherd told me with great wonder of its size: "Anyone who enters it young comes out old, because of the amount of time it takes him to cross its whole length."

FIG. 89. PILLAR IN CAVE OF MOTHER OF TWINS

13 / THE UPPER CHAMBERS OF THE MAIDENS

East of Beit Shemesh, in the cliffs which rise above a deep gorge, there is a large cave which bears traces of having once served as an abode for hermits. For sometime past it has been called Samson's Cave, for it was said that here the hero found shelter after he burned the cornfields of the Philistines.

Farther east, along the steep and rocky mount overlooking the Jerusalem–Lod railway, there is a row of several smaller cells which also appear to have been used as hermitages. They are known in Arabic as *Alali el-Benat*— Upper Chambers of the Maidens.

Local tradition holds that in bygone days these caves, too high up to be reached except by ropes, were full of beautiful maidens who, having vowed to remain virgins, had withdrawn there. The necessities of life were lowered to them daily from the top of the cliffs and their seclusion appeared to be of the strictest.

After some years, however, children were seen running from one cave to another, and it was found that the girls had lowered a rope into the valley and brought up a handsome hunter, whom they had espied from their aerie.

It is said that the incensed villagers starved them to death for their deceit.[201]

XVIII

YAVNEH—

THE SEAT OF WISDOM

Yavneh, today a townlet in the coastal plain, is located on the site of an important center of learning established after Jerusalem fell into the hands of the Romans.

Yavneh, Jamnia in Greek, was formerly the main town of the area known as the South, and headed the many surroundings villages, the hometowns of numerous famous scholars.

1 / YAVNEH—THE ABODE OF LEARNING

When Jerusalem was slowly being strangled by the Roman siege, there lived in the town Rabbi Yohanan ben Zakkai, the most important scholar of his time, whose teachings have molded Jewish thought and consciousness to this very day.

When it became clear that the physical power of the Jews would be shattered, Rabbi Yohanan made up his mind to save the spiritual strength of his people. To this end he left the doomed city and proceeded to the Roman camp.

When he was brought before Vespasian, the commander in chief, he hailed him with the words: "Peace be upon thee, great emperor!" Vespasian exclaimed angrily: "Thou deserveth death for calling me emperor when I am not."

The sage replied: "But thou must be, for if thou were not, God would not deliver Jerusalem into thine hands. For thus did Isaiah prophesy: 'Lebanon [a designation of the Holy Temple] shall fall by a mighty one.' "*

At this very moment a messenger brought the news of the Roman emperor's death and of Vespasian's election to the throne.

Considerably elated by the good tidings the new emperor turned to Rabbi Yohanan and said: "I see that thou art a prophet. Since thy words have been fulfilled, make a wish and it shall be granted."

Rabbi Yohanan asked for the town of Yavneh and its scholars, and it was accorded to him.

The town of Yavneh took the place of destroyed Jerusalem. It became the religious and national center of Israel, the abode of learning where the spirit of Judaism was nurtured for many generations.[202]

2 / THE VINEYARD OF YAVNEH

The Great Sanhedrin, the Supreme Court of Israel, was transferred from Jerusalem to Yavneh. Here several new schools of study were established, the cradle of many great scholars and sages who developed the mishnaic literature, a collection of legal traditions supplementing the Law of Israel.

The great school of Yavneh was known by the name *Kerem de-Yavneh*—Vineyard of Yavneh—because the scholars "sat there in rows like vines in a vineyard."

The expression is all the more appropriate since the vineyard is a symbol of Israel. The prophet Isaiah said:

---

* See *Legends of Jerusalem*, p. 109.

"For the vineyard of the Lord of hosts is the house of Israel."[203]

3 / THE CITY OF WISE MEN

One of the wise men of Yavneh related: "Once while wandering from place to place I met a Roman high official. He greeted me, although he knew me not; he asked me: 'Rabbi, from what place are thou?'

"I said: 'I am from the great city of Yavneh, the town of wise men and rabbis.'

"He said: 'Rabbi, come and settle in the place I will show thee, and I shall provide thee with wheat, barley, lentils, and all kinds of beans.'

"I answered: 'My son, if thou give me thousands of thousands of silver denarii, I shall not relinquish the Torah and set my home where the Torah is not found.'

"'And why is that so?' he wondered.

"I replied: 'Our world has been destroyed because we neglected the learning of the Torah and this is the source of all the hardships that have befallen Israel.' "[204]

4 / AN ECHO IN ANCIENT YAVNEH

Once great scholars were assembled in the school of Yavneh, when they heard an echo, saying: "There is one here who deserves that the divine Presence should rest upon him, but his generation is not worthy of it!"

And all eyes turned to Rabbi Shemuel Hakatan—Samuel the younger. And when he died the people mourned: "Woe to the humble! Woe to the pious!" And when they laid Rabbi Shemuel in his grave, they enclosed with him his key and his notebook, saying: "The loss of this man we must cry and mourn. When kings die, they leave their crowns to their children; when rich men die, they leave their wealth to their heirs; but Rabbi Shemuel Hakatan has taken all the beauties of the world with him!"

The key symbolized the entrance to the gate of paradise.

"God the Almighty," says a legend, "has many keys and among them the key to resurrection and the key to the Garden of Eden."[205]

5 / A SCHOLARS' DISPUTE IN YAVNEH

Once in Yavneh some Jewish scholars were arguing about the Law. A quarrel broke out between them with regard to a certain ruling (halakha). Rabbi Eliezer, who was in the right, rose and cried in anger: "You are wrong, the Law is as I say! Let this carob tree be my witness!" and the carob tree uprooted itself and was thrown one hundred ells away. Said his companions: "A tree is not a lawful witness!"

So Eliezer said: "The waters in the aqueduct will prove it!" And the waters of the aqueduct flowed backwards. But his companions again said: "Water is not a lawful witness."

Then the sage cried in yet greater wrath: "If the Law be as I say, let the walls of the house of study prove it!" And the walls trembled and the stones shifted their position as though ready to fall. Rabbi Joshua rebuked the walls, saying: "If scholars argue among themselves about the points of law, why do you presume yourselves entitled to interfere?"

So the walls did not fall apart out of respect to Rabbi Joshua but did not straighten themselves out of respect for Rabbi Eliezer, and they remain leaning to this day.

Rabbi Eliezer called out: "If the Law be as I say, let the heavens prove it!" And an echo from above was heard, saying: "Why do you argue with Rabbi Eliezer? His ruling is right always and in all places!"

Rabbi Joshua arose and countered: "The echo does not deserve our attention. The Torah which was given on Mount Sinai already ruled: 'The Law is according to the majority.'"

The Almighty God smiled in the heavens and said: "My children have had the better of me!"[206]

6 / THE MORAL OF THE YAVNEH RABBIS

"A favorite saying of the rabbis of Yavneh was: I am God's creature and my fellow [layman] is God's creature. 'My work is in the town and his work is in the country./ I rise early for my work and he rises early for his work./ Just as he does not presume to do my work, so I do not presume to do his work./Will you say, I do much and he does little?'

"We have learnt that one may do much or one may do little: it is all one, provided he directs his heart to heaven!"[207]

7 / JACOB'S SHIP IN YAVNEH YAM

Yavneh had its own harbor town on the Mediterranean: Yavneh Yam—Yavneh on the Sea. Today its ruins are buried under the sand dunes, but here and there remains of the past can still be recognized by the discerning eye.

Yavneh Yam gained repute at the time of the Maccabean revolt. Judah Maccabee set fire to Greek ships in the harbor, and the blaze could be seen as far as Jerusalem from the mountain heights.

Legend repeats the following fable allegedly told by Naphtali, one of Jacob's twelve sons: "After seven days I saw our father standing on the shore of Yavneh Yam, and we were with him. And behold, there came a ship sailing by, without sailors or pilot; and there was written upon it 'the ship of Jacob.'

"And our father said to us: 'Come, let us embark on our ship.' And when he had gone on board, there arose a vehement storm and a mighty tempest of wind; and our father, who was holding the helm, departed from us. And we, being tossed with the tempest, were borne along over the sea; and the ship was filled with water, and was pounded by mighty waves, until it was broken up. . . . And when the storm ceased, the ship reached the land as it were in peace."[208]

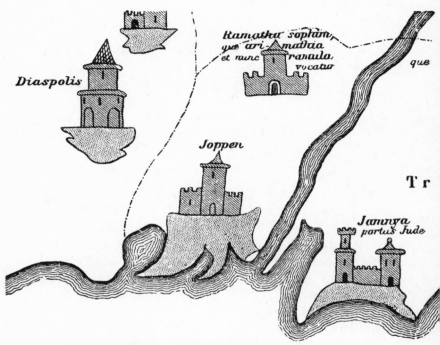

FIG. 90. YAVNEH YAM ON ANCIENT MAP (c. 1300)
Bottom left is "Joppen"—Jaffa. To right is "*Jamnya portus Jude*"— Yavneh, port of Jews. Above is "Diaspolis" (Diospolis)—Greek-Roman name for Lod (Lydda). Nearby is "Ramathu"—Ramla.

XIX
ASHKELON IN THE OLDEN DAYS

Ashkelon is a new city called by a very old name that is often mentioned in the Bible, but is of obscure origin. The ancient town, one of the main cities of the Philistines and the only one on the Mediterranean shore, was turned into a heap of ruins following the savage battles fought by Crusaders and Moslems in the Middle Ages (fig. 91).

The prophecies of Zephaniah—"Ashkelon a desolation" —and of Zechariah—"Ashkelon shall not be inhabited"— were fulfilled.

The town, neglected for many generations, has come to life again. Today it spreads around the old ruins, and the site of the ancient city and its remains have been turned into a national park.

1 / JEWS AND THEIR NEIGHBORS IN ASHKELON

Two rich brothers lived in Ashkelon. They had evil neighbors who used to say: "When these Jews go to Jerusalem to pray, we will enter their houses and take away their possessions."

There came a time when the brothers journeyed from Ashkelon to Jerusalem, and the Lord sent two angels in their image; in their absence the angels went to and from the houses.

When the brothers returned they sent to their neighbors gifts that they had brought with them from Jerusalem. The neighbors said: "Where have you been?" "To Jerusalem," they answered. "When did you go?" "The other day," answered the brothers. "When did you return?" "Yesterday." "Whom did you leave in your houses?" "No one."

The neighbors understood then that it was the hand of the Lord and exclaimed: "Blessed be the God of the Jews, who never deserts them, nor is deserted by them."[209]

2 / HONORING PARENTS IN ASHKELON

The sages ponder: "How far does the honor of parents extend?" And they answer: "Go forth and see what a certain heathen, Dama son of Netinah by name, did in Ashkelon."

Once the priests of the Temple sought to purchase precious stones for the ephod, the ceremonial breastplate worn by the high priest. They went to Dama son of Netinah in Ashkelon, and made an offer "at a profit of 600,000 [gold denarii]. Rabbi Kahana taught: At a profit of 800,000, but as the key was lying under his father's pillow, he did not trouble him." A different version says that Dama found his father asleep with his feet on the chest containing the merchandise.

Another story tells of the honor he extended to his mother: "[He] was once wearing a gold embroidered silken cloak and sitting among Roman nobles, when his mother came, tore it off from him, struck him on the head, spat in his face, yet he did not shame her."[210]

FIG. 91. RUINS OF ASHKELON (1818)

3 / THE PIOUS AND THE RICH OF ASHKELON

In Ashkelon there lived a pious man and a rich man. The pious man consecrated all his life to the study of the Torah, and the rich man was always busy collecting more wealth and feeding himself grossly to such an extent that he was nicknamed "The Bowels."

When the pious man died, no one took any notice. When the rich man died, all work stopped in the town and all went to his funeral.

A friend of the pious man was very wroth to see the honor which was given to the rich man as opposed to the neglect which was the share of the pious man in this world.

At night in a dream his dead friend appeared to him and appeased him as to his fate. When he himself died in turn, he met his friend in the next world, strolling peacefully amid cool and spacious gardens watered by flowing springs and fountains. And the rich man lay on the ground tortured with excruciating thirst—his tongue outstretched toward the waters which all his desperate efforts could not bring within his reach.[211]

4 / HOW WAS ASHKELON RID OF ITS WITCHES?

When Rabbi Shimon son of Shetah was appointed a prince in Israel, people came to him and said: "In the city of Ashkelon there is a certain cave inhabited by eighty witches."

One rainy day Rabbi Shimon gathered together eighty stalwart young men and gave each one a new case, a clean robe being folded in each. The young men accompanied Rabbi Shimon to Ashkelon, bearing the cases on their heads, so that their clothes would not be spoiled by the rain. Rabbi Shimon said to them: "I will enter the cave myself. If I whistle once, put on your robes; and if I whistle a second time, all of you together rush into the cave and each of you seize a witch and lift her up from the ground, for such is the nature of witches that if you raise them from the ground they lose all their power."

When Rabbi Shimon arrived at the entrance to the cave, he shouted: "Witches, witches, open for me, I am one of you!" They said to him: "How is it your clothes are so dry in this time of rain?" "I walked between the drops of rain!" he answered. And they asked again: "What have you come for?" He replied: "To learn and to teach. Let each one of you show me what you can do, and I will show you what I can do." One witch uttered an incantation and bread appeared. Another brought forth meat in a similar way; a third, dishes; and a fourth, wine. Then the witches said to him: "And now, what can you do?" To which he replied: "I can whistle twice and cause to appear eighty young men, clad in dry robes, who will make merry with you and you with them." He whistled once, and the boys donned their robes; he whistled a second time and they all rushed into the cave. Shimon said to them: "Let each one choose his partner!" And according to their in-

structions, each of the young men lifted up a witch and
so they carried them away to be hanged.

Thus was Ashkelon rid of its eighty witches.[212]

5 / ABRAHAM'S WELL IN ASHKELON

In the Middle Ages a well named for the patriarch
Abraham was shown in Ashkelon. The famous Jewish traveler Benjamin of Tudela, who visited Eretz Israel about
1173, mentioned it for the first time: "And there in the
town there is a well which is called the Well of Abraham.
He dug it at the time of the Philistines."

Legend holds that the waters of this well come from the
Pool of Siloam in Jerusalem.*

Rabbi Yaacob son of Nataniel, who was in Eretz Israel
in the twelfth century, related: "Once Christian priests
were bathing in the waters of Siloam. A bowl fell from the
hands of one of them. Later it was found in the well of
Abraham in Ashkelon and recognized through the engrav-
ings it bore."[213]

6 / WHERE WAS SEMIRAMIS BORN?

Beautiful Semiramis of Greek mythology was the daughter of Derketo, a goddess well beloved by the pagan inhabitants of ancient Ashkelon.

Derketo was represented in the shape of a fish, as Dagon
of the Philistines, the god of the inhabitants of Ashkelon
and its surroundings in times past, allegedly had been.

It is told that Derketo fell in love with a beautiful youth
who had come to worship at Aphrodite's temple. She gave
birth to a girl whom she called Semiramis and forthwith
threw herself into a pool in Ashkelon, where she was transformed into a fish.

Her daughter was cared for by doves. She grew up to

---

* See *Legends of Jerusalem*, p. 277.

become a famous princess in the land of Assyria. At her death she was transformed into a dove. Therefore fish and doves were venerated by the inhabitants of Ashkelon.

Some ancient coins from that city carry the image of a dove, and the head of a dove made of marble was found among the ruins of the town.

In his *Metamorphoses* Ovid, the Roman poet of the first century, told the story of Derketo and concluded: "According to the faith of the people who live in Palestine, she was transformed into a fish covered with scales, and swimming in a pool . . . and her daughter became a dove, white and pure."[214]

7 / THE MIRACULOUS PILLAR OF ASHKELON

Numerous beautiful pillars of marble are scattered to this day among the ruins of Ashkelon, the remains of the splendid palaces which adorned the town in ancient days. At various periods many of them were carried away to decorate new buildings in various places of the Holy Land.

The famous Moslem traveler of the Middle Ages Ibn Battuta, who visited Palestine in 1326, described the ruins of Ashkelon (in Arabic, Askalan) and its numerous marble columns: "Among them is a red pillar. The Christians took it on a boat away to their country. On the way the pillar disappeared and afterwards it was found again at its former place in Ashkelon!"[215]

8 / THE TREASURE OF ASHKELON

It was a widespread belief among the native peasants that amid the ruins which dot the landscape of the Holy Land great treasures of the former inhabitants are buried. They looked with suspicion at the foreign archaeological expeditions which came to excavate the historical sites. It was whispered that the excavators' true intention was to uncover these treasures. But in order to keep their purpose secret, before they started to dig they uttered a special magic prayer, which turned all the treasures buried in the ruins into pieces of clay and pottery. They carried these away to their own countries, where another incantation turned the sherds back into precious gold and silver.

In the beginning of the nineteenth century, Lady Hester Lucy Stanhope, the daughter of the third earl of Stanhope, went to the East. Her bounties had attached to her the bedouin Arabs; and it is said that they wished to proclaim her queen and do homage to her as such. A ceremony which bore a strong resemblance to the coronation of the sovereign Queen of the Desert was prepared for her at Tadmor, the ancient Palmyra, when she went to visit its ruins.

When Lady Stanhope lived on Mount Lebanon, a manuscript was put into her hands. It disclosed the repositories of immense hoards of money buried in certain spots in the city of Ashkelon.

After having formed an agreement with the central Turkish government, to whom a part of this money was promised, Lady Stanhope decided to proceed to the ruins of Ashkelon.

With the governor of Jaffa and other notables of the country, she arrived at Ashkelon and started to excavate, employing in her service more than 150 peasants. Lady Stanhope's medical attendant, Dr. Lewis Meryon, who accompanied her in her travels, wrote: "The men worked with great animation. The idea of discovering immense heaps of gold seemed to have an effect upon them, although they could not hope for a share in it. . . . On the fifth day the outline of the foundation of the entire building was made out. . . . On the outside of the west foundation three subterraneous places were opened, which at first, it was thought, would lead to the object we were in

FIG. 92. ROMAN STATUE FROM ASHKELON (1815)
Drawing of statue found by Lady Hester Stanhope.

search of. But they proved to be cisterns and reservoirs for rain water. . . .

"Signor Antonio Damiani [an English agent at Jaffa] affected an air of mystery in everything, and soberly advised her ladyship, if she wished to succeed, to sacrifice a cock of a particular colour, and at a particular hour of the day, to ensure success. . . .

"Digging in the line of the west wall . . . about four feet under the surface, they found four gray granite columns, closely packed to each other, as if done methodically. This discovery revived the people's hopes; for it was supposed that huge masses of granite could not have fallen in such a position accidentally, and would not be laboriously placed so, unless to conceal something. . . . They found also a statue of marble [fig. 92]. . . . Reports were circulated that the chest of the statue was found full of gold, half of which was given to the Pasha and the other half kept by Lady Hester. . . .

"But, when every research was fruitless, after a fortnight from the commencement, Lady Hester came to the conclusion that Jazzar Pasha, the governor of the city of Acre, by digging for marble and other materials in the ruins of Ascalon, had been fortunate enough to discover the treasure."

Here is Lady Hester's own account of these excavations, which she sent to Lord Bathurst, then secretary of state:

"My Lord,

"A curious document, once in the hands of the Church, fell by accident into mine. It was an indication to considerable treasure in Syria. . . . I proceeded . . . to Ascalon . . . and after digging for several days . . . we came to the under-ground fabric we were looking for: but, alas! It had been rifled. It was, as nearly as one could calculate, capable of containing three millions of pieces of gold—the sum mentioned in the document. . . . We found a superb colossal Statue without a head. . . . Knowing how much it would be praised by English travellers, I ordered it to be broken into a thousand pieces that malicious people might not say I came to look for statues for my countrymen and not for treasures for the Turkish Port.

"This business has taken up a good deal of my time for these three months past. . . . The authenticity of the paper I do not doubt, but, as many centuries have elapsed since the Christians hid treasure there, it is not very surprising that it should have been removed. . . .

"I have the honour, etc.

"H. L. Stanhope"[216]

9 / WHERE DOES THE SHALLOT ORIGINATE?

The shallot is an excellent species of onion which was grown in the fertile gardens of Ashkelon.

Pliny, the Roman historian of the first century, mentioned the tasty Ashkelonian onion. The Talmud tells of a woman who lived in Ashkelon and was named Miriam, Bat Alei Bezalim—Daughter of Onion Leaves.

The Ashkelon onion was much appreciated by the crusaders, who spread its use in the European countries, where it was called by the name of its place of origin corrupted in various ways. The Spanish called it *escaluna*, the Italians *scalogno*, the French *échalotte*, the Germans *Schalotten*, the English shallot or Ascalonian garlic. In botany it is known as *Allium ascalonicum* or *Porrum ascalonicum*.[217]

10 / THE VALE OF THE ANTS

The First Book of Kings says: "And God gave Solomon wisdom and understanding exceeding much. . . . He spoke also of beasts . . . and of creeping things." Legend adds that the learned king also understood the language of all creatures.

"Once King Solomon crossed a small vale where ants were busy; and he heard the voice of a black ant hurrying the others, saying: 'O ants, enter ye into your habitations, lest Solomon and his armies tread you under foot.'

"Solomon sent after the ants and said: 'Which one of you didst say: "Enter ye into your habitations, lest Solomon and his armies tread you under foot?"'

"The same black ant said: 'I did.'

"He asked her: 'Of all the ants, why wert thou the one to talk?' She said: 'I am the Queen!' 'What is thy name?' 'Akhsanna.'

"He said: 'I wish to ask thee one question.' She said:

'It is not proper that the one who questions should be sitting while the one who is questioned is on the ground. Lift me onto thy hand, and I shall answer thee.'

"He lifted her onto his hand. She looked into his face and said: 'Ask.'

"He said: 'Is there in the world one more powerful than myself?' She said: 'Yes.' 'Who?' he asked; she said: 'I!' He said: 'And how dost thou reckon thyself more powerful than me?' She said: 'If I were not more powerful than thee, the Almighty, blessed be He, would not have sent thee here to carry me up on the palm of thine hand!'

"When King Solomon heard these words, his heart filled with anger, and he threw her on the ground, saying: 'Ant, dost thou not know who I am? I am Solomon the son of David the king, peace be on his soul!' "

The Koran has a similar story in the chapter "*En-Namel* —the Ants": ". . . until when [Solomon and his men] came to the Valley of Ants. An ant said: 'O ants, enter your houses lest [Solomon] and his hosts crush you while they know not.' So he smiled, wondering at her words, and said: 'My Lord, grant me that I may be grateful for Thy favor.' "

The legend does not locate the site where this encounter took place, neither does the Koran, where this tale first appears. But Moslem folklore of the Middle Ages situates the Vale of the Ants next to Ashkelon. And to this day the Arabs of the vicinity know the place and tell this story.[218]

XX
TALES
OF THE SOUTH

1 / WISDOM IN THE SOUTH

In olden times the inhabitants of the South were noted for their wisdom, as those of north Galilee were for their wealth.

Therefore the sages used to say: "For wealth to the North you must go,/But wisdom in the South you find;/Choose South, for wisdom you know/Will bring wealth, and so peace of mind."

In the Temple the table with the shewbread faced the north and the candlestick was directed toward the south, because the first is suggestive of wealth while the second, light, is a symbol of wisdom.[219]

2 / THE FLOWERY LANGUAGE OF THE JUDEANS

The Judeans were renowned for their precise and florid language. For instance, a Judean once announced that he had a cloak to sell.

"What," he was asked, "is the color of your cloak?" "Like that of spinach on the ground," he replied.[220]

3 / THE HERMIT FROM THE SOUTH

The sages of Israel relate that the people of the South are tender of heart and obedient to the words of the holy Law.

Shimon the high priest related the following. "Once a hermit came to me from the South. I saw that his eyes were beautiful and his appearance handsome, but his hair hung in long curls, untended.

"I said to him: 'Why do you neglect yourself and do not tend your beautiful body?' He answered: 'I was a shepherd to my father in my city. Once I went to fetch water from a spring and saw my image on the surface of the water. Mad impulses stirred within me and I was nearly overcome. . . . It was then that I decided to become a hermit and to devote myself to God.' "[221]

4 / THE INNKEEPER OF THE SOUTH

In the settlements of the South, especially in those which flanked the roads, there were inns to serve travelers.

Once there was a certain innkeeper in the South who at night would dress and say to all his guests: "Time to go —a caravan is passing."

And they would go out, and highwaymen would overpower them, rob them, and go back to share the loot with the innkeeper.

Once Rabbi Meir was a guest there. The innkeeper, as usual, dressed and said: "Time to go—a caravan is passing." "I have a brother for whom I am waiting," said Rabbi Meir. "Tell me his name," said the innkeeper, "and I will go call him." "His name is Ki-Tov," answered Rabbi Meir.

All that night the innkeeper called at the gate of the synagogue: "Ki-Tov, Ki-Tov"; but no one answered him. In the morning at sunrise Rabbi Meir arose, placed his baggage on his donkey, and prepared to go.

"But where is your brother?" asked the innkeeper. "Here he is," was the answer. "And God saw the light and it was good"—in Hebrew, *ki-tov.*[222]

5 / THE SYCAMORES IN THE LOWLAND

The Shephela—the Lowland—is the southern section of the coastal plain, stretching toward the approaches of the Negeb and the Sinai Desert. Many of the famous cities of the Holy Land were built in the Shephela. Today new Israeli towns established in this vicinity have redeemed the ancient names.

The sycamore (in Hebrew, *shikma*) is the typical tree of the Lowland (fig. 93). It is a member of the fig family, unrelated to the plane tree which is commonly called a sycamore in the United States. In the olden days it was found in great numbers on the hills and along the brooks which drain the area.

It is told that King David appointed a special man to be in charge of the sycamores of the Shephela: ". . . and over . . . and the sycamore trees that were in the Lowland was Baal Hanan."

The profusion of sycamores in the Shephela became a symbol of plenty: "And the king [Solomon] made silver to be in Jerusalem as stones, and cedars made he to be as the sycamore trees that are in the Lowland, for abundance."

The sages list every section of the land of Israel according to its characteristic vegetation and they say: "An indication of lowland is the sycamore tree."

The sycamore grows wild and gives a generous yield of fruit, but of low quality and little taste. Only the poorest collect it. When the prophet Amos wished to stress his humble origin he said: "I was no prophet, neither was I a prophet's son; but I was a herdman, and a dresser of sycamore trees."

FIG. 93. SYCAMORE TREE IN LOWLAND

In ancient Hebrew the expression *"gerofit shel shikma —branch of a sycamore"* came to designate an ordinary uncultured person.[223]

6 / HOW DID THEY BORDER THEIR FIELDS?

The sea onion—in botany, *Urginea maritima*—is a wild scilla commonly found both in plains and on mountainsides (fig. 94). In the spring its cluster of pointed leaves grows erect from a large bulb deeply buried in the soil, and in autumn its tall stem carries a sheaf of tiny blooms.

Its Hebrew name is *hazuva* or *hazav*, and thus also is designated a new settlement in the South, where the sea onion grows profusely.

From ancient times it was customary to mark the borders of fields with a row of sea onions, and until recently rows of this plant could be observed along the sides of land plots, mainly in the South.

Legend says that when Joshua divided the land of

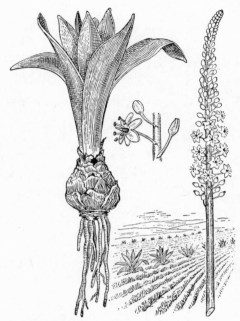

FIG. 94. SEA ONION—URGINEA MARITIMA

Israel between the tribes he indicated their borders by
growths of sea onions. "It was asked: What is *hazuva*?—
the plant with which Joshua marked the boundaries of
the tribes in the land."

The sea onion grows deep, straight roots into the soil.
If an evil man wishes to enlarge his plot at the expense of
his neighbor, he goes out at night, uproots the sea onions,
and replants them farther away. In the morning when the
wronged man notices this, he can prove it easily, for the
wicked man never succeeds in taking out all the roots of
the plants to their very tips, and his bad deed is soon
exposed.

Thus it was said: "The sea onion cuts off the feet of the
criminals."

Legend adds: "In this world borders are marked with
stones and sea onions, but in the world to come they will
be made out of precious stones and pearls."[224]

XXI
CITIES
IN THE SOUTH

1 / BEROR HAIL—THE HOME OF RABBI YOHANAN

Beror Hail, a Jewish village mentioned in talmudic literature, was situated in the South. The origin of the name is unknown.

Beror Hail gained renown as the home of Yohanan ben Zakkai, one of the greatest sages of Israel who lived at the end of the first century.

"Our Rabbis taught: [When the Torah says] justice, justice shalt thou follow; this means: Follow the scholars to their academies . . . , Rabbi Yohanan ben Zakkai to Beror Hail."

The sages recount that when Rabbi Yehoshua went to meet Rabbi Yohanan in Beror Hail, the inhabitants of the surrounding villages welcomed him all along the way with baskets of freshly picked figs.[225]

2 / BEROR HAIL AND BURNI

In the olden days Beror Hail and its neighbor Burni, like other villages throughout the country, suffered from persecution at the hands of the foreign rulers.

The inhabitants were forbidden to perform circumcision

and to hold the wedding ceremony prescribed by the
Jewish faith. They were compelled to carry them out in
secret, and they informed the community of the celebra-
tions by special signs. To this end they made use of Jeremiah's saying: "The voice of mirth and the voice of
gladness, the voice of the bridegroom and voice of the
bride, the sound of the millstones, and the light of the
lamp."

The sound of the millstone meant a circumcision, or,
as they said cryptically, the week of a son. The light of the
lamp in daytime indicated a feast held at the occasion of
a wedding. As it was said: "The noise of grindstones at
Burni [announced that] a circumcision [was being per-
formed], and the light of a candle [by day] at Beror Hail,
showed that a feast [was being celebrated] there."

Probably Burni was located on the site of the ruin called
Burnet in Arabic, next to the kibbutz Galon of today; Beror
Hail was near the new settlement of the same name situ-
ated on the highway to Gaza.

Or Haner—the Light of the Candle—a village next to
Beror Hail, symbolizes Jewish determination to fulfill the
commandments of the Law at all costs.[226]

3 / BEIT GUVRIN IN THE END OF TIME

The land of Edom or Seir, a part of the southern section
of Jordan, is often mentioned in the Bible. Its inhabitants
were descendants of Esau, son of the patriarch Isaac, and
among them lived the Horites: ". . . and the Horites in
their Mount Seir."

In the postbiblical period many of the Horites and the
Edomites migrated to southern Judah and reached the
surroundings of Beit Guvrin, known in Greek-Roman literature as Eleutheropolis.

Our sages expound: "And the Horites in their mount
Seir—that is Eleutheropolis." And they go on: "When Isaac

blessed his son Esau and promised him: 'Behold, of the fat places of the earth shall be thy dwelling,/And of the dew of heaven from above'—that is Beit Guvrin."

"Again, when Jacob says: 'Until I come into my lord unto Seir'—this too indicates Beit Guvrin."

According to legend, Beit Guvrin will be the last town to fall into the hands of the Messiah, and with its liberation "his kingdom will be complete."[227]

4 / VILLAGES IN THE KING'S MOUNTAIN

The King's Mountain, in Hebrew *Har Hamalekh*, was a section of the southern mountains of Judea. It was named after King Alexander Jannaeus (Yannai), one of the main rulers of the Hasmonean dynasty.

The sages report with obvious exaggeration: "King Yannai had sixty myriads of cities in the King's Mountain and in each of them was a population as large as that of the exodus,* save in three of them, which had double as many. These were Kefar Bish, Kefar Shikhlayim, and Kefar Dikraya.

"Kefar Bish, Evil Village—because they never gave hospitality to visitors.

"Kefar Shikhlayim, Cress Village—because they made their living from watercress.

"Kefar Dikraya, Males' Village—because women used to bear males first and finally a girl and then no more."[228]

5 / THE DESTRUCTION OF THE KING'S MOUNTAIN

"Because of a cock and a hen,
the King's Mountain was destroyed."

There was a custom in that place of carrying a cock and a hen before a bridal procession as a symbol of the

---

* According to the Bible, the Israelites who took part in the exodus numbered "six hundred thousand and three thousand and five hundred and fifty."

commandment of the Lord: "Be fruitful and multiply."

One day some Roman soldiers took away the cock and the hen, whereupon they were attacked by the Jews. The soldiers charged the Jews with rebellion against the Roman emperor, who came at once with a large army to subdue them. There was one among the Jews named Bar-Deroma (the Son of the South), who was very nimble and strong withal; he sprang upwards of a mile at a bound and slew several thousands of the Romans. The emperor then took off his crown, placed it upon the ground, and said: "Lord of the universe! May it please Thee not to deliver me into the hands of this man or my empire into the hands of one individual!"

Bar-Dorema was then killed by a serpent. When the emperor heard of his death and the extraordinary manner in which it occurred, he said: "Since such a great miracle has been wrought on my behalf I will spare the city this time." And he at once began to withdraw his army. The Jews began to dance and make merry in the evening, and the city was so brightly illuminated that one could read the engraving of a seal at the distance of a mile. The emperor, thinking that the Jews were doing this to mock him, suddenly returned and assaulted the city.

Three hundred thousand swordsmen went up to the King's Mountain and there slaughtered the people for three days and three nights, and yet while on the one side of the mount they were mourning, on the other they were merry; those on the one side did not know the affairs of those on the other.[229]

6 / WHY WAS IT CALLED GAZA?

The town of Gaza, located on the southern seacoast, is one of the oldest cities in the world. It appears in ancient Egyptian hieroglyphic records prior to the Israelite conquest of the promised land. The Bible often mentions it as one of the major Philistine cities.

FIG. 95. GAZA (1863)

Gaza was an important station on the Way of the Sea,
the lifeline of the Fertile Crescent, the link between the
great powers of the ancient Middle East: Egypt and
Assyria.

From the dawn of civilization down to the present many
decisive battles which shook the world and molded its
history have been waged here.

The origin of the name Gaza (in Hebrew, Aza) is unknown. Some say it derives from the Hebrew *az*, meaning
"strong," because whoever held Gaza never failed to fortify
it considerably against enemy incursions.

In early times Greek merchants settled in the town and
altered its name to Gaza, meaning "treasure" in their language.* They told that when the town was built, great
treasures belonging to primeval man were found buried
in its soil.

Another Greek legend connects the name Aza with
Azon son of Hercules, who allegedly established the
town.[230]

* The word *gaza* in the sense of treasure was also adopted by the Talmud.

FIG. 96. GAZA (1598)
From Hebrew manuscript. Above is written: "The village of Gaza is the town of Samson, a beautiful city."

7 / SAMSON AND THE GATES OF GAZA

It came to pass that Samson the hero came to Gaza and spent the night there, as it is related: "And Samson lay till midnight and arose at midnight and laid hold of the doors of the gate of city and the two posts, and plucked them up bar and all; and put them upon his shoulders and carried them up to the top of the mountain that is before Hebron."

The sages elaborate: "Between the shoulders of Samson was a distance of sixty ells. . . . It proves that the doors of Gaza were less than sixty ells wide."[231]

8 / THE FATE OF SAMSON IN GAZA

The Philistines caught Samson, brought him to Gaza, tortured him, and gouged out his eyes. And then they assembled to sacrifice to their god Dagon. "And it came to pass, when their hearts were merry, that they said: 'Call for Samson, that he may make us sport.' . . .

FIG. 97. SAMSON CARRYING PORTALS OF GAZA
This twelfth-century mosaic is from floor of church in Cologne, West
Germany.

"Now the house was full of men and women, and all
the lords of the Philistines were there; and there were upon
the roof about three thousand men and women, that beheld while Samson made sport. And Samson called unto
the Lord, and said: 'O Lord God, remember me, I pray
Thee, and strengthen me.' . . .

"And Samson took fast hold of the two middle pillars
upon which the house rested, and leaned upon them, the
one with his right hand, and the other with his left. And
Samson said: 'Let me die with the Philistines.' And he
bent with all his might; and the house fell upon the lords,
and upon all the people that were therein."

In the Middle Ages, the ruins of the edifice which Samson the hero destroyed were shown in Gaza. Some of the
pilgrims mentioned it. A Jewish traveler who visited Gaza
in 1481 told about the Jewish quarter of this town and "the

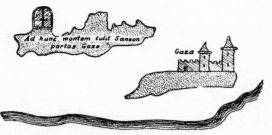

FIG. 98. GAZA AND VICINITY (C. 1300)
From Latin map of Holy Land preserved in Florence, Italy. Right: Gaza. Left: mountain with portals of Gaza carried to this spot by Samson: *"Ad hunc montem tulit Sanson partas Gaze."*

house of Delilah, where Samson the hero lived. And next to it, at a distance of about an eighth of a mile, on the top of a hill, I saw the courtyard where stood the big building which he felled in his vigor and vehemence. And the houses around are destroyed and desolate, but according to what one sees to this day the courtyard must have been then a really big thing."[232]

9 / WHAT IS THE ORIGIN OF GAUZE?

Gauze, the very thin transparent stuff made of cotton or linen and used since antiquity, was originally brought to Europe from Gaza. In Latin it was called *gazzatum*, and it is generally agreed that this name is derived from that of the city.*[233]

10 / WHAT IS METHEG AMMAH?

The Philistines were at all times King David's bitterest enemies: "It came to pass, that David smote the Philistines, and subdued them; and David took Metheg Ammah out of the hand of the Philistines."

Apparently Metheg Ammah is a place-name, and one commentator, assuming that *ammah* means "channel," offered the following explanation of the name: "The water channel passed through the town and it was built to lead the water from outside the town into its precincts."

* Similarly, muslin (in French, *mousseline*; in Italian, *misolino*) was named after the town of Mosul, today in Iraq.

Legend has a different interpretation. It says that *metheg* is a bridle and *ammah* an ell, and goes on to say that Abimelech, king of the Philistines, met the patriarch Isaac and said: "We have indeed seen that God is with thee. We know indeed that God Almighty has determined to give all these lands to thee and thy seed; make with us a covenant that thou will not inherit the land of the Philistines."

What did Isaac do? He took an ell out of the bridle of the ass he was riding and gave it to Abimelech as a testimony of the oath they had both taken.

When King David wished to invade the land of the Philistines, he first took out from their hand the "ell of the bridle—*metheg ammah*" to free himself from the oath. Only then could he prevail upon them.[234]

11 / ZENAN—HADASHAH—MIGDAL GAD

In the portion of Judah were the towns "Zenan and Hadashah and Migdal Gad," as mentioned in the description of his inheritance.

Zenan is the same as Zaanan which Micah mentions: "The inhabitant of Zaanan is not come forth." The name is derived from the Hebrew *zon*, which means "flock," as this vicinity was pasture for herds of sheep and goats. It was most likely situated not far from the present settlement of Negba, on the site of the village called in Arabic Irak es-Suidan.

Hadashah, which means "new" in Hebrew, was situated where the village of Hatta lies, eastward from Irak es-Suidan.

Migdal Gad—the Tower of Gad—was named after the god of fortune of the Semites. The prophet Isaiah recalls it: "But ye that forsake the Lord,/That forget My holy mountain,/That prepare a table for Fortune [Gad]."

The legend elaborates on the names of these towns:

Zenan from *Zinah*, shield—God is its shield.

Hadashah, the new—God will restore it in the end of time.

Migdal Gad—here God will cut out [in Hebrew, *gadad*] the foundations of the idolatrous nations.[235]

12 / KABZEEL—EDER—YAGUR

Other towns of the inheritance of Judah were "Kabzeel and Eder and Yagur."

The name Kabzeel is probably composed of the two Hebrew words, *kabez*—gather—and *El*—God, for it was a place where shepherds gathered their flocks.

Kabzeel probably stood on the site of the ruins of Kaseifa at the southern end of Judah. It was the home of one of the great heroes of King David: "And Benaiah the son of Jehoiada, the son of a valiant man of Kabzeel, who had done mighty deeds."

The expression "a man of mighty deeds of Kabzeel" was adopted by the rabbinical literature. And when a rabbi from a small place wanted to draw attention on his many social and literary achievements, at the same time depreciating them, he added to his name "the one of the mighty deeds from Kabzeel," pretending a semblance of humility. Kabzeel is derived from the Hebrew *kabzan*, meaning "poor man."

The town of Eder stood in the neighborhood of Gaza, on the site of the ruined el-Ader, which has clearly preserved the ancient name.

Yagur likely stood on the site of the village Agur, formerly Ajur, on the border of the Judean mountains. The name Yagur derives from the Hebrew *gur*—dwelling.

And thus the sages of Israel comment on these three names: "Whoever gathers [*kabez*] his flock [*eder*] to the study of the Torah shall dwell [*yagur*] in the portion of God [*El*]," that is, in the Garden of Eden.[236]

XXII
BEERSHEBA
AND ITS VICINITY

1 / WHY WAS IT CALLED BEERSHEBA?

Beersheba has been the capital of the Negev since the most ancient times. The Hebrew name Beersheba is explained in two ways: Well of Seven and Well of Oath. It is written: "And it came to pass at that time, that Abimelech . . . spoke unto Abraham, saying: 'God is with thee in all that thou doest. Now therefore swear unto me here by God that thou wilt not deal falsely with me.' . . . And Abraham said: 'I will swear.' And Abraham took sheep and oxen, and gave them unto Abimelech; and they two made a covenant. And Abraham set seven ewe lambs of the flock by themselves. And Abimelech said unto Abraham: 'What mean these seven ewe lambs which thou hast set by themselves?' And he said: 'Verily, these seven ewe lambs shalt thou take of my hand, that it may be a witness unto me, that I have digged this well.' Wherefore that place was called Beersheba, because there they swore both of them."

Isaac, the son of Abraham, also made a covenant with Abimelech at this place: "And he made them a feast, and they did eat and drink. And they rose up betimes in the morning, and swore one to another. . . . And it came to pass the same day, that Isaac's servants came, and told him concerning the well which they had digged, and said unto him: 'We have found water.' And he called it Shibah. Therefore the name of the city is Beersheba unto this day."

The Aramaic translation of the Torah explains that the name Beersheba, meaning "the Well of Seven," refers to the seven ewe lambs.[237]

2 / ABRAHAM'S TAMARISK IN BEERSHEBA

Our father Abraham, while wandering in the Negev, came to Beersheba. "And Abraham planted a tamarisk tree in Beersheba and called there on the name of the Lord, the Everlasting God."

The sages of Israel add: "When God gave the land to Abraham our father, He gave it to him such as it was . . . and Abraham improved it, as it is written: 'And Abraham planted.' "

The tamarisk is a common tree in the Negeb. Its planting indicates a new period in the life of man in the Negev, the transition from nomadic to settled life, from shepherd to peasant. Today shady tamarisk trees grow beside the small hamlets of the bedouins who settled in the Negev.

The tamarisk tree is the symbol of hospitality in Jewish tradition. Its Hebrew name is *eshel*. Some find in this name the initials of the three Hebrew words:

E, for *akhila*—food*

Sh, for *shetiya*—drink

L, for *lina*—sleep.

Because the tamarisk tree stands out conspicuously in the flat Negev, it became symbolic of a man outstanding in his community. In the olden days the Aramaic expression

---

* In Hebrew both *eshel* and *akhila* start with the letter alef. The difference lies in the vowel, which appears as a sign below the alef.

FIG. 99. ANCIENT WELL AND BEDOUIN TENT OF BEERSHEBA
This ancient well, extant in Beersheba to this day, is named after
Abraham. Stones at mouth are deeply grooved from centuries of
rubbing by ropes of those who come to draw water.

was born: *"talya be-eshel ravravei*—to hang on to a big
tamarisk tree"—meaning to support one's words or one's
deeds upon the words or deeds of a great and famous man.

In the late medieval Hebrew literature, the title Ha-
Eshel ha-Gadol—the Great Tamarisk Tree—is used in a
complimentary way to designate learned and renowned
rabbis.[238]

3 / ABRAHAM'S CEDARS IN BEERSHEBA

The Bible calls the patriarch Jacob by the name Israel:
"Thy name shall be called no more Jacob, but Israel
[shall be thy name]," and it adds: "And Israel took his
journey with all that he had, and came to Beersheba."
What was the purpose of this journey? Legend says: "He
went to cut down the cedars which his grandfather Abraham had planted in Beersheba."[239]

4 / THE HOSPITALITY OF ABRAHAM IN BEERSHEBA

The sages of Israel comment on the tamarisk tree which Abraham the patriarch planted in Beersheba. They say that Abraham planted an orchard with trees bearing the most tasty fruits. In the middle he put an inn stocked with food and drink, and opened four gates to the four corners of the world. And he received wayfarers and invited them into his house.

Why did Abraham open a gate on every side? So as not to trouble the visitor by making him walk around the walls.

After they had eaten and drunk to their satisfaction, the guests arose to thank Abraham and bless his name. And he said to them: "Verily, you did not eat from mine, but from the God of the universe." When they heard these words, they asked: "And how shall we bless Him?" He said to them: "Say: 'Blessed be the God of the world, from whose food we ate. Blessed be the One who provides bread to all flesh.' "[240]

5 / THE FEAST OF SUKKOTH IN BEERSHEBA

Tradition holds that Abraham celebrated the first Sukkoth (Feast of Tabernacles) in Beersheba, and he built here an altar to the Lord who had delivered him, and who was making him rejoice in the land of his sojourning: "And he celebrated a festival of joy in this month seven days, near the altar which he had built at Beersheba. And he built booths for himself and for his servants on his festival and he was the first to celebrate the Feast of Tabernacles on the earth."[241]

6 / SAMUEL'S SONS IN BEERSHEBA

The prophet Samuel had two sons, Joel and Abijah: "And it came to pass, when Samuel was old, that he made his sons judges over Israel . . . they were judges in Beer-

FIG. 100. STATUE OF ALLENBY IN BEERSHEBA (1935)

sheba. And his sons walked not in his ways, but turned aside after lucre, and took bribes, and perverted justice."

The sages wonder: "Is it possible that the sons of the righteous Samuel acted thus?" And they expound: "A trading caravan passed through Beersheba, whereupon they [Samuel's sons] would neglect their communal duties and go about their own business, and on account of such behavior the Holy One, blessed be He, stigmatized them as though they took bribes."[242]

7 / THE MONUMENT TO ALLENBY IN BEERSHEBA

In the public garden of Beersheba there stands a statue of Lord Edmund Allenby, the commander in chief of the British army that conquered the Holy Land from the Turks in the First World War (fig. 100). Beersheba was the first town to fall into their hands—in October 1917.

The native Arabs commonly believed that if there came a day when the waters of the Nile streamed to the Holy Land and a prophet (in Arabic, *en-nebi* or *al-nebi*) appeared, these would be omens of their deliverance from the Turkish yoke.

To provide water to their troops proceeding through the desert of Sinai, the British laid a pipeline from Egypt to the Holy Land. For the Arabs this was a divine sign.

When they further heard that the British were led by a man called Allenby, a name that to their ears sounded like *al-nebi*, they knew that redemption was assured.[243]

8 / BEERSHEBA IN THE END OF TIME

Beersheba is called in Arabic Bir es-Seba—Well of Seven —or es-Seba, for short.

A Moslem geographer of the thirteenth century described Bir es-Seba and its seven wells, and he told of the important part it will play in the end of time, according to Moslem tradition: "This is the place where all the people will gather on the Day of Resurrection," which is called "*Yaum es-Seba*—Day of es-Seba."

He ended with a short legend. A wolf seized a lamb but the shepherd rescued it from between his teeth. Said the wolf to the shepherd: "Woe to you on the Day of es-Seba!"[244]

9 / ABRAHAM THE PATRIARCH IN GERAR

The people of Sodom were known for their wickedness and their inhospitality. Hence Abraham pitched his tents close to their town to shelter the wayfarers who chanced to wander in that vicinity. When God unleashed His wrath on Sodom and laid it waste, no more travelers came that way. So Abraham thought in his heart: "Sodom lies destroyed, but I shall not forfeit my custom of hospitality."

"And Abraham journeyed from thence toward the land of the South [Negev], . . . and he sojourned in Gerar."

Gerar is today a forsaken hill covered with ruins in the environs of Beersheba.[245]

10 / ARAD AND THE WAY OF ATHARIM

Arad is a new city east of Beersheba, named after an old biblical town that once stood in this vicinity but today is a mound of ruins. The Arabs have preserved its name exactly.

Possibly Arad is derived from the Hebrew *arod*—a wild ass commonly found in the land of Israel in the earliest times.

When the tribes of Israel attempted to penetrate into the promised land from the south, the king of Arad and his men warded them off: "And the Canaanite, the king of Arad, who dwelt in the South, heard tell that Israel came by the way of Atharim; and he fought against Israel, and took some of them captive."

The sages say: "He was called Arad because he resembled an *arod*, the wild ass of the wilderness."

In the past, as it does today, Arad stood at an important crossroads. It commanded the entrance north toward the heart of the country and also the road south to the desert of Sinai. This latter is the way of Atharim mentioned above.

Atharim possibly contains the Arabic word *athar*, meaning "footprints," for the track could be easily followed owing to the marks left by the numerous camel caravans plodding along this way from the most ancient times.[246]

11 / THE ASCENT OF SCORPIONS

The ancient highway from Jerusalem through Beersheba to Edom and to Eilat on the Red Sea ran down the steep rocky slope called *Maaleh Akrabbim*—Ascent of Scorpions. This height was part of the mountain range which marked the border of the land promised to the Israelites: "This shall be the land that shall fall unto you for an inheritance . . . and your border shall turn about southward of the ascent of Akrabbim."

It also indicated the end of the inheritance of Judah: "And it went out southward of the ascent of Akrabbim."

In the rabbinic literature of the Middle Ages the name *Maaleh Akrabbim* became an idiomatic description of the stinging pain caused by the accumulation of troubles and increasing debts that the impoverished Jewish communities could not meet. A Jerusalem rabbi of the seventeenth century, complaining to his overseas brethren of the hardships assailing his community, wrote: "Our debts have increased on the Ascent of Scorpions exceedingly high."[247]

XXIII
THE NEGEV
AND ITS PEOPLE

1 / AT A WELL IN THE NEGEV

In the south of Eretz Israel stretches the Negev. Its rainfall is very scanty; hence its name, which in Hebrew means "dry." The Negev was the cradle of Israel. In its arid areas grazed the flocks of the patriarchs Abraham, Isaac, and Jacob, the fathers of the twelve tribes.

Some very ancient wells are found in the expanses of the Negev. In all of them the topmost layer of stones, which form the mouth of the well, are worn down, and the continuous rubbing of the ropes against the side during the many centuries have cut deep crevices into them (fig. 69).

Many of these wells were used by our forefathers to water their flocks. Occasionally disputes flared up around them—more often than not between the Philistine shepherds and those of Abraham the patriarch.

Our sages relate: "The shepherds of our father Abraham quarreled with the shepherds of Abimelech. The shepherds of Abraham said: 'This well is ours!' And the others countered: 'This well is ours.'

"The shepherds of Abraham suggested that for whomever's flocks the waters shall rise of their own accord from the bottom of the well, his shall it be.

"When the waters saw the flocks of Abraham the patriarch, forthwith they rose up."[248]

2 / THE SPIES IN THE NEGEV

When Israel went out of Egypt, they neared the borders of the Negev from the south and planned to enter the land through its open areas. The spies who came up from the Sinai Desert to explore the country crossed the Negev first and then went up the mountains, northward.

"And Moses sent them to spy out the land of Canaan, and said unto them: 'Get you up here into the South [Negev] and go up into the mountains; and see the land, what it is; and the people that dwelleth therein.' "

The legend explains why the spies were made to cross the barren Negev first before they climbed the fertile slopes of the mountains. The Almighty, blessed be His name, wanted to insure that the spies were favorably impressed by the mountains, which form the greatest part of the land.

Why to the Negev first? Because that is the way of the tradesman, first to produce his poorest wares and only afterward his choicest ones.[249]

3 / THE TRIBE OF SIMEON IN THE NEGEV

When Eretz Israel was divided among the twelve tribes, almost all the Negev fell to the portion of the children of Simeon, the southernmost tribe of the country. As it was weak, it found protection in its strong neighbor, the tribe of Judah. "This is the inheritance of the tribe of the children of Simeon according to their families. Out of the allotment of the children of Judah was the inheritance of the children of Simeon, for the portion of the children of Judah was too much for them; therefore the children of

Simeon had inheritance in the midst of their inheritance."

The difficult conditions of life in the Negev gave the children of Simeon no possibility of riches.

The sages comment on the words of Jacob the patriarch:

" 'I will divide them in Jacob'—that is the tribe of Levi.

" 'And scatter them in Israel'—that is the tribe of Simeon."

"The poor were mostly from the tribe of Simeon."

"There are no poor people, writers and teachers, but from the tribe of Simeon."²⁵⁰

4 / ALEXANDER THE GREAT AND THE WISE MEN OF THE NEGEV

Alexander of Macedonia, at the head of his troops, crossed the whole length of the western Negev on his way from Eretz Israel to Egypt, in 332 B.C.E.

Legend relates his meeting with the elders of the Negev. The sages of Israel say: "Ten questions did Alexander of Macedonia ask the wise men of the Negev.

"He asked: 'Is it farther from the earth to the sky than from the east to the west?'—The wise men answered: 'O king, is it not known to thee that when the sun stands in the east or in the west he is so far away that man can look upon his brightness, but when he stands overhead he is so near that his brightness dazzles the eyes of man? Therefore it must be farther from east to west than it is from the earth to the sky.'

"The king asked again: 'Were the skies created first or the earth?'—They answered: 'The skies were created first, as it is written [in the Torah]: "In the beginning God created the heaven and the earth." '

"He questioned: 'Was light created first or darkness?' They said: 'Darkness was created first.'

" 'Who is a wise man?'—'He who can foresee that which is to come.'

" 'Who is a hero?'—'He who conquers his desires.'

" 'Who is a rich man?'—'He who is contented with his lot.'

"The king said further: 'What must a man do to be beloved of the people?'—The wise men answered: 'He must hate the government and its ruler.'

"Alexander asked the wise men again: 'Is it better to be on sea or on land?'—'On land,' they replied, 'for they who sail on the sea find no ease of heart and mind till they reach the land.'

" 'Who is the wisest of you all?' he said to them.—'We are all equal in wisdom for we have answered your questions as one man.'

"Alexander then clad them in purple robes, and gave them necklaces of gold."[251]

SAMARIA

XXIV
IN THE MOUNTAINS
OF SAMARIA

1 / THE LAND OF JOSEPH: EPHRAIM AND MANASSEH

The fruitful land of Samaria was in the hands of the tribes of Ephraim and Manasseh, the children of Joseph. Moses, the man of God, blessed the children of Israel before his death: "And of Joseph he said: 'Blessed of the Lord be his land.'"

The sages of Israel explain: "The land of Joseph was the most blessed in the world."

"'For the precious things of heaven, for the dew'—at all times and seasons did the dew live upon the ground.

"'And for the deep that coucheth beneath'—fresh springs and fountains were always to be found in the depths of the ground.

"'And for the precious fruits brought forth by the sun'—the land was ever bathed in bright sunshine.

"'And for the precious things brought forth by the moon'—brightly did the moon shine upon it.

"'And for the chief things of the ancient mountains and for the precious things of the earth and the fulness thereof'—the land of Joseph was full of blessings. The man who had his lot in this land could desire nothing better."[252]

2 / THE FLAGS OF JOSEPH AND HIS SONS

While wandering in the desert to the promised land each tribe had its own flag, whose color corresponded to the color of the stone representing it in the breastplate of the high priest.

"Joseph's stone was an onyx and the color of his flag was jet black. The embroidered design thereon for both princes Ephraim and Manasseh was Egypt, because they were born in Egypt.

"On the flag of Ephraim was embroidered a bullock, in allusion to the text [of the blessing of Moses]: 'His firstling bullock.'"

"On the flag of the tribe of Manasseh was embroidered a wild ox, in allusion to the text: 'And his horns are the horns of the wild ox.' "[253]

3 / SHILOH—CENTER OF THE TRIBES OF ISRAEL

After Joshua son of Nun conquered the land, Shiloh became the center of the people of Israel. Here the land was divided among the different tribes, and to each was apportioned his inheritance. In Shiloh was put up the tabernacle, the foremost religious sanctuary of Israel before the erection of Jerusalem's Temple.

"And the whole congregation of the children of Israel assembled themselves together at Shiloh, and set up the tent of meeting there; and the land was subdued before them."

On the verse of the Torah, "Come to the rest . . . which the Lord your God giveth thee," the sages say: " 'The rest' —that is Shiloh."

The legend relates: "In four places did the divine Presence [Shechinah] rest on Israel, and one of them was Shiloh."

Shiloh was later destroyed and laid waste, as the psalmist

FIG. 101. RUIN IN SHILOH

sang: "For they provoked Him with their high places,/And moved Him to jealousy with their graven images./God heard, and was wroth,/And He greatly abhorred Israel;/And He forsook the tabernacle of Shiloh/The tent which He had made to dwell among men;/And delivered His strength into captivity/And His glory into the adversary's hand."

The ruins of Shiloh are known to the Arabs as *Seilun*; they lie between Jerusalem and Shechem in the mountains of Samaria.

In about 1322 Rabbi Ashtori ha-Parhi told about these ruins: "Till this day there is a dome called [in Arabic] *Koubet es-Sakina* [Dome of the Shechinah], and next to it there is a place named [in Arabic] *Maida Bnei Israel*— that is to say, the tablets* of the children of Israel."

* In Arabic *maida* really means "table."

A Moslem geographer of the thirteenth century described the ruins of Shiloh and "the mosque of the Shechinah [*Masjad es-Sakina*], where stands the stone table Hajar el-Maida."[254]

4 / THE PILGRIMS TO SHILOH

The Israelites used to go up to the sanctuary in Shiloh to prostrate themselves before the Lord.

Among the pilgrims were Elkanah and his barren wife, Hannah, inhabitants of the mountains of Ephraim: "And this man went up out of his city from year to year to worship and to sacrifice unto the Lord of hosts in Shiloh. . . . And it came to pass, when the time was come about, that Hannah conceived and bore a son; and she called his name Samuel."

Why did the Lord Almighty fulfill Elkanah and Hannah's prayer for a son? Legend offers this answer.

Elkanah with his wife and all his relatives went up to Shiloh every year. On the way he always encamped within towns; and people would come up and ask: "Where art thou heading?" And he would say: "To the house of God in Shiloh, whence the Torah of the Lord shines forth and where all good deeds are conceived. Why should thou not join us and we shall all go up together?" Forthwith their eyes would overflow with tears and they would say joyfully: "Indeed, we shall go up with thee."

Every year Elkanah chose a different route for his pilgrimage until it came to pass that all of Israel had journeyed with him to Shiloh. Said the Lord to Elkanah: "Thou have brought Israel to good deeds and thou have taught them to fulfill the pilgrimage to my sanctuary. I will bring out of thy loins a son which will lead all Israel in the path of righteousness." "And the Lord appeared again in Shiloh; for the Lord revealed himself to Samuel in Shiloh."[255]

FIG. 102. OLD MOSQUE IN SHILOH, BUILT OF ANCIENT STONES
AND PILLARS

5 / SHILOH AND GEREB

In Shiloh stood the tabernacle of God and within it
burnt the sacrificial fire.

Not far from Shiloh was a place called Gereb, where the
image of Micah was worshiped. As the Bible records: "And
they passed thence unto the hill country of Ephraim, and
came unto the house of Micah . . . and [they] said unto
their brethren: 'Do ye know that there is in these houses
an ephod, and teraphim and a graven image, and a molten
image?'"

The smoke rising from the offerings made in Shiloh
mixed with that of the sacrifice in Gereb. The angels of
the Lord endeavored to push back the idolatrous fumes
discharged in Gereb. Said God the merciful, blessed be

He: "Let it be, for there the weary wayfarer is offered shelter and food."

Thus in recognition of their generous hospitality the Lord forgave the inhabitants of Gereb their pagan customs.

Possibly Gereb of Micah stood on the site of the ruins called in Arabic *Ghuraba*, on top of a mountain overlooking Shiloh, by the side of the main Jerusalem–Shechem highway.[256]

6 / A COIN HONORING JOSHUA

The grateful Israelites honored their leader Joshua son of Nun by minting a coin carrying on one side the image of a bullock and on the other a wild ox, the two symbols used by Moses when he blessed Joseph, Joshua's ancestor: "His firstling bullock, majesty is his;/And his horns are the horns of the wild ox;/With them he shall gore the peoples all of them, even the ends of the earth."

Not only did Joshua conquer the land of Canaan for the tribes of Israel, he also, say the sages, expressed his loving care for his people by paving roads throughout the land for their welfare.[257]

7 / TIMNATH HERES—THE CITY OF JOSHUA

Timnath Heres was a small town in the mountains of Ephraim, in Samaria. There, as it is written, Joshua son of Nun was interred: "And they buried him in the border of his inheritance in Timnath Heres in the hill country of Ephraim."

With the slight shift of a vowel, legend modified the name into *temunath heres*—picture of the sun—and adds that a picture of the sun adorned the tomb of Joshua as a reminder of the miracle that he wrought in the Valley of Ayalon when he bid the sun to stand still.*[258]

* See legend VII:10.

FIG. 103. RUINS OF TIMNATH HERES—ANCIENT BURIAL CAVE

8 / TIMNATH HERES—TIMNATH SERAH

The story of Joshua's burial appears twice in the Bible, but the second time with a variation: "And they buried him in the border of his inheritance in Timnath Serah, which is in the hill country of Ephraim."

Why both Timnath Serah and Timnath Heres? This, it was said, is meant to reflect the miraculous improvement in the quality of the fruit which followed Joshua's conquest of the land of Canaan. Before the conquest the land bore fruit of little goodness, small and as dry as pottery sherds—*heres* in Hebrew; after the conquest it became large, succulent, and odoriferous—*serah* in Hebrew.[259]

9 / MOUNT GAASH NEAR TIMNATH HERES

"And they buried him in the border of his inheritance in
Timnath Serah, which is in the hill country of Ephraim,
on the north of the mountain of Gaash."

Very likely here was *nahal Gaash*—the river of Gaash,
whence mighty men came to King David's army.

The legend tells that when Joshua died, the Israelites,
busy at dividing the land among the tribes and engaged in
their inheritance, did not pay homage to his bodily remains
nor did they mourn him as he deserved. Therefore God the
Almighty, provoked to anger by their neglect, caused a
mountain to shake and quake, intending to overturn it on
their heads. Then the people realized that they had not
fulfilled their duty to Joshua, and henceforward the mountain was called Har Gaash—Mount Volcano.[260]

10 / THE PRIESTLY PAIRS IN GOFNA

The Arab village of Jafna lies in the mountains of
Samaria, close to the Jerusalem–Shechem highway. Here
once stood Gofna, named after the rich vines (in Hebrew,
gefen) which have covered the slopes of the mountains
since the most ancient times.

Legend has a story to tell about this place. "There was
a town in Eretz Israel and its name was Gofna. There
lived in the city eighty pairs of brothers, all priests, who
married eighty pairs of sisters."[261]

11 / IN THE HOSTEL OF YASSUF

On the side of the Jerusalem–Shechem highway, in the
mountains of Samaria, lies the Arab village of Yassuf,
which is mentioned in Samaritan literature. The story is
told of two brothers, Ephraim and Menashe, who lived in
Yassuf. Once a Jew passed the village on his way to Jerusalem and with him were a pair of young pigeons, an offer-

ing to the Great Temple. The Jew spent the night in Yassuf. The two brothers stole the pigeons from his basket and replaced them with two rats.

In the middle of the night the Jew arose and proceeded on his way. In the Temple he handed the basket as an offering. When the priest opened the basket and saw the rats, he took hold of the man to kill him. But the latter cried out: "Lo! I have been swindled! I slept in a hostel in Yassuf, and there were none there but two Samaritan youths. And I left the place in the middle of the night for fear of being late and of forfeiting the offering which I must present to atone for my sins; and I did not notice that I had been swindled."

Men were sent to the hostel and they caught the Samaritan brothers, who confessed their guilt.

Some of the judges of the law court passed sentence thus: "It is advisable that these youths should remain in the Temple and serve it all the days of their life, and eat thistles and drink water and sleep on the ground."[262]

12 / SAMARIA—CAPITAL OF THE KINGDOM OF ISRAEL

"The head of Ephraim is Samaria."

The town of Samaria, which was once the most important capital of the kingdom of Israel, is now an Arab village called Sebustia. Omri, king of Israel, built Samaria as his capital. "And he bought the hill Samaria of Shemer for two talents of silver; and he built on the hill, and called the name of the city which he built, after the name of Shemer, owner of the hill, Samaria [Shomron]."

"Why did Omri become king of Israel?" ask the sages. "Because he added another city to the kingdom, that is Samaria."

Samaria was also the capital of Ahab, the son of Omri.

FIG. 104. RUINS OF SAMARIA—CAPITAL OF ISRAEL (1835)

It is said of Ahab that for the seventy children he had in Samaria he had seventy children in the city of Jezreel, and each one had two palaces, one for the summer and one for the winter.

It is written: "And Ahab did more to provoke the Lord God of Israel to anger than all the kings of Israel that were before him."

Said Rabbi Yohanan: "Because he wrote on the gates of Samaria, 'Ahab denies the God of Israel.'"

"There was not a furrow in the land of Israel on which Ahab did not erect an idol and worship it.

"Therefore Ahab, king of Israel, has no portion in the God of Israel!"[263]

13 / THE PLACE OF THE FIRE

Near the ruined city of Samaria, on the slope of the mountain which looks down on the village of Sebustia, there is to this day a holy place dedicated to Sheik Shaaleh

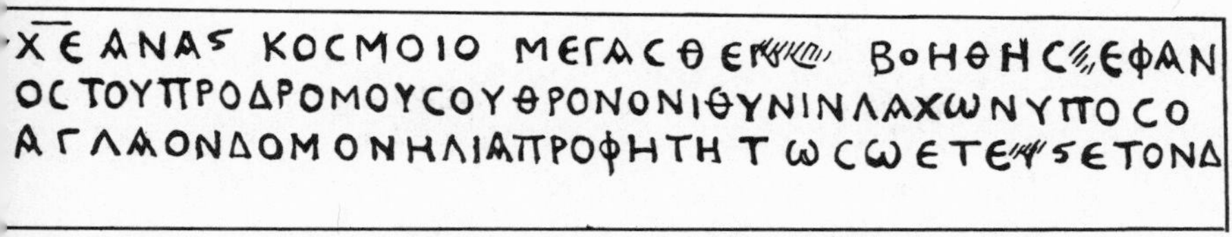

XEANAS KOCMOIO METACΘ εκ☩κα, ΒοΗΘΗC☩,ΕΦΑΝ
OCTOYΠPOΔPOMOYCOYΘPONONIΘYNINΛAXωNYΠOCO
AΓΛΛONΔOMONHΛIAΠPOΦHTH TωCωετεκψsετoΝΔ

FIG. 105. GREEK INSCRIPTION FOUND AT SHEIK SHAALEH
Translated, this reads: "Jesus, great ruler of the world, help Stefan
. . . who built this magnificent house to honor your prophet Elijah."

—Sheik of the Fire. Here, it is said, the fire descended and burned the messengers of the king of Israel in the time of Elijah the prophet. A Greek inscription from the fourth century which was discovered here tells about a magnificent building which was erected on this spot in memory of Elijah the prophet (fig. 105).

"And Ahaziah [the king of Israel] fell down through a lattice in his upper chamber that was in Samaria, and was sick; and he sent messengers, and said unto them: 'Go, inquire of Baal-zebub the god of Ekron whether I shall recover of this sickness.' But an angel of the Lord said to Elijah the Tishbite: 'Arise, go up to meet the messengers of the king of Samaria, and say unto them: Is it because there is no God in Israel, that ye go to inquire of Baal-zebub the god of Ekron? Now therefore thus saith the Lord: Thou shalt not come down from the bed whither thou art gone up, but shalt surely die. . . .' Then the king sent unto him [Elijah] a captain of fifty with his fifty. And he went up to him; and, behold, he sat on the top of the hill, and he spoke unto him: 'O man of God, the king hath said: Come down!' And Elijah answered and said to the captain of fifty: 'If I be a man of God, let fire come down from heaven, and consume thee and thy fifty.' And there came down fire from heaven, and consumed him and his fifty."[264]

14/ THE PIT OF JOSEPH IN SAMARIA

Amid the mountains of Samaria stretches the Valley of Dothan, named after the town of Dothan or Dothain, which is today a hill of ruins on the side of the high road leading from Sebustia to Jennin.

In the Valley of Dothan the shepherd sons of Jacob, pastured their flocks. It is written: "And Joseph went after his brethren, and found them in Dothan. . . . And they took him and cast him into a pit—and the pit was empty, there was no water in it. And they sat down to eat bread; and they lifted up their eyes and looked, and, behold, a caravan of Ishmaelites came from Gilead . . . and they drew and lifted up Joseph out of the pit, and sold Joseph to the Ishmaelites."

To this day in the Valley of Dothan is a pit named after Joseph—in Arabic, *Jib Yusef.* A Jewish traveler in 1847 told of this pit and described the caravan trail and a praying place built next to it.

Some medieval Moslem travelers mentioned another pit of Joseph in the south of Samaria near the village of Sinjil, on the way to Jerusalem. In Galilee, too, a Joseph's pit was shown.[265]

15 / KING SAUL, BEZEK, AND TELAIM

Amid the Samarian mountains rises a high summit: Mount Bezek. On its slope lies a ruin named in Arabic *Ibzeik,* the site of the ancient Bezek where King Saul gathered his warriors when he first went out to war against the Ammonites across the Jordan. The Bible says: "And he numbered them in Bezek; and the children of Israel were three hundred thousand, and the men of Judah thirty thousand."

The origin of the name Bezek has remained obscure. According to the Hebrew legend, the Bezek mentioned in the Bible is not a place-name, but the Aramaic word *bazka* —small stone.

And legend continues that whereas it is prohibited to number people even for a beneficial purpose, Saul ordered each of his men to present a stone so that by counting the stones he knew the number of his fighters. So instead of reading "numbered them in Bezek," the sages of Israel read "numbered them with stones."

About another of Saul's wars which he waged much later in his life, it is related: "And Saul summoned the people, and numbered them in Telaim, two hundred thousand footmen, and ten thousand men of Judah."

Telaim is situated in the south of Judah amid pasture lands; hence its name, which means "lamb."

In this case too legend holds that Telaim is not a place-name and, repeating the same pattern as above, it says that when King Saul wished to ascertain the number of his warriors he had each one present a lamb; by counting the lambs he could appraise the strength of his army.

Thus it appears that King Saul counted his men first with stones and later with lambs; therefore it was said: "At the beginning the Israelites were poor and could bring naught but stones; later when the kingdom was strengthened they became affluent and therefore brought lambs."[266]

FIG. 106. SHECHEM AND MOUNT GERIZIM (c. 1884)
Above are Mount Gerizim with tombs of Joseph and his sister,
Dinah, at its foot. On top of mount is tomb of Hamor, father of
founder of Shechem, whose name is mentioned in Bible: "And
Hamor and Shechem his son came unto the gate of their city"
(Genesis 34:20).

XXV
SHECHEM
AND ITS VICINITY

1 / SHECHEM AND SIMEON'S STANDARD

In the desert of the wanderings, each tribe of Israel carried its standard: "The children of Israel shall pitch by their fathers' houses; every man with his own standard."

The standard of the tribe of Simeon pictured the town of Shechem on a green background. Why was this standard bestowed upon Simeon? In memory of his deeds in Shechem: "And it came to pass . . . that two of the sons of Jacob, Simeon and Levi, Dinah's brethren, took each man his sword, and came upon the city unawares, and slew all the males. And they slew Hamor and Shechem his son with the edge of the sword, and took Dinah out of Shechem's house and went forth. The sons of Jacob came upon the slain, and spoiled the city, because they had defiled their sister."

Tradition shows the tomb of Hamor on the top of nearby Mount Gerizim (fig. 106).[267]

2 / SHECHEM IS CALLED NABLUS

Next to ancient Shechem the Romans built a new town which they called Neopolis—New City. This the Arabs

came to call Nablus, the contemporary Arabic name of
Shechem.

A Karaite pilgrim of the year 1641 found in the name
Nablus the Hebrew word *nebala*—shameful deed—be-
cause of the Nablusites' disgraceful behavior toward
Dinah, the daughter of Jacob.

The Arabs, on the other hand, hold that Nablus is a contraction of two words: *nab*—teeth—and *lus*—a species of
large snake. There is a tale that in the valley next to
Shechem lived a gigantic and dreadful snake. Once the
inhabitants caught it and beat it to death. They extracted
its teeth and hung them on the main gate of Shechem and
said proudly: "Here are the teeth [*nab*]of the giant snake
[*lus*]." Hence the name Nablus, which has remained to this
day.[268]

3 / JACOB THE PATRIARCH IN SHECHEM

The Torah reports: "And Jacob came in peace to the city
of Shechem, which is in the land of Canaan . . . and encamped before the city. And he bought the parcel of
ground, where he had spread his tent . . . and he erected
there an altar and called it El-elohe-Israel [God of Gods of
Israel]."

The sages of Israel explain: " 'And Jacob came in peace
[in Hebrew, *shalom*, also meaning intact, entire] to the
city of Shechem'—he came entire in body, his fortune
intact, and with his complete knowledge of the Torah.

" 'And encamped before the city'—he minted them [the
residents] coins, built them marketplaces, and butcher
shops."

Some surmise that the Hebrew word *shalom*, which is
translated "in peace," refers to a place in the neighborhood
of Shechem. So instead of reading, "And Jacob came in
peace to the city of Shechem," they read: "And Jacob came
to Shalom of the city of Shechem." Indeed, not far from

Shechem there is an Arabic village named Salem, which is Shalom in Hebrew.*269

4 / THE MOSQUE OF JACOB'S MOURNING

In the town of Shechem, next to the old Samaritan quarter, stands a Moslem mosque which the Arabs call the Great Mosque.

It is built on the site of a Samaritan synagogue of the Middle Ages. On its minaret, which overlooks all Shechem, is set a stone which bears the Ten Commandments in the Samaritan script.

Inside the mosque the Arabs show the place where Jacob the patriarch was sitting when the messenger brought him the tidings of his favorite son Joseph's untimely end. There came his treacherous sons and produced the striped shirt stained with blood and said: " 'This have we found. Know now whether it is thy son's coat or not.' . . . And Jacob rent his garments, and put sackcloth upon his loins, and mourned for his son many days."

Therefore the Arabs also call this mosque by the name *Hizen Ya'acub*—the Mourning of Jacob. And for that reason it is sacred to the Moslem inhabitants of Shechem to this day.270

5 / THE MIGHTY NIMROD IN SHECHEM

Of Nimod, the hunter who appeared after the great flood, the Book of Genesis says: "And the sons of Ham: Cush and Mizraim . . . and Canaan. . . . And Cush begot Nimrod; he began to be a mighty one in the earth. He was a mighty hunter before the Lord; wherefore it is said: 'Like Nimrod a mighty hunter before the Lord.' And the beginning of his kingdom was Babel." The prophet Micah calls Babel "the land of Nimrod."

---

* Since Shalom is another name for Jerusalem, the Torah adds, to avoid confusion, "Shalom of Shechem."

A Moslem geographer who visited Palestine about 1250 wrote: "The Jews say that it was here that Nimrod the son of Canaan threw Abraham into the fire. The learned, however, say this took place at Babylon, in Iraq, and Allah alone knows the truth!"

Another Moslem who was in Shechem in 1689 told of a building like a cellar, buried in the ground, and "they say that here lies Nimrod"—*Nimrud* in Arabic.[271]

6 / HOW MANY SPRINGS ARE THERE IN SHECHEM?

Shechem is situated in a fertile valley watered by numerous springs of exceptional sweetness, which pour out their blessing into the rich gardens and luxuriant orchards of the vicinity.

It was said that 360 fountains emerge within the Valley of Shechem, a number equal to the sum of the letters composing its name: Sh = 300, ch = 20, m = 40.

The Jerusalemite rabbi Abraham Rosanes, who visited Shechem in 1867, was the first to mention this story. He reportedly told it in the name of the sages in the olden days, although there is no trace of it in ancient Hebrew literature.[272]

7 / THE WELL OF JACOB

Close to Shechem is the Well of Jacob, over which a Greek church has been built. At this well Jesus of Nazareth met the Samaritan woman.

The well is named after Jacob the patriarch of Israel. Tradition holds that Jacob dug it when he bought this parcel of ground, as related in the Holy Scriptures.

Christian pilgrims flocked to the well at all times. One wrote in 1180: "Jacob's Well changes its color four times a year, being muddy, blood red, green, and clear." A Frenchman in 1697, wishing to ascertain its depth, "took a stone and threw it in the well and started to say in Latin

FIG. 107. JESUS AND SAMARITAN WOMAN AT WELL OF JACOB.
This painting is from old catacomb in Via Dino Campagni, Rome.

the well-known Christian prayer 'Glory be to the Father
and to the Son and to the Holy Spirit, as it was in the
beginning, is now, and ever shall be'; and when he said
the last word he heard the fall of stone in the water of
the well."

The well has been explored since, and it was found to be
seventy-five feet deep.[273]

8 / THE FOUNTAIN OF SOCHER

To the east of the city of Shechem, at the foot of Mount
Ebal, lies the Arab village of Askar. Here stood the town

of Sychar. Once, Jesus was passing through Samaria: "So he came to a city of Samaria, called Sychar, near the field that Jacob gave to his son Joseph."

The Jews called this town Ein Socher—Spring of the Lock. Around it stretches a beautiful and fruitful valley which in springtime is covered with rich fields of wheat and barley.

One year, in the days of the Temple, the corn of the districts around Jerusalem failed and there was not sufficient wheat even for the shewbread in the Temple. The priests did not know where to obtain the choice wheat necessary for the preparation of the shewbread in accordance with the injunctions of the holy Law: "Ye shall bring out of your dwellings two wave-loaves . . . ; they shall be of fine flour, they shall be baked with leaven, for firstfruits unto the Lord."

There appeared in the courtyard of the Temple a dumb man who stood before the priests of the Lord. He placed one hand upon his eye (in Hebrew, *ein*) and his other hand upon the lock of a door (in Hebrew, *socher*), but the priests did not know what the afflicted of God meant thereby.

So they brought him to the overseer of the Temple, who looked at the dumb man and, turning to the priests, said: "Do you not see where his movements lead? They lead to *ein* [eye or spring] and to *socher* [a lock]. Tell me, therefore, is there such a place as Ein Socher—Spring of the Lock?"

And the priests answered: "Yes, there is." And he said to them: "Go to the valley near Ein Socher and you will find wheat for the shewbread for the Temple."*[274]

9 / THE WELL OF JOB

Several medieval pilgrims mentioned the existence of a

* See legend XVI:7.

well or fountain called after Job the righteous, in the surroundings of Shechem in the Samarian mountains.

An English writer tells of Samaria in about 1336: "And between the hills of the country, there is a well that . . . changes its color: sometimes clear and sometimes troubled; and men call that the Well of Job."

In 1499 a German pilgrim who ventured into Samaria recorded a similar story. "We went from this town of Basten down the mountain where we found a fine fountain called after Job, which changes its color four times yearly, at one time it is green, the second red, the third time yellow, the fourth dark, as we were told."

In the Samarian mountains of today there is no well or fountain named after Job, or Ayub, as the Arabs call him.*[275]

* See *Legends of Jerusalem*, p. 282.

XXVI
MOUNT GERIZIM AND MOUNT EBAL

1 / MOUNT OF BLESSING AND MOUNT OF CURSE

The town of Shechem is situated in a narrow valley enclosed between two mountains: Mount Gerizim to the south and Mount Ebal to the north. Both are famous in the tradition of Israel.

Before the tribes of Israel entered the promised land, Moses, the man of God, ordered his servant Joshua son of Nun in these terms: "And it shall come to pass, when the Lord thy God shall bring thee into the land whither thou goest to possess it, that thou shalt set the blessing upon Mount Gerizim, and the curse upon Mount Ebal."

"And Moses charged the people the same day, saying, 'These shall stand upon Mount Gerizim to bless the people, when ye are passed over the Jordan: Simeon, and Levi, and Judah, and Issachar, and Joseph, and Benjamin; and these shall stand upon Mount Ebal for the curse: Reuben, Gad, and Asher, and Zebulun, Dan, and Naphtali.'"

In the days of Israel's conquest of the land, the tribes came to Shechem: "Then Joshua built an altar unto the Lord, the God of Israel, in Mount Ebal. . . . And all Israel, and their elders and officers, and their judges, stood on this side of the ark and on that side . . . half of them in front of Mount Gerizim and half of them in front of Mount Ebal. . . . And afterward he read all the words of the law, the blessing and the curse."

The sages of Israel picture the scene thus: "Six tribes went up to the top of Mount Gerizim and six tribes went up to the top of Mount Ebal. And the priests and the Levites were standing below, the holy ark in their midst. The priests circled round the ark and the Levites circled round the priests and all Israel stood on either side . . . then they faced toward Mount Gerizim and solemnly recited: 'Blessed be the man that maketh not a graven or molten image!' And the people on both side answered 'Amen.'

"Then they faced toward Mount Ebal and cursed solemnly: 'Cursed be the man that maketh a graven or molten image!' And the people on both sides answered 'Amen.' "

And so they continued until they had said all the blessings and all the curses.

Therefore Mount Gerizim is called *Har ha-Beracha*— Mount of Blessing—and Mount Ebal, *Har ha-Kelalah*— Mount of Curse.[276]

2 / MOUNT GERIZIM AND THE GREAT FLOOD

An ancient Samaritan tradition relates: "When the whole world was flooded in the time of Noah the righteous, Mount Gerizim, as a token of its sanctity, was projected above the surface of the waters. It is told that when Rabbi Yonathan went up to Jerusalem to pray, on his way he passed Mount Gerizim. A Samaritan saw him and asked: 'Where art thou going?' He answered: 'To Jerusalem to pray.'

"He said: 'Is it not worth thy while to pray on the Mount

of Blessing [Gerizim], and not in that house of corruption!'

"Rabbi Yonathan asked him: 'And why is that mountain blessed?'

"The Samaritan answered: 'Because it was not under the waters of the Great Flood.' "277

3 / MOUNT GERIZIM—THE ANCIENT MOUNTAIN

Mount Gerizim is also called by the Samaritans *Har ha-Kedem*—Ancient Mountain.

The Samaritan poet Marqah, who lived about 100 B.C.E, wrote: "Why was it called *Har ha-Kedem*? Because this mountain and the Garden of Eden appeared before the appearance of the dry earth.

"From here was taken the dust for the creation of Adam.

"Adam is the glory of the creation and the blessed mount is the splendor of the earth."

On Mount Gerizim the Samaritans still show the place where the altar was built by Adam and his son Seth, the altar built by Noah after the flood, and the rock on which Abraham was about to sacrifice Isaac, his son.

On Mount Gerizim are shown also the stones which were brought up from the Jordan by Joshua son of Nun. As it is written in the holy Law: "And Moses . . . commanded the people . . . 'When ye are passed over Jordan, that ye shall set up these stones . . . in Mount Ebal [in the Samaritan version, Mount Gerizim]. . . . And thou shalt write upon the stones all the words of this law very plainly.' "

The sages of Israel comment: " 'Very plainly'—in seventy tongues."

To the Samaritans, Gerizim is the most holy of mountains. They face toward it in their prayers, and on its top they celebrate their Passover and offer their sacrificial lambs to this very day.

The holiness of Mount Gerizim is one of the foundations

of the Samaritan faith. Therefore the rabbis said: "When shall a Samaritan be accepted in the community of Israel? When he rejects Mount Gerizim and recognizes Jerusalem as the most holy mount."[278]

4 / MOUNT CAIN AND MOUNT ABEL

In medieval times there was a common belief among Christian pilgrims, founded upon the similarity of names, that Abel, the son of Adam, lived on Mount Ebal.

Theodoricus wrote in 1172: "Near Shechem are two mountains; one whereon Cain is said to have offered sacrifice to God of the fruits of the earth, the other whereon Abel likewise offered sacrifice to God of the fatlings of his flock."

In 1231, the French chronicler Ernoul called Mount Gerizim Mount Cain, and Mount Ebal he called Mount Abel.[279]

5 / WHY WAS IT CALLED EBAL?

The origin of the name Ebal is unknown. A Samaritan tradition relates this name to the Hebrew word *evel*—mourning. Here Enoch father of Methuselah was mourned: "And Enoch walked with God, and he was not; for God took him."

Samaritans believe that the window to the next world and the gate of heaven open above that place of mourning.[280]

6 / THE DOVE ON MOUNT GERIZIM

On the summit of Mount Gerizim was erected the temple of the Samaritans. Yohanan, the king of the Hashmoneans, destroyed it in 129 B.C.

The sages of Israel tell that in this temple the Samaritans kept the image of a dove, to which they paid divine honor instead of to the Almighty Lord of the universe.

"The Samaritans circumcise in the name of the image of a dove."

"Others say that the Samaritans have an image like the form of a dove, and they pour out libations to this."[281]

7 / THE SPEAKING FOWL ON MOUNT GERIZIM

When the Romans spread their rule over the land of Israel in ancient days, they oppressed the Samaritans, persecuted them, and forbade them to ascend Mount Gerizim and pray on the site of their ancient synagogue.

A Samaritan legend says that the Romans also prevented the Samaritans from ascending the mountain (Gerizim) and decreed that everyone who climbed this mountain would be put to the sword.

The Romans erected on the top of the mountain the image of a fowl made of brass, which faced the sun and followed it around its course. And if a Samaritan went up the mount, the fowl shouted: "A Hebrew!" to inform the Romans that a Samaritan was ascending. Then the Romans would come up and put him to death.[282]

XXVII
THE PLAIN OF SHARON

1 / THE PRAYER OF THE SHARONITES

There were many Jewish villages in Sharon in days gone by. Many of the inhabitants were herdsmen, breeding flocks of sheep and herds of cattle. The slopes of the hills and the banks of the brooks made pleasant pasture. The calves of Sharon were among the best in the land of Israel.

The houses of the Sharon villages were built from bricks made of mud and clay. Job said about them: "Houses of clay,/Whose foundation is in the dust/Who are crushed before the moth!"

The sages of Israel did not value the clay houses of the Sharonites. To the prescription of the Torah, "What man is there that hath built a new house, and hath not dedicated it? Let him go and return to his house, lest he die in the battle, and another man dedicate it," they added: "He also that builds a house of bricks in Sharon may not return," because their houses were so weak that they had to renew them very often: repair the crevices and replace the fallen mortar.

In years of plentiful rain these houses would crumble and fall, and many of the Sharonites would meet death in the collapse of their houses. The Arabs still tell of such villages, destroyed by furious storms and rain.

In the olden days the men of Sharon besought the high priest to mention their straits when he entered the holy of holies on the Day of Atonement and prayed for the people. The high priest would say: "May it be Thy will, O Lord our God and God of our fathers, that Thou send not upon us exile and that this year may be a year of low prices, a year of plenty, a year of trade, a year of rain, heat and dew." And for the men of Sharon he said: "May it be Thy will, O Lord our God and God of our fathers, that their houses shall not fall on them and become their graves!"[283]

2 / THE FORESTS OF SHARON

Till about a century ago the whole width of Sharon, from Jaffa to Tul Karem, was covered with great thick forests of oaks.

Sheik Abd al-Latif, who dwelt in Jaffa, told this tale.

"When my grandfather was young, he used to travel on business from Jaffa to Tul Karem and back by way of the forest. When he came to denser parts he could not ride upright upon his donkey, but had to bend low because of the thickly growing branches and foliage. Even when he was old, blind, and weak, he would still come to stay with his sons at Tul Karem.

"Once when he was about a hundred years old and totally blind he ordered his sons to take him to Jaffa to visit his many relatives and friends. He was put on a donkey, and I, then a youngster, was told to ride with him. When we came to the broad Plain of Sharon, my grandsire lay flat along his donkey. I asked: 'Grandsire, why do you not ride upright?' He answered 'My dear grandson, I still remember this district from my boyhood

when it was a wild thicket. I always had to ride thus, and
even now I fear the multitude of branches.' I answered:
'O grandsire, you err indeed. Times are changed. There
is no more forest in Sharon; ride upright and never fear.
For lack of care and with so many wars, the woods have
disappeared during the years.' "[284]

3 / THE SYCAMORE OF KEFAR SABA

Near the town of Kefar Saba in southern Sharon there
was in ancient times a Jewish village of the same name.
A sycamore tree (*shikma*) was there, and all who
touched it became unclean. Though men sought for a
reason and examined it and the ground around, they could
find no cause for the impurity of this tree.

But one day this tree was uprooted in a high wind; and
they found a dead man's skull amid its roots. Then they
understood why that sycamore made people unclean.[285]

4 / THE BATTLE WITH THE SUN

In the southern part of the Plain of Sharon, next to the
settlement of Raanana, was a small Arab village called
Khirbet 'Azun—Ruins of Azun. And indeed the village
looked like its name: its houses were poor and tumble-
down, its courtyards deserted, and its inhabitants few.
But it was not so of old.

Formerly a large, flourishing village spread across a
great area here and hummed with many men and much
cattle. The villagers were all well-to-do and possessed
their own property, for their lands were fruitful and gave
their produce for the sustenance of man and beast. The
spot had only one shortcoming: it lay directly in the path
of the rising sun, for it was situated on the slopes of the
hills of Ephraim. Each morning when the fellahin went
out to labor and the rays of the rising sun struck their eyes,
it blinded them and caused them mortal anguish. And

when they returned at evening the rays of the setting sun
lay in ambush to blind them anew, spoiling their understanding and upsetting their thoughts.

The anger of the men of Azun against the sun, for its
interfering and plaguing habits, grew and grew. One fine
day they called a meeting of all the villagers to discuss
how they could deal with the sun's obstinacy. It was a
very long, stormy meeting, for they were boiling with
indignation. Many fiery addresses were given, and at
length they unanimously decided to go out armed together
and to wage war with the sun and drive it from the Lord's
heavens, so that it could no longer mock the fellahin or
disturb their labor. And the call went forth: *"Ta'alu nit-
harab m'a esh-shams*—Come battle with the sun!"

And so they did.

At dawn the next day all the able-bodied men gathered
together. They went armed from head to foot, and, bearing
bows and marching in file like soldiers, at the command of
their sheik they set out to do battle with the sun. As soon
as it began to shine over the hills of Ephraim they joined
battle, shooting their arrows and casting their spears
directly at the heart of the sun with mighty shouts, as one
does in war.

And the sun rose ever higher, seeming to pay no attention to their brave deeds. Its shafts of light flashed and
burned ever more fiercely, blinding them; its fire was
poured upon the ground around them, and the weary men
sank powerless to the ground.

Then they thought: "It is very hard to wage war while
the sun rises and grows ever stronger. Let us wait till it
begins to set. Then it will easily be finished off."

They gathered their strength all day, waiting for the
sun to go down. As it sank toward the sea they roused
themselves and renewed their onslaught. But now the
battle proved easy, for the sun was close and had little

power; and they continued till they saw it drown and disappear into the sea.

Then they were very happy that they had at last vanquished their mighty foe. "The sun will not rise again after the way we have beaten it. It is drowned and has set forever." And they went home rejoicing in victory and told their womenfolk of their great valor; they spent the night in dancing and song.

But when the sun rose anew next day as of old they were very perplexed. Its rays shone right upon them and there was no sign of the mortal wounds they had inflicted the day before. And they were very downcast, for they saw that their battle with the sun had been of no avail.

Then the old sheik, silencing them, rose and proposed that they send to the holy dervish who lived at the tomb of Sidi 'Ali ibn 'Ulem at the nearby ruins of Arsuf, to ask for counsel.

His plan was adopted with one voice, and a deputation of the gentlefolk of the village and their donkeys, laden with the best of the land's produce, went to visit the holy dervish.

When the men came to the dervish they put the gift before him and, falling on their faces, told him of their trouble. They also told him of the battle which had belied their hopes; tears in their eyes, they asked for counsel.

The dervish listened and, shaking his head, said: "In open battle the sun cannot be defeated; but if you pay two hundred pieces to the holy grave, I shall give you whatever good counsel Allah puts in my mouth."

The men agreed to pay the large sum, for they were greatly troubled by their foe, which made their lives a misery. And the dervish bade them come again on the morrow bringing the sum he asked.

On the morrow, after they had paid, the dervish entered the grave, where he stayed long in prayer, bowing and prostrating. When he came forth with beaming face he gave them this counsel from Allah.

He told them to remove their village to beyond the hills where their lands were, and let the village site serve them for farmland. And he promised to pray to Allah to take the curse of the sun from them so that it would no longer dazzle and blind them on the way to and from the fields.

And the men did so. They forsook their village and took their tents, their cattle, and their property to the hills to the east. And the prayer of the holy dervish stood them in good stead, for the sun no longer shone in their eyes when they went to and from work, and troubled them no more. And they praised Allah and the faithful dervish.

The village amid the hills grew and prospered; it was named Azun, like the first settlement. But what is left of the old village in Sharon is called even today Hirbet Azun —Ruins of Azun.[286]

5 / THE TEST STONE IN SIDNA ALI

On the shore of the Mediterranean Sea, near Herzliya, there is a large building topped with a turret on the site of the grave called, in Arabic, *Sidna Ali*—Our Master Ali. In the late Middle Ages the Jews and the Samaritans believed this to be the burial place of the famous judge Eli of Shiloh. The tomb is on the edge of the ruins of Arsuf—ancient Appolonia.

The gravestone of Our Master Ali lies in a large courtyard paved with stones, inside a room whose ceiling is gone. In a wall outside this room a black stone is fixed, and this stone is used by the Arabs to test the deeds of men. The testee stands several feet from the stone, extends his arms, and with his eyes closed slowly approaches it. If the palm of his hand touches the stone, it is a sign that he is innocent of all sin and worthy of paradise. But if, God forbid, his hand should touch some other stone, it is a sign that he is weighed down by iniquity. He must pray and take a vow, and perhaps then Allah the merciful and compassionate will take pity on him, and deliver him from the tortures of hell, and install him in the paradise of the virtuous.*[287]

6 / SHEIK HILLU NEAR HADERA

On one of the hills next to Hadera, hidden under the foliage of some trees, is a tomb sacred to the Arabs, named after Sheik Hillu. It is said that Hillu, which means "Sweet" in Arabic, is only the nickname of this saintly personage. Sheik Hillu was the chieftain of a bedouin tribe bearing his name which encamped in these parts.

And for what reason did Sheik Hillu become sanctified? Sheik Hillu owned a she-camel named Sharkah. They used to load her with corn, and she would go all by herself to the mill and kneel in front of the miller; he would unload the sacks of corn, mill it, and then load her up again with the flour. And Sharkah would return to Sheik Hillu. That was her custom.

It happened once that when Sharkah was on her way back, loaded with flour, some fellahin dwellers of the hills crossed her path. They seized her and led her quickly to their village. There they slaughtered her and made of her meat a plenteous meal. But her head they did not eat; they buried it whole in the ground. It is the way of the Moslems not to eat the camel's head, because when a caravan nears a sacred shrine the first to perceive it is the lofty head of the camel, and so it is sacred and not to be eaten.

Meanwhile, Sheik Hillu was waiting for his camel which had tarried. He went to the mill to ask after her and was told: "Verily, Sharkah was here, but after she was loaded

---

* The Englishman C. Wilson, who engaged in research on ancient Jerusalem in 1865, spoke of a stone fixed in the wall of the Mosque of Aksa, on Mount Moriah, by which the Arabs foretold their fate in the hereafter.

with flour, she set her face homeward as she was wont to do always." Then Sheik Hillu followed her tracks eastward and came to the village at the limit of the mountains. And he approached the villagers and said: "Peace be upon you, men of Gath! How I do worry. Two days are past already and Sharkah has not returned yet; maybe you saw her? And the blessing of Allah will be upon you."

"We have not seen or heard anything," answered the men.

But Sheik Hillu knew the evil deed they had done and called in a loud voice: "O Sharkah, O Sharkah, awake and get up!"

He had just uttered these words when Sharkah's head appeared hovering in the air, her mouth open, her nostrils quivering; she was groaning in great pain.

The men of Gath threw themselves at his feet, begging forgiveness; they knew Sheik Hillu then to be a man of Allah and venerated him greatly.

After his death his tomb was sacred to the men of his tribe and to all the Arabs around.[288]

7 / THE RIVER OF THE CROCODILES

In the Plain of Sharon, near Caesarea and Benyamina, there flows a river from the mountains of Samaria which is called in Hebrew *Nahar Hataninim*—River of the Crocodiles—because of the many crocodiles which once thrived in its waters. Near this river was once a town called *Crocodilopolis*—City of the Crocodiles. In 1877 a female crocodile was caught measuring ten feet in length and bearing forty-eight eggs.

The pilgrim Fetellus wrote in 1148 c. e.: "In the river of Caesarea are crocodiles, horrible serpents. The mouth of the crocodile is distinguished from all mouths in this respect that its upper jaw is movable, while its lower is fixed. . . . The crocodile hates man above all animals. . . .

FIG. 108. CROCODILE (1547) ¹

How crocodiles came to be at Caesarea I shall state shortly. In ancient days two brothers reigned at Caesarea with equal authority; the elder of them, because he was not reigning alone, plotted for the death of his brother, who was afflicted with leprosy, thinking to himself that if he could get two pairs of crocodiles from the Nile to the aforenamed river, his brother, who frequented the river baths in the summertime, would perhaps be killed and he would obtain the kingdom. This actually happened and so the elder reigned alone. And from that time many crocodiles appeared in the river."[289]

8 / THE SPRING OF MOUNT SINA

The anonymous pilgrim from the city of Bordeaux, France, who visited the Holy Land in 333 described his journey from Caesarea to the Valley of Jezreel. About three miles from Caesarea he came to the mountain of Sina. This is likely the southernmost end of the Carmel Range, which stands out on the border of Sharon, close to Benyamina of today.

The pilgrim told about a spring in the vicinity of Mount Sina which has a remarkable virtue. Any sterile woman who bathed in its waters would bring forth a child.

The spring he refered to is probably one of the sources of the River of the Crocodiles, which streams westward to the Mediterranean Sea.[290]

9 / THE DRUM AND ITS STICK

Not far from the ruins of ancient Athlit, the "Castle of the Pilgrims" of the crusaders, along the seashore, there is carved on the leveled surface of a rock wall a big circle with a thick line on its side (fig. 109). Some scholars surmise that these are the two characters "A" and "T" of the ancient Canaanite script and the first two letters of the name Athlit.

In the eyes of the Arabs the circle is like a drum and the line is like a drummer's stick. And if you ask one how they happen to be drawn on the rock, he will tell you that once from the village of Athlit, which was situated in the ruins of the ancient fortress, a happy procession went out eastward to lead a bride to the house of her bridegroom in the village of Ein Ghazal, at the foot of the Carmel Range. The procession proceeded gaily and noisily. Sacred dervishes danced around, whirling their long robes along the way and beating their drums ecstatically.

Suddenly the head of the dervishes' band noticed that the bride did not behave becomingly. He was very angered at her and with all his might he threw the drum and stick which were in his hands. These whirled through the air till they encountered a projecting rock, into which they sank and disappeared. And they left on the rock the graven drawing of a circle and line.[291]

10 / RAHASH STREET IN HADERA

Hadera, one of the first pioneering settlements in Israel, is today a lively, bustling town in the northern part of the Valley of Sharon. It stretches on land formerly covered in part by malarial swamps and in part by sand dunes.

One of the streets of Hadera is named Rahash Street. What is the origin of the name?

During the First World War, on the quiet evening of a

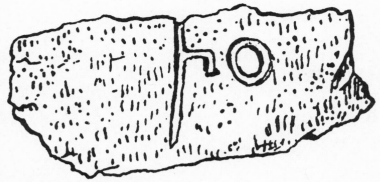

FIG. 109. DRUM AND ITS STICK

Sukkoth (Feast of Tabernacles) day, the small community of Hadera—men, women, and children—went out in carriages and on horseback to spend the time of day on the shore of the sea.

This gay party stayed a few hours on the sands of the beach; the young even kindled a few bonfires and the jollity was complete.

The happenings of that day reached the ears of Abdul Latif Abu Hantash, the sheik of the neighboring townlet of Kakun and a sworn foe of Hadera. He hurried to the Turkish administrator and slandered the inhabitants of Hadera, accusing them of conspiring against the Turks, going out on the beach to contact enemy boats, and even providing them with wheat presumably transported to the shore on the floor of the carriages.

On the Sabbath, the first day of the month of Shevat 1915 (in Hebrew, *Rosh Hodesh Shevat*), Hadera was surrounded by Turkish soldiers with the governor of Jennin at their head. They were followed by large crowds of Arab peasants from Kakun and the surrounding villages, led by Sheik Abu Hantash, who were eager to take part in the looting of Jewish property that they intended to carry out after the arrest of the settlers.

The investigation started in the style of those days, with

insults and blows and flogging on the soles of the feet. The settlers of Hadera were finally handcuffed and put in irons.

Fortunately the story quickly reached Sheik Ahmed Abdallah of the village of Anabta, on the highway to Shechem, a friend of Hadera and an enemy of Sheik Abu Hantash.

He forthwith set out to see the Turkish governor of Shechem, who luckily was spending the day in nearby Tulkarem, and told him of Abu Hantash's evil deeds and of the large military expedition which had gone out to punish Hadera.

The governor speedily proceeded to Hadera to intervene in favor of the settlers, and by the end of the day these were released and Abu Hantash and his wicked, greedy companions were put in chains and thrown into prison in Tulkarem.

From that time *Rosh Hodesh Shevat*—Rahash for short —became a day of rejoicing in Hadera and a street was named for it.[292]

XXVIII
CAESAREA
IN OLDEN DAYS

1 / THE JEWISH NOTABLES OF CAESAREA

Caesarea was the Roman capital of Eretz Israel, the seat of the administration and the headquarters of the army. It had a large, prosperous Jewish community. To the words of the psalmist, "I shall walk before the Lord/In the lands of the living," the sages add: "This refers to Caesarea and its daughter villages where it is cheap to live and hunger unknown."

One of the famous sages of Caesarea was Rabbi Abahu, in the third century. It is said that when he proceeded from the house of study to the house of Caesar, the mothers went to meet him singing his praises: "The greatest of his nation, and the speaker of his people,/The torch bearer, may thy coming be blessed with peace!"

On the day of Rabbi Abahu's death the very columns of Caesarea shed tears.

Once two other important scholars, Rabbi Hanina and Rabbi Joshua son of Levi were invited to meet the governor of Caesarea in his residence. The governor stood up respectfully in front of them. His astonished friends wondered: "You, the representative of the great Roman Empire stand up for these Jews?" Said the governor: "The faces of angels did I see, and I stood up."[293]

2 / THE JEWISH MARTYRS IN CAESAREA

Many of the Jewish rebels who fought against the Romans were imprisoned in Caesarea. Of these the most famous are the Ten Martyrs of Israel (in Hebrew, *Aseret Harugei Malkhut*), among whom was Rabbi Akiba.

The Jewish traveler Yaacov son of Nathanael, who came to Eretz Israel in the twelfth century, wrote: "In Caesarea there is the cave of the Ten Martyrs, and near the entrance is to be found the tomb of a heathen. Once this man appeared in a dream to the elders of the city and cried: 'Take me away from my burying place, for I am being scourged with lashes of iron which are red hot. . . . In the cave near me, there are men wearing white robes and they are like angels.'"

Today there is no sign of this cave; but in the Roman hippodrome of Caesarea lies a big square stone. It is likely the stone that Yaacob the son of Nataniel mentions: "In Caesarea there is a great stone of marble, which is said to have been the throne of Caesar, and on the spot where the martyrs were slain no blade of grass has ever grown."[294]

3 / ROMAN SOLDIERS IN OLD CAESAREA

Once Antoninus, emperor of Rome, came to Caesarea and invited Rabbi Yehuda Hanassi, who lived in Zippori (Sepphoris) in Galilee. He came accompanied by Rabbi Shimon and Rabbi Hiyya the great.

Rabbi Shimon noticed a strong and handsome legionary, whose head reached to the capital of the pillars.

He said to Rabbi Hiyya: "Look how well fattened are the calves of Esau [the nickname of the Romans]."

Rabbi Hiyya took him to the market and, pointing out

FIG. 110. RUINS OF CAESAREA (1850)

to him a basket of grapes and figs covered with flies, he said: "The flies and that legionary are alike one unto the other!"[295]

4 / ON THE COAST OF ANCIENT CAESAREA

It is told that Rabbi Izhak son of Eliezer, while strolling along the coast of Caesarea, saw a bone lying on the ground. He pressed it into the sand with his foot, but it kept rolling out. He pressed it back again and said: "This bone has a purpose."

One day the messenger of Caesar passed the same way. The bone rolled between his feet; he stumbled and fell down dead.

He was searched and was found to be carrying decrees against the Jews of Caesarea.[296]

5 / THE WAYS OF JUSTICE IN ANCIENT CAESAREA

"There was once a governor who used to put to death

the receivers [of stolen property] and release the thieves, and all used to find fault with him, saying that he was not acting correctly.

"What did he do? He issued a proclamation throughout the province saying: 'Let all the people go out to the campus!'

"What did he do then? He brought some weasels and placed before them portions of food. The weasels took the portions and carried them to their holes.

"The next day he again issued a proclamation, saying: 'Let the people go out to the campus!' Again he brought weasels and placed portions of food before them, but stopped up all holes. The weasels took the portions and carried them to their holes, but finding these stopped up, they brought their portions back to their places. [He did this] to demonstrate that all the trouble is due to receivers."

There was a saying in old Hebrew literature: "It's not the mouse that steals, but the hole!"[297]

6 / IN THE THEATERS OF ROMAN CAESAREA

Among the views of Roman Caesarea one can see a hippodrome and a theater on the seashore (fig. 111). The masses of the foreign population used to come here to enjoy the horse racing and the performances. Jews looked with hatred upon these establishments and their sages decreed: "Do not go to the theater and to the circus because admiration for them serves as manure for the growth of idolatry!"

The Jews used to pray thus: "I am thankful to Thee, God my Lord, and the Lord of my fathers, that Thou hast put my share with those who rejoice in the house of study and in the house of prayer and not with those who waste their lives in circuses and theaters."

When the news of the fall of Jerusalem into the hands

FIG. 111. ROMAN THEATER IN CAESAREA

of the Romans reached Caesarea, its notables were enjoy-
ing themselves in its theaters and circuses; and they poked
fun at the miserable Jews whom poverty compelled to
live on the carob's fruit (St.-John's-bread) and on thorns
and thistles, the food of camels.

A sage of Caesarea expostulated: "The people of the
world sit in theaters and circuses and play music and drink
to excess; and while they wallow in food and intoxicate
themselves they sit and mock me saying: 'God forbid that
we shall ever eat carobs like the Jews.' And they bring
into their theater a camel . . . and they ask among themselves: 'Why does it look so mournful?' And they answer:
'These Jews . . . have no vegetables and they have eaten
up all his thistles; therefore he is grieving.'"

On the ruins of Roman Caesarea a new Jewish Caesarea

stands. Its rows of bright houses surrounded with green are built over the remnants of the proud theaters and hippodrome which lie at their feet in the dust.[298]

7 / THE RIVALRY BETWEEN CAESAREA AND JERUSALEM

Jerusalem has been the capital of Israel and its spiritual center from its earliest days. Caesarea was the metropolis of Roman rule and the center of its influence in Palestine. The foreign Caesarea was built upon the destruction of the Israelites' Jerusalem, and she was hostile to its Hebrew culture.

The sages of Israel said: "Caesearea and Jerusalem—if anyone should tell thee that both are destroyed, do not believe him; if he says both are peopled, believe him not.

"If he says Caesarea is destroyed and Jerusalem is peopled, or Jerusalem is destroyed and Caesarea is peopled, believe him.

"When the one is replenished the other must be waste; both cannot flourish or be desolate at the same time."

In our days Jerusalem flourishes as the capital of Israel and the spiritual center of the Hebrew culture, and on the ruins of Roman Caesarea, a newly built Jewish Caesarea prospers.[299]

8 / EKRON—CAESAREA

Rabbi Abahu of Caesarea chose to designate his city by the name Ekron, after the famous Philistine town and one of the main centers of hostility toward Israel in the past; wherefore the prophet cursed her and predicted her bitter end: "And Ekron shall be rooted up./Woe unto the inhabitants of the seacoast./. . . I will even destroy thee, that there shall be no inhabitant."

As for Rome, Rabbi Abahu called her Edom, for the two vied in power and in their hatred for the Israelites, and he said: "Ekron shall be rooted up; this is Caesarea the daughter of Edom [Rome], which is situated among the sands, and which was a thorn in the side of Israel since the days of the Greeks."[300]

9 / THE GOOD LIFE IN CAESAREA

Here are two stories from the Midrash about a baker and a cook.

"It happened that a woman took her son to a baker in Caesarea and said to him: 'Teach my son the trade.'

"He replied to her: 'Let him stay with me five years and I will teach him five hundred confections with wheat.'

"He stayed with him five years and was taught five hundred confections with wheat.

"The baker said to her: 'Let him stay with me another five years and I will teach him a thousand confections with wheat!' "

"A woman of Caesarea once took her son to a cook and said to him: 'Teach my son the trade.'

"He replied to her: 'Let him stay with me four years and I will teach him a hundred dishes made from eggs.'

"He stayed with him four years and was taught a hundred dishes made from eggs.

"The cook said to her: 'Let him stay with me another four years and I will teach him another hundred dishes from eggs.'

"Rabbi [Yehuda Hanassi] heard this and exclaimed: 'We do not know what good living is!' "[301]

10 / WHO BUILT THE AQUEDUCT OF CAESAREA?

If you wander around Caesarea you are sure to see a great aqueduct stretching from the foothills of the Samarian mountains to the town. Should you follow this aqueduct from the hills to the town, you will find it starting gaily off with three conduits. Go farther, and first one, then a second conduit disappears, and only one forlorn watercourse reaches the town.

Presumably being of an inquiring turn of mind, you may ask the reason. It is as follows.

In the days of old the daughter of the king of Caesarea had no peer for beauty in the whole land. And she had three suitors: a Moslem, a Jew, and a Christian. She was much perplexed, for she was equally fond of them all; so she went to her father for counsel. He was a wise man and answered: "My child, we must act in the best interests of the city. Whichever of the three you choose, the other two sections of the dwellers in the land will be displeased. So you cannot choose arbitrarily but must eliminate two of your suitors without giving offense. You can do it this way: the water pits of the city are salty and brackish, but in the foothills are fountains of fresh living water. Let him who brings this fresh water to Caesarea first win your hand."

So the three youths went out to the hills and began to build three conduits. But soon one grew tired and forsook the labor, leaving the others to continue. So they went on with two conduits. But when the second one saw that the first was working much more rapidly, he too gave up the work in despair. So only one was left and he was the first to bring living water to Caesarea. He was lucky and married the princess and they lived happily ever after.

But do not ask whether it was the Jew, the Moslem, or the Christian who won the bride. For I swear there is no one who can tell you.[302]

11 / HOW WAS CAESAREA RID OF ITS BAD SMELLS?

In 1130 the Christian pilgrim Fetellus, who visited the Holy Land during the Crusades, told the following story.

"In the circuit of the city, among gardens, were various small caves, constructed of sawn stones, in which spices

FIG. 112. ROMAN AQUEDUCT IN CAESAREA

and aromatics were mingled in the fire. Hence the whole city was redolent of the combining wafted odors, shutting out all bad smells and causing exhilaration in the countenances of the citizens."[303]

THE ANCIENT SOURCES

THE BIBLE. It is divided into three parts: Torah or Pentateuch, Nebiim (Neviim) or Prophets, and Ketubim (Ketuvim) or Writings (Hagiographia); hence the Hebrew name of the Bible: *Tanakh*. The English translation used in the series The Sacred Land is by the Jewish Publication Society of America, Philadelphia.

RASHI. The most popular commentator on the Bible. Rashi is the acronym taken from his full name: Rabbi Shelomo Izhaki. He lived at the end of the eleventh century in France.

RADAK. Another commentator on the Bible. Radak is contracted from Rabbi David Kimchi. He lived in the thirteenth century in Narbonne, France.

JOSEPHUS. The Jewish historian Joseph ben Mattitiahu Hacohen. He was born in Jerusalem about 38 C. E. and took part in the revolt against Rome. His various treatises on the history of the Jews have survived in Greek and have been widely translated. His main works are *Antiquities of the Jews* and *Wars of the Jews against the Romans*.

MISHNAH. From the Hebrew *shano,* "to study." This is a literary creation written in Hebrew, mainly in the second century, and compiled in the Galilee in 200 c. e. The Mishnah, sometimes called in the plural Mishnayot, is divided into six orders (Hebrew *Shisha* Sedarim, which gave rise to the contracted name: *Shas*). Each order (*seder*) contains various tractates (*masekhot*), sixty-three tractates in all. The English translations used here are by H. Danby (Oxford, 1933) and P. Blackman, (New York, 1965).

TOSEFTA. The Aramaic form of the Hebrew *tosefet,* which means "supplement." It is an addition to the Mishnah, which was compiled and edited in Eretz Israel at the end of the fourth century.

TALMUD. From the Hebrew *lamod,* "to learn"; Talmud-learning. A vast collective literary creation to which hundreds of sages contributed during the course of several generations. There are two Talmuds, each produced by a different school of study, one in Eretz Israel and the other abroad:

Talmud Yerushalmi was compiled in Eretz Israel, mainly in the Galilee; it is named Yerushalmi (Jerusalemite) as an expression of longing for the capital then held by foes. It is sometimes called the Palestinian Talmud. It was completed at the end of the fourth century, under Byzantine rule. Mainly written in Aramaic, it is about one-third the size of the Talmud Babli. The only existing translation was by M. Schwab into French, eleven volumes, published in 1871–89, Paris.

Talmud Babli (or *Bavli*), the Babylonian Talmud, was compiled in Babylon (Hebrew *Babel* or *Bavel*) at the end of the fifth century. Written in Aramaic and Hebrew, it is a comprehensive treatise of Judaic laws and a treasury of Jewish folklore. The English translation of the whole Babylonian Talmud was done by a number of scholars under the editorship of I. Epstein and published in 1935–52 by Soncino Press, London.

ABOTH DE-RABBI NATHAN. A collection of folk tales concerning the forefathers, *aboth* or *avot* in Hebrew, and named after its compiler, Rabbi Nathan, who lived in the third century. There are two versions of the work, A and B. They were published by S. Schechter in 1887. The English translation of version A was published by A. Goldin in 1955, New Haven.

MECHILTA DE-RABBI ISHMAEL. *Mechilta* is Hebrew-Aramaic for "collection." This *mechilta* is named for the sage mentioned in its opening sentence: "Rabbi Ishmael says. . . ." It is a collection of interpretations of the Book of Exodus, written in approximately the eighth century. An English translation by J. Z. Lauterbach was published by the Jewish Publication Society in 1933–35, Philadelphia.

MECHILTA DE-RABBI SHIMON BAR-YOHAI. A collection of commentaries on Exodus compiled about the fifth century and attributed to the famous rabbi of the second century who lived in Eretz Israel. His tomb, in the Galilee, is venerated to this day.

MIDRASH TANAIM. The Hebrew word *midrash* is derived from *darosh*, to inquire, to investigate. *Tanaim* (singular *tana*) is the title accorded to the sages of the Mishnah period. *Midrash Tanaim* is a collection of exegeses to Deuteronomy.

TANHUMA. A collection of legendary explanations to the Torah (Pentateuch) written by Tanhuma son of Abba, in the fourth and fifth centuries.

PESIKTA DE-RAB KAHANA. *Pesikta* is Hebrew-Aramaic for "portion." This was written in the sixth and seventh centuries and attributed to Rabbi Kahana. The English translation by W. G. Braude, published in New Haven, was used here except where otherwise indicated;

the Jewish Publication Society's English translation by
Braude was published in 1975.

MIDRASH RABBA. *Rabba* is similar to *Rabbati*. This is
a large collection of various homiletics on Torah quota-
tions (Five Books of Moses) and the Five Scrolls. It
was composed by various rabbis who lived from the
fourth to the twelfth centuries.

Its first five volumes deal with the Five Books of
Moses: *Bereishith Rabba* is about Genesis, approximately
fifth century; *Shemot Rabba* is about Exodus, approximately tenth century; *Va-Yikra Rabba* is about
Leviticus, approximately seventh–ninth centuries; *Ba-
Midbar Rabba* is about Numbers, approximately eighth–
ninth centuries; *Debarim Rabba* is about Deuteronomy,
approximately eighth–ninth centuries.

The next five volumes deal with the Scrolls: *Shir
ha-Shirim Rabba* is about the Song of Songs, approximately seventh–eighth centuries; *Ruth Rabba* is about
the Book of Ruth, approximately seventh–tenth centuries; *Eicha Rabba* is about the Book of Lamentations,
approximately fifth century; *Koheleth Rabba* is about
the Book of Ecclesiastes, approximately seventh century; *Esther Rabba* is about the Book of Esther, approximately fifth century.

An English translation was prepared under the editorship of H. Freedman and M. Simon and published
in ten volumes, in 1939, by Soncino Press, London.

MIDRASH TEHILLIM. Relates to the Book of Psalms
(Hebrew *Tehillim*), *Shoher Tov* (Hebrew for "seeketh
good") is another name of *Midrash Tehillim* because
it opens with the following verse: "He that diligently
seeketh good seeketh favor" (Proverbs 11:27). *Midrash
Tehillim* was composed in the ninth–tenth centuries
approximately, probably in Eretz Israel. The English
translation was prepared by W. G. Braude and published in two volumes in 1957, New Haven.

PIRKE RABBI ELIEZER. *Pirke* is Hebrew for "chapters." This is attributed to Eliezer son of Hyrcanos, a prominent sage. It is a collection of homiletics and tales and was written about the ninth century in Eretz Israel. The English translation done by G. Friedlander appeared in 1916, London.

ZOHAR. Hebrew for "splendor." This is a collection, written partly in Aramaic and partly in Hebrew, of mystical commentaries on the five books of the Torah, the Pentateuch. It is attributed to the above-mentioned Rabbi Shimon bar-Yohai, although in fact it was composed in Spain, in the thirteenth century by Rabbi Moses de Leon, probably from earlier sources.

The *Zohar* is the fundamental book of the Cabala—Jewish mysticism. Its adepts are called Cabalists. *Cabbala* is Hebrew for "reception." Every generation was supposed to receive the secrets of mysticism from the generation preceding it. The English translation of the *Zohar* was done by H. Sperling and M. Simon and published in five volumes by Soncino Press in 1931–34, London.

YALKUT SHIMONI is a comprehensive collection (in Hebrew, *yalkut*) of legendary commentaries and rabbinical sayings covering all the books of the Bible. It was edited by Rabbi Shimoni, "chief of the preachers" of Frankfurt, Germany, in the thirteenth century.

BEIT HA-MIDRASH. Hebrew for "the house of study"; the name of a modern publication of various small Hebrew tractates of later periods, edited by A. Yellinek. The six volumes of *Beit ha-Midrash* were originally published in 1853–77, Germany.

ABBREVIATIONS

JJS—*Journal of Jewish Studies*

JQR—*Jewish Quarterly Review*

MGWJ—*Monatsschrift für Geschichte und Wissenschaft des Judentums*

MPCC—*Migne, Patrologiae Cursus Completus*

PEQS—*Palestine Exploration Fund, Quarterly Statement*

PPTS—*Palestine Pilgrims Text Society*

QDAP—*Quarterly of the Department of Antiquities in Palestine*

REJ—*Revue des Études Juives*

ZDPV—*Zeitschrift des Deutschen Palästina Vereins*

SOURCES OF THE LEGENDS

1. *WHERE THE PROPHET ELIJAH RESTED:* 1 Kings
   19:3. *Descriptiones Terra Sancta* (ed. Tobler), VII, p.
   105. E. Suriano, *Il Trattaro di Terra Santa* [Treatise on the
   Holy Land], 1949, p. 119.
2. *THE WELL OF THE STAR:* Matthew 2:1–2, 8–10.
   Theodosius, in *PPTS*, II, 1893, p. 17. *The Pylgrymage of
   Sir Richard Guylforde*, 1506, p. 35.
3. *THE FIELD OF THE PROPHET HABAKKUK:* Bernar-
   dus Monachus, in *Itinerarium* (ed. Tobler–Moliner), I,
   p. 317. Bonifacius de Stephanis, *Liber de perenni cultu
   Terrae Sanctae*, 1875. *Yosifon*, 1896–1913 ed., p. 25.
4. *THE FIELD OF THE PETRIFIED PEAS:* Ricoldes de
   Monte Crucis, in Laurent, *Peregrinatores medii aevi qua-
   tuor*, 1864, p. 110. Genesis 25:33. Theodoricus, *Libellus de
   Locis Sanctis* (ed. Tobler), p. 76. *Travels of the Late
   Charles Thompson*, III, 1752, p. 156. Flavius Josephus,
   Wars, 12, 5, 2.
5. *THE FIELD OF FLOWERS—CAMPUS FLORIDUS:*
   Odoricus de Foro Julii, in Laurent, *Peregrinatores*, p. 153.
   "The Voiage and Trauaile of Syr John Maundevile Knight,"

1832, p. 69 (from a manuscript in the British Museum, Cotton Titus c.XVI). *The Pylgrymage of Sir Richard Guylforde*, p. 36.

6. *THE BIRTHPLACE OF BENJAMIN:* Genesis 35:16–20.

7. *THE HOUSE OF JACOB THE PATRIARCH:* Reyzen van Cornelius de Bruyn, 1681; T. Ehrenstein, *Das Alte Testament im Bild*, 1923.

8. *THE WELL OF DAVID IN BETHLEHEM:* 2 Samuel 23:14–17.

9. *THE MILK GROTTO IN BETHLEHEM:* An article by an anonymous pilgrim, in *PPTS*, VI, 1894, p. 16. Ludolphus of Suchem (Sudheim), "Descriptio terrae sanctae," *PPTS*, XII, 1895, p. 95. W. Lithgow, *The Totall Discourse of the Rare Adventures & Painfull Peregrinations*, 1906, p. 247. Mark Twain, *The Innocents Abroad*.

10. *THE FIELD OF BOAZ AND RUTH:* Ruth 2:1.

11. *WHERE IS ANCIENT RAMAH?* Jeremiah 31:15. J. Doubdan, *Le Voyage de la Terre-Sainte*, 1666, p. 170. *Two Journeys to Jerusalem*, 1687, p. 97. Henri Maundrell, *Journey from Aleppo to Jerusalem*. R. Pococke, *A Description of the East*, II, 1745, p. 45.

12. *THE POOLS OF SOLOMON:* Ecclesiastes 2:4–6. Flavius Josephus, *Antiquities*, VIII, 3. F. Troilo, *Orientalische Reis-Beschreibung*, 1717, p. 425.

13. *SOLOMON'S TEMPLE AND THE SPRING OF EITAM:* Babli, Yoma 31a; Zebahim 54b. Deuteronomy 33:12.

14. *THE SPRING OF EITAM AND THE HIGH PRIEST:* The commentary of Rashi to Babli, Shabbath 148b. J. Schwarz, *A Descriptive Geography of Palestine*, 1850, p. 269.

15. *THE CLOSED GARDEN AND SEALED FOUNTAIN:* Song of Songs 4:1, 4, 12–15. *Midrash Zuta* (ed. Buber), p. 6.

16. *THE POOLS OF SOLOMON AND RACHEL'S SON:* Mujir ed-Din, *Kitab al-Uns ej-Jalil be-Taarikh al-Kuds wal-Khalil*.

17. *THE SPRING OF EITAM AND THE EUPHRATES*

RIVER: Yerushalmi, Taanith 4:8. Babli, Shabbath 145b and Rashi's commentary.

18. *EL-KHADER—THE EVERGREEN:* I heard this story from one of the villagers.

19. *MIGDAL EDER AND THE MESSIAH:* Genesis 35:21 and the Aramaic translation. Micah 4:8.

20. *WHERE DOES THE MESSIAH COME FROM?:* Song of Songs 2:8. *Shir ha-Shirim Rabba* 2. *Midrash Sechel Tov, Vaishlah,* 1900, p. 200. Yerushalmi, Berachoth 2. *Eicha Rabba* 1:16.

21. *BEITAR IN ITS GREATNESS:* Babli, Yebamoth 122a; Gittin 58a. Yerushalmi, Taanith 4. *Eicha Rabba* 2:2. *Beit Eked ha-Agadoth* (ed. Horowitz–ha-Levi) I, 1881, p. 40.

22. *WHAT CAUSED THE DESTRUCTION OF BEITAR?* Babli, Gittin 58a. *Eicha Rabba* 2:2.

23. *BAR-KOKHBA—THE HERO OF BEITAR:* Yerushalmi, Taanith 4. Numbers 24:17.

24. *THE FATE OF BAR-KOKHBA: Otzar Massaoth* (ed. Eisenstein), 1926.

25. *EMPEROR HADRIAN DESTROYED BEITAR: Eicha Rabba* 2:2.

26. *IN MEMORY OF THE MARTYRS OF BEITAR:* Babli, Berachoth 48b.

27. *BEITAR AND ITS NEIGHBOR KOBI:* Babli, Sanhedrin 95b. 2 Samuel 21:17.

28. *HEBRON IS KIRYAT ARBA: Aboth de-Rabbi Nathan* (B) 43. Isaiah 41:8. Babli, Eirubin 53a; Sottah 13a. N. Shapira, *Tuv Haarez,* 1655.

29. *THE FIELD OF ADAM:* Genesis 2:7, 3:19. *Yerushalaim* (ed. Lunz), VII, 1906, p. 91. Yaacob ben Nataniel (ed. Gruenhut), 1905. Fettelus (Frettelus), in *PPTS,* V, 1897, p. 9. John of Würzburg, in *PPTS,* V, 1896, p. 58.

30. *THE CAVERN OF ADAM AND EVE:* Maundrell, in T. Wright, *Early Travels in Palestine,* 1848, p. 490. N. Poggibonsi, *Libro d'Oltramare,* 1945. Suriano, *Il Trattaro di Terra Santa,* p. 149.

31. *THE FIELD OF ABEL'S DEATH:* Genesis 4:8. *Pirke*

Rabbi Eliezer 21. V. Aptowitzer, *Kain und Abel in der Agada*, 1922. *The Pilgrimage of Arnold von Harff*, 1946, p. 231. Eusebius Hieronymus (Saint Jerome), *Commentarii Ezekiel* 27:18.

32. *THE HOUSE OF ABRAHAM: Travels of Rabbi Benjamin of Tudela*, 1840, p. 42.
33. *THE SYNAGOGUE OF ABRAHAM:* Naphtali Elhanan, *Emek Hamelech*, p. 14a. Shneur Zalman, *Zichron Yerushalaim*, Jerusalem, 1876, p. 10.
34. *JEWISH PENITENTS IN HEBRON:* Yeshaya Horowitz (Shiloh Hakadosh), *Shenei Luhot Haberit*, "Perek Yoma," "Amud Hateshuva," p. 227b.
35. *THE MIRACLE AT HEBRON:* L. A. Fraenkl, *Nach Jerusalem*, II, 1858, p. 475. J. Meyuhas, in *Yerushalaim* (ed. Lunz), IX, 1911, p. 322.
36. *PURIM OF HEBRON: Yerushalaim* (ed. Lunz), IX, 1911, p. 323.
37. *THE OAK OF ABRAHAM:* Genesis 18:1–2, 8. Josephus, *Wars*, IV, 9, 7. Idem, *Antiquities*, 1, 10, 4. Arculfus, in *PPTS*, III, 1897, p. 39. John of Würzburg, in *PPTS*, V, 1896, p. 59. "The Voiage and Trauaile of Syr John Maundevile Knight."
38. *THE TENT OF ABRAHAM: Sibub Rabbi Petahia* (ed. Gruenhut).
39. *THE VINEYARD OF NOAH:* Genesis 9:20–21. *A Spanish Franciscan's Narrative of a Journey to the Holy Land* (ed. H. C. Luke), 1927, p. 37. Z. Vilnay, *Mazevot Kodesh be-Erez-Israel*, 1963, p. 68.
40. *THE PLACE OF THE CERTAIN TRUTH:* Genesis 19:27–28. Al-Mukaddasi, *Ahsan al-Takassim fi Muarif al-Akalim*, 1906, p. 178.
41. *BOR SIRAH—THE CRUSE AND THE THORNY BURNET:* 2 Samuel 3:26–27, 32. Babli, Sanhedrin 49a. Yerushalmi, Sottah 1:7. 1 Samuel 26:7.
42. *DAVID THE SHEPHERD IN THE WILDERNESS:* Psalms 63:2. *Bereishith Rabba* 39:8. *Shemot Rabba* 2:2.
43. *THE ROCK OF DISPUTE:* 1 Samuel 23:28. *Yalkut Shimoni, 1 Samuel* 133.

44. *DAVID THE SHEPHERD AND THE WILD OX:* *Midrash Tehillim* (Lekah Tov) 22:28 (ed. Buber), p. 98. Psalms 22:22, 78:69. *Yalkut Shimoni, Job* 926.

45. *THE WILDERNESS IN THE MESSIAH'S TIME: Beit ha-Midrash* (ed. Yellinek), IV, p. 125; II, p. 61. *Sefer Zerubbabel.*

46. *THE ASCENT OF ADUMMIM:* Joshua 15:7, 18:17. Eusebius Hieronymus, *Onomastikon,* 1904, p. 25. Ricoldes de Monte Crucis, *Itinerarius* (ed. Laurent), p. 108.

47. *FROM THE ASCENT OF ADUMMIM:* Babli, Rosh ha-Shana 22b. Tosefta, Rosh ha-Shana 1:15. Yerushalmi, Rosh ha-Shana 2:1.

48. *THE ROCK OF THE BACKS:* F. G. Carpenter, *The Holy Land and Syria,* 1923, p. 124.

49. *ELIJAH IN THE BROOK OF CHERITH:* 1 Kings 17:5–6. *Bereishith Rabba* 5:5. Babli, Hullin 5a.

50. *THE BUBBLING FOUNT:* T. Canaan, "Haunted Springs and Water Demons in Palestine," *JPOS,* 1921, p. 4.

51. *THE HAUNTED FOUNTAIN: Tanhuma, Kedoshim* (ed. Buber), II, p. 39. *Midrash Tehillim* (Shoher Tov), 20:7, 1891, p. 176. *Yalkut Shimoni, Tehillim* 580.

52. *THE CAVE OF THE SHEPHERD:* L. Bauer, *Das Palestinische Arabish,* 1913, p. 212.

53. *THE CLIFF OF THE SCAPEGOAT:* Leviticus 16:10, 21–22. Babli, Yoma 67b. Radak, *Sefer Hashorashim,* s.v. "Ez." Tosefta, Yom ha-Kippurim 4:13.

54. *HOW WAS THE SCAPEGOAT CHOSEN?:* Leviticus 16:5, 10–22. Mishnah, Yoma 4:1.

55. *THE FATE OF THE SCAPEGOAT:* Babli, Yoma 67b. Tosefta, Yom ha-Kippurim 4:13.

56. *THE SCAPEGOAT IN THE TIME OF SHIMON THE JUST:* Yerushalmi, Yoma 4:3.

57. *MIRD—THE CITY OF NIMROD:* C. Clermont-Ganneau, *Archaeological Researches in Palestine,* I, 1899, p. 301.

58. *THE LAND OF BENJAMIN:* Joshua 18:11–12. Genesis 49:27.

59. *THE DIVINE PRESENCE IN BENJAMIN:* Deuteronomy 33:12. Babli, Zebahim 118b.
60. *WHERE ARE THE THOUSAND BENJAMINITES?:* Judges 20:15. The commentary of Radak to Judges 20:15. The commentary of Rabbi Isaac Abarbanel. Zacuto, *Sefer Yohasin Hashalem,* 1857, p. 7. Gedaliah ben Yihya, 1877, p. 19. N. Brüll, *Jahrbücher fur Jüdische Geschichte,* III, 1877, pp. 34–40.
61. *JACOB'S VISION AT BETHEL:* Genesis 28:10–13, 16–19. Babli, Hullin 91b.
62. *JACOB'S PILLOW IN WESTMINSTER ABBEY: Encyclopaedia Britannica,* s. v. "Westminster."
63. *BETHEL IS JERUSALEM:* Genesis 28:16. John of Würzburg, in *PPTS,* V, 1896, p. 14.
64. *BETHEL WAS FIRST CALLED LUZ:* Genesis 28:19. *Bereishith Rabba* 69:8. *Yalkut Shimoni, Shoftim* 38. Judges 1:22. Babli, Sottah 46b.
65. *THE ASCENT OF BETH HORON:* Joshua 18:14, 10:10–11. Babli, Berachoth 54a, Nidah 61a.
66. *THE MIRACLES IN THE ASCENT OF BETH HORON:* Babli, Sanhedrin 32b. Tosefta, Nidah 8:7.
67. *JOSHUA'S VICTORY IN THE VALLEY OF AYALON:* Joshua 10:12–14, 24:30. Babli, Baba Bathra 75a; Berachoth 58a. *Pirke Rabbi Eliezer* 49.
68. *THE CAVE OF THE GORGE:* L. Haefeli, *Syria und sein Lebanon,* 1926, p. 12.
69. *JERICHO—THE TOWN OF THE MOON:* Deuteronomy 4:19. *Yosifon* 38. Josephus, *Wars,* I, 6, 6. The commentary of Rashi to Ezekiel 27:17.
70. *JERICHO—THE TOWN OF PERFUME: Yosifon* 38. Babli, Yoma 39b.
71. *THE HOUSE OF RAHAB IN JERICHO:* Joshua 2:1. *Yalkut Shimoni, Joshua* 9. *Pesikta de-Rab Kahana,* p. 115a.
72. *THE SPIES IN THE STREETS OF JERICHO:* Joshua 2:1. *Ba-Midbar Rabba* 15:1. *Ruth Rabba* 2:1.
73. *WHY HAS THE BULL NO HAIR ON HIS NOSE?: Alpha-Beitha de-Ben Sira, Otzar Midrashim* (ed. Eisen-

stein), p. 47. *Midrash Tanaim*, p. 218. *Bereishith Rabba* 39:11. Deuteronomy 33:17.

74. *"WHOEVER SEES THE WALL OF JERICHO . . .":* Babli, Berachoth 54a. R. Rabbinovicz, *Dikdukei Sofrim*, I, 1868, p. 146. *Yalkut Shimoni, Joshua* 11. Joshua 24:11.

75. *SEVEN TIMES AROUND THE ALTAR:* Yerushalmi, Sukkah 4:3. *Midrash Tehillim* (Shoher Tov) 17 (ed. Buber), p. 65. Eliezer of Gremiza, *Harokeah Hagadol*, 1960, p. 124, n. 221.

76. *THE FATE OF HIEL, WHO BUILT JERICHO:* Joshua 6:26. 1 Kings 16:34. Babli, Sanhedrin 113a. *Seder Eliyahu Zutta* (ed. Ish-Shalom), 1904, p. 185.

77. *"GO TO JERICHO!"—"STAY IN JERICHO!":* J. A. H. Murray, *Oxford Dictionary*, s. v. "Jericho." 2 Samuel 10:5.

78. *JERUSALEM VOICES IN JERICHO:* Babli, Yoma 20b, 39b. Mishnah, Tamid 3:8. Yerushalmi, Sukkah 5:3. *Midrash Zuta, Koheleth* (ed. Buber), p. 127.

79. *THE SPRING OF THE PROPHET ELISHA:* 2 Kings 2:19. Yerushalmi, Berachoth 5:1. Babli, Berachoth 58b.

80. *THE MOURNING PLACE OF JACOB:* Genesis 50:9–12. Babli, Sottah 13a. *Bereishith Rabba* 96. Eusebius Hieronymus, *Onomastikon*, pp. 8–9. Poggibonsi, *Libro d'Oltramare*.

81. *GOG IN THE VALLEY OF JERICHO:* Ezekiel 38–39. Babli, Berachoth 58a. *Sifri, Debarim*, 357.

82. *THE SNAKES OF JERICHO:* Antonini Placentini (ed. Geyer), p. 165. Al-Mukaddasi, *Ahsan al-Takassim*, p. 175. Ibn Keisarani, *Al-Ansab al-Mutafaka*, 1865, p. 33. "Ernoul's Account of Palestine," *PPTS*, VI, 1896, p. 58. Ludolphus of Suchem, "Descriptio terrae sanctae."

83. *THE ROSE OF JERICHO:* Moshe Hess, *Rome und Jerusalem*, 1863, (Hebrew translation, David Zemah, 1899), p. 85. A. H. Langbank, *Ha-Magid*, XXI, no. 36, 1877, p. 329.

84. *JACOB THE PATRIARCH ON THE JORDAN:* Genesis 32:10–11 and the commentary of Rashi on Genesis 32. "Midrash Yelamdenu," *Beit ha-Midrash* (ed. Yellinek) VI, p. 81. *Bereishith Rabba* 76:5.

85. *THE JORDAN OF JERICHO:* Psalms 114:1, 3. Babli, Berachoth 54a. Joshua 3:14–17. Ashtori ha-Parhi, *Kaftor Va-Perah* (ed. Lunz), p. 119.
86. *THE STONES ON THE BANK OF THE JORDAN:* Joshua 4:5–9. Tosefta, Sottah 8:6. Babli, Sottah 34a. Yerushalmi, Sottah 7:8. Antoninus Martyr, in *PPTS*, II, 1896. Arculfus, in *PPTS*, III, 1897.
87. *THE HOLY FIELD OF GILGAL:* Luke 19:1. Theodosius, in *PPTS*, II, 1893, pp. 7, 14. Antoninus Martyr, in *PPTS*, II, 1896, p. 12.
88. *THE PRAYER ON THE JORDAN:* Babli, Berachoth 54a. Ha-Parhi, *Kaftor Va-Perah* (ed. Lunz), p. 121.
89. *ADAM IN THE WATERS OF THE JORDAN: Vita Adae* 1:17. Louis Ginzberg, *Legends of the Jews*, I, p. 87.
90. *ELIJAH AND ELISHA ON THE JORDAN:* 2 Kings 2:7–14, 6:1–7.
91. *JEREMIAH ON THE BANKS OF THE JORDAN: Eicha Rabba, Petihta,* 24. *Yalkut Shimoni, Eicha* 986.
92. *"LET THE JORDAN BE THY BORDER":* Jeremiah 12:5, 49:19. Zechariah 11:3. Yerushalmi, Moed Kattan 2.
93. *TWO FISHERMEN IN THE JORDAN:* Tosefta, Yebamoth 14:6. Babli, Yebamoth 121a.
94. *FISH FROM THE JORDAN AND THE MEDITERRANEAN: Aboth de-Rabbi Nathan* (A) 40.
95. *THE JORDAN AND THE MEDITERRANEAN SEA:* Babli, Baba Bathra 74b. Florent Goujon, *Histoire et Voyage de la Terre Sainte*, 1671, p. 225.
96. *THE LION ON THE BANKS OF THE JORDAN:* Ludolphus of Suchem. "Descriptio terrae sanctae."
97. *THE JORDAN FLOWS INTO THE BEHEMOTH:* Job 40:15–23. *Ba-Midbar Rabba* 21:18. Babli, Bekhoroth 55a; Baba Bathra 74b; Zebahim 113b. *Pesikta Rabbati*, 1880, p. 194b. *Yalkut Shimoni, Job* 926, 40.
98. *"NO MAN EVER DROWNED IN THE DEAD SEA":* Babli, Shabbath 108b. Josephus, *Wars*, IV, 8, 4. R. Steele, *Mediaeval Lore*, 1905, p. 172.
99. *"TAKE IT TO THE DEAD SEA!":* Mishnah, Abodah Zarah 3:3; Nazir 4:4. Yerushalmi, Abodah Zarah 1:4.

100. *THE DEAD SEA IN THE END OF TIME:* Zechariah 14:2, 8. Ezekiel 47:8–9, 10–12. Yerushalmi, Shekalim 6:2. Tosefta, Sukkah 3:9.

101. *THE MIRACLE OF THE ARNON RIVER:* Babli, Berachoth 54a, 58a. Numbers 21:14–15. *Ba-Midbar Rabba* 19:25.

102. *THE TWO LEPERS IN THE BATTLE OF THE ARNON:* Numbers 21:14 and Aramaic translations. Babli, Berachoth 54a.

103. *THE BATTLE OF THE ARNON—A "MIGHTY DEED":* *Mechilta*, II, p. 151. Deuteronomy 3:24. 1 Chronicles 29:10.

104. *THE POOL OF ABRAHAM THE PATRIARCH:* I heard this story from a bedouin while I was touring the banks of the Dead Sea in 1925.

105. *THE FATE OF LOT'S WIFE:* Genesis 19:1, 12–26. *Bereishith Rabba* 51:7. *Sefer Hayashar.*

106. *LOT'S WIFE—PILLAR OF SALT:* Babli, Berachoth 54a. Josephus, *Antiquities,* I, 11, 4. *Travels of Rabbi Benjamin of Tudela.*

107. *EIN GEDI—A VINEYARD IN CYPRUS:* Wilbrandi de Oldenborg, in Laurent, *Peregrinatores,* p. 181. Song of Songs 1:14.

108. *ZOAR AND ITS SPRING:* Genesis 14:2, 19:20. *Bereishith Rabba* 50:10. Deuteronomy 34:3. Al-Mukaddasi, *Ahsan al-Takassim.*

109. *THE OVERTHROW OF SODOM AND GOMORRAH:* Genesis 18:20–23, 19:24–28. Amos 4:11. Lamentations 4:6.

110. *THE FATE OF THE CITIES OF THE PLAIN:* Genesis 10:19. Deuteronomy 29:22. Babli, Baba Bathra 24b; Shabbath 109a.

111. *THE KINGS OF SODOM AND GOMORRAH:* Genesis 14:2. *Bereishith Rabba* 42:5.

112. *JUDGES IN SODOM AND ITS NEIGHBORHOOD:* *Bereishith Rabba* 50:3. *Midrash Agadah* (ed. Buber), p. 29.

113. *THE RULING OF SODOM'S JUDGES:* Babli, Sanhedrin 109a; Nidah 69a.

114. *THE EVIL ANGELS DWELL IN SODOM:* Babli, Shabbath 67a.
115. *THE ARROGANT INHABITANTS OF SODOM:* Job 28:6–7. *Pirke Rabbi Eliezer* 28. Babli, Sanhedrin 109a.
116. *THE PEOPLE OF SODOM WERE EVIL SINNERS:* Genesis 13:13. Babli, Sanhedrin 109a. Mishnah, Aboth, V, 10.
117. *WOE TO THE GUEST IN SODOM: Midrash Agadah,* p. 43.
118. *THE TREATMENT OF A GUEST IN SODOM:* Ibid.
119. *AT A WEDDING IN SODOM:* Ibid.
120. *THE GOOD MAID OF SODOM:* Genesis 18:20. *Midrash Agadah,* p. 42.
121. *THE FATE OF A BEGGAR IN SODOM: Midrash Agadah,* p. 42.
122. *THE PIOUS DAUGHTER OF LOT IN SODOM:* Babli, Sanhedrin 109b. *Midrash Agadah,* p. 42. Genesis 18:21.
123. *THE FRUITFUL TREES OF ANCIENT SODOM:* Psalms 60:8. *Pesikta de-Rab Kahana* (ed. Buber), p. 187b.
124. *THE EAST WIND IN SODOM:* Job 4:9. *Bereishith Rabba* 51:3.
125. *AN ANGEL OVERTHROWS SODOM AND ITS SISTER CITIES:* Genesis 19:1. Job 28:9. *Bereishith Rabba* 50:2. *Midrash Agadah,* p. 45.
126. *THE ANGEL STRUCK AT DAWN: Midrash Agadah,* p. 45.
127. *THE STONES WHICH FELL ON SODOM:* Genesis 19:24. Koran, Hud 9:84, 15; Al-Hejr, 74. Al-Mukaddasi, *Ahsan al-Takassim.*
128. *THE CURSED PLANTS OF SODOM:* Genesis 19:25. Deuteronomy 32:32. *Bereishith Rabba* 51:4.
129. *SODOM REDEEMED:* Ezekiel 16:53–56. *Tanhuma,* p. 47.
130. *WHERE DID THE NAME MOZAH COME FROM?:* Joshua 18:26. Mishnah, Sukkah 4:5. Yerushalmi, Sukkah 4:3. Babli, Sukkah 48a.
131. *WHERE DID GOLIATH FALL?:* J. Zuallart, *Il Devotissimo Viaggio di Gierusalemme,* 1587.

132. *THE STONES OF BEIT HAKEREM:* Exodus 20:22. Mishnah, Middoth 3:4.

133. *THE MIRACULOUS STONE OF EIN KAREM:* Bertrandon de la Broquiere, in Wright, *Early Travels in Palestine*, p. 287.

134. *MONTJOIE—THE MOUNT OF JOY:* "The Voiage and Trauaile of Syr John Maundevile Knight." *Joinville Chronicle: Memoirs of the Crusades* (trans. F. Marzials), 1908, p. 275.

135. *THE PROPHET JEREMIAH IN ABU GHOSH:* Denis Possot, *Le Voyage de la Terre Sainte*, 1890, p. 161. W. R. Wilson, *Travels . . . and the Holy Land*, 1824, p. 105.

136. *KIRYAT YEARIM—ABODE OF THE ARK OF THE LORD:* Joshua 15:9–10. 1 Samuel 7:1. 1 Chronicles 13:6. Psalms 132:6. Koran, The Cow 2:261.

137. *THE HOLY UZEIR IN ABU GHOSH:* Koran, The Cow 2:264. Dumeiri, *Hayat el-Hayuan*, p. 220. Clermont-Ganneau, *Archaeological Researches*, II, 1896, p. 26. Vaux-Steve, *Fouilles a Qaryat el-Enab*, 1950, p. 114.

138. *IMAM ALI AND THE PLATE OF CREAM:* This tale was told to me by an Arab from the village of Abu Ghosh in 1928.

139. *LATRUN—THE HOME OF THE GOOD THIEF:* Mark 15:27. Luke 23:39–43. Yakut, *Mujam al-Buldan,* I, p. 310.

140. *RABBI YOHANAN AND THE JEWISH MAIDEN:* Mechilta, Yitro, 1931, p. 203.

141. *KING SOLOMON AND THE VILLAGERS OF KEBAB:* E. Pierotti, *Customs and Traditions of Palestine*, 1864, p. 62.

142. *THE ROOFLESS CAVE OF GEZER:* Clermont-Ganneau, *Archaeological Researches in Palestine*, II, p. 235.

143. *THE OVEN OF MOTHER EVE:* This legend was told to me by an Arab while visiting the site in 1925.

144. *THE ORIGIN OF THE NAME ABU SHUSHA:* This tale was heard by me in 1925. Warren-Conder, *The Survey of Western Palestine*, II, 1882.

145. *THE HEROIC BROTHERS OF KEFAR HARRUBA:*

Yerushalmi, Taanith 4. *Eicha Rabba* 2:2. Deuteronomy 32:30.

146. *THE PROPHET SALEH OF RAMLA:* Koran 7:73–78. P. Kahle and H. Schmidt, *Volkserzählungen aus Palatina,* 1918, pp. 3–9.

147. *THE OVERTURNED CISTERN:* I heard this story in 1928. M. van Berchem, *Inscriptions Arabes de Syrie: Memoires . . . de l'Institut Egyptien,* III, 1896, no. 422.

148. *RAMLA—A CHRISTIAN CITY:* Ludolphus of Suchem, "Descriptio terrae sanctae," p. 65.

149. *THE WISE MEN OF LOD:* This tale was told to me in 1925.

150. *THE GREAT RABBI ELIEZER IN LOD:* Zephaniah 1:10. Deuteronomy 16:20. *Pesikta Rabbati,* p. 29b. Yerushalmi, Shabbath 2. *Shir ha-Shirim Rabba* 1:3.

151. *RABBI AKIBAH ON A WELL IN LOD: Aboth de-Rabbi Nathan* (B) 12. Job 14:19.

152. *THE MARTYRS OF LOD:* Babli, Pesahim 50a and the commentary of Rashi. *Eicha Rabba* 13:9. *Megillath Taanith* 12; *Semahoth* 8. *Koheleth Rabba* 9:10. *Midrash Zuta, Koheleth* 9:10 (ed. Buber), p. 122.

153. *LOD'S MARTYRS IN PARADISE:* "Seder Gan Eden," *Beit ha-Midrash* (ed. Yellinek), III, p. 135.

154. *THE PIOUS WOMEN OF LOD:* Lamentations 2:10. *Eicha Rabba* 2:14.

155. *"WHICH WAY LEADS TO LOD?":* Mishnah, Aboth 1:8. Babli, Eirubin 53b.

156. *THE CAVE OF LOD: Pesikta Rabbati* (ed. Ish-Shalom), p. 148b. *Pesikta de Rab Kahana* (ed. Buber), p. 136a.

157. *THE DISCOURSE IN LOD'S CAVE: Zohar,* I, Va-Yehi, p. 284b. Va-Yikra, p. 15a. Tazriah, p. 42b.

158. *SAINT GEORGE IN LOD:* Theodosius, in *PPTS,* II, 1893, p. 9. Arculfus, in *PPTS,* III, 1897.

159. *WHERE DID SAINT GEORGE KILL THE DRAGON?:* Clermont-Ganneau, *Archaeological Researches in Palestine,* II, p. 108.

160. *THE ANTICHRIST AT THE GATE OF LOD:* Al-Muka-dassi, *Ahsan al-Takassim,* p. 176. Tabari, *Taarich el-Russul*

wael-Muluk, I, p. 2463. Yakut, *Mujam al-Buldan*, IV, p. 354.

161. *BETWEEN LOD AND KEFAR ONO:* Babli, Ketuboth 111b. *Midrash Shir ha-Shirim* (ed. Gruenhut), 14:7.

162. *WHERE DID NAHUM OF GIMZO COME FROM?:* 2 Chronicles 28:18. Babli, Taanith 21a.

163. *WHY IS IT CALLED JAFFA?:* Plinius, *Naturalis Historia*, 10, 14. M. Reisher, *Shaarei Yerushalaim*, 1879, p. 20. "The Voiage and Trauaile of Syr John Maundevile Knight."

164. *HOW JAFFA WAS CAPTURED:* E. A. Wallis-Budge, *Facsimiles of Egyptian Hieratic Papyri in the British Museum* (no. 10060), second series, 1923, plate 47.

165. *AT JAFFA "THY PROUD WAVES BE STAYED":* Job 38:10–11. Yerushalmi, Shekalim 6:1. *Bereishith Rabba* 23:7.

166. *KING SOLOMON'S WINEPRESS IN JAFFA:* Zechariah 14:10–11. *Pesikta de-Rab Kahana*, p. 143b. *Shir ha-Shirim Rabba* 7:5.

167. *THE MIRACLE AT JAFFA'S HARBOR:* Mishnah, Middoth 3:10. Tosefta, Yom ha-Kippurim 2:4. Yerushalmi, Yoma 3:8. Babli, Yoma 38a. *Midrash Zuta, Shir ha-Shirim* (ed. Buber), p. 24.

168. *THE SEA OF JAFFA:* Abraham Azulai, *Hesed Le-Abraham*, Mayan 3, Nahar 22 (ed. Amsterdam), p. 34.

169. *THE ROCK OF ANDROMEDA:* Strabo XVI, 2, 28. Plinius, *Naturalis Historia*. Josephus, *Wars*, III, 9, 3. Ovid, *Metamorphoses* (trans. F. J. Miller), 4, 670–760, 1916, pp. 225–33. "The Voiage and Trauaile of Syr John Maundevile Knight." F. Fabri, *Evagatorium in Terrae Sanctae*, 1484.

170. *THE ROCK OF ADAM:* The account by an anonymous traveler, in *PPTS*, VI, 1894, p. 36. Odoricus de Foro Julii, in Laurent, *Peregrinatores*, p. 156. Dimashki, *Nuhbat ed-Daher fi Ajaib el-Bar wael-Bahr* (ed. Mehreen), 1866.

171. *GOING TO JAFFA:* K. Raumer, *Palaestina*, 1860, p. 205.

172. *THE CURSE OF THE GOVERNOR:* This legend I heard from an Arab in Jaffa in 1925.

173. *"IF YOU WILL IT IS NOT A LEGEND":* The name Tel Aviv is taken from the prophecy of Ezekiel 3:15.

174. *WHY IS A FLYING CAMEL THE EMBLEM OF TEL AVIV'S FAIRS?:* This story was told at the opening of the first Tel Aviv fair.

175. *WHERE DID THE NAME NAHLAT BINYAMIN COME FROM?:* This tale was one told by the first settlers along the street.

176. *KEREM HATEIMANIM—VINEYARD OF THE YEMENITES:* This legend was told by one of its inhabitants in 1930. Song of Songs 7:9. Psalms 92:13.

177. *WHO WAS SHEIK SALAMEH?:* This story was told to me by an Arab of the village in 1925.

178. *THE MOUNT OF NAPOLEON:* This legend is current among the inhabitants of the surroundings.

179. *THE FERTILITY OF BNEI BERAK:* Babli, Ketuboth 111b.

180. *RABBI AKIBAH IN BNEI BERAK:* Deuteronomy 16:20. Babli, Sanhedrin 32b.

181. *THE VINEYARDS OF BNEI BERAK: Midrash Tanaim,* 1909, p. 173. Yerushalmi, Peah 7:6.

182. *THE FATE OF THE DESCENDANTS OF HAMAN:* Babli, Sanhedrin 96b. Esther 3–9.

183. *THE MEETING AT ANTIPATRIS:* Babli, Yoma 69a. *Megillath Taanith* 9. According to Josephus, Alexander met the high priest in Sapha (that is, Mount Scopus in Jerusalem), *Antiquities,* X, 8, 5.

184. *WHY IS IT CALLED BEIT DAGON?:* Joshua 15:41. 1 Samuel 5:4–5. The commentaries of Rashi and Radak.

185. *ZERIFIN'S OFFERING TO THE TEMPLE:* Leviticus 23:10. Mishnah, Kelim 1:6; Parah 2:1. Babli, Minahoth 64b; Sottah 49b; Baba Kama 82b.

186. *HOW DID THEY BRING THE OMER?:* Leviticus 23:20. Babli, Minahoth 64b.

187. *THE LOT OF THE PEACHES OF DORON:* Yerushalmi, Peah 7:4. Psalms 107:34.

188. *WHERE DID THE NAME ZARNUKA COME FROM?:* Babli, Sanhedrin 26a. The legend was told to me in this village in 1924.

189. *THE INHERITANCE OF DAN:* Joshua 19:40. Genesis 49:16, 18. Judges 13:5. *Ba-Midbar Rabba* 2:2.
190. *ZORAH—THE BIRTHPLACE OF SAMSON:* Judges 13:19–20, 24. Psalms 84:12.
191. *BETWEEN ZORAH AND ESHTAOL:* Babli, Baba Bathra 91a. Yerushalmi, Sottah 1:8. Judges 13:25, 16:4. Babli, Sottah 9b.
192. *SAMSON THE HERO IN RAMAT LEHI:* Judges 15:9–17. 2 Samuel 23:11. 1 Chronicles 11:13. *Shemuel Rabba* 20.
193. *SAMSON'S SPRING IN BEIT GUVRIN:* Judges 15:18–19. Antoninus Martyr, in *PPTS*, II, 1896, p. 25.
194. *THE ROCK OF DESTRUCTION:* Z. Vilnay, *Hartuv we-Sevivoteha*, 1928, p. 11.
195. *THE ARK OF GOD IN BEIT SHEMESH:* 1 Samuel 6:12–19. *Bereishith Rabba* 54:4. Babli, Abodah Zarah 24b; Horayot 12a. Exodus 25:10.
196. *THE BATTLEFIELD OF DAVID AND GOLIATH:* 1 Samuel 17:1–3, 40–42, 49.
197. *GOLIATH'S BURIAL PLACE:* Antoninus Martyr, in *PPTS*, II, 1896, p. 25.
198. *THE CAVE OF ADULLAM—THE SHELTER OF DAVID:* Psalms 142:2. 1 Samuel 22:1–2. Psalms 57:3 and the Aramaic translation. *Encyclopaedia Britannica*, s. v. "Adullam."
199. *DAVID AND THE SPIDER'S WEB: Alpha-Beitha de-Ben-Sira* (ed. Schteinschneider), p. 24.
200. *THE CAVE OF THE MOTHER OF TWINS:* I heard this from an Arab shepherd in the vicinity in 1926.
201. *THE UPPER CHAMBERS OF THE MAIDENS:* This story was told by Arabs living in the vicinity.
202. *YAVNEH—THE ABODE OF LEARNING:* Babli, Rosh ha-Shana 31a. Isaiah 10:34.
203. *THE VINEYARD OF YAVNEH: Shir ha-Shirim Rabba* 8:9. Isaiah 5:7.
204. *THE CITY OF WISE MEN: Beit Eked ha-Agadoth* (ed. Horowitz–ha-Levi), II, 1882, p. 32.
205. *AN ECHO IN ANCIENT YAVNEH:* Tosefta, Sottah 13:4.

206. *A SCHOLARS' DISPUTE IN YAVNEH:* Babli, Baba Mezia 59b. Exodus 23:2.
207. *THE MORAL OF THE YAVNEH RABBIS:* Babli, Berachot 17a, 59b.
208. *JACOB'S SHIP IN YAVNEH YAM:* R. H. Charles, *The Apocrypha and Pseudepigraphia*, II, 1913, p. 331.
209. *JEWS AND THEIR NEIGHBORS IN ASHKELON:* Zephaniah 2:4. Zechariah 9:5. *Shir ha-Shirim Rabba* 7:2. Yerushalmi, Peah 3:8.
210. *HONORING PARENTS IN ASHKELON:* Babli, Kidushin 31a. Abodah Zarah 23b.
211. *THE PIOUS AND THE RICH OF ASHKELON:* Yerushalmi, Hagigah 2:2.
212. *HOW WAS ASHKELON RID OF ITS WITCHES?:* Mishnah, Sanhedrin 6:4. Yerushalmi, Hagigah 2:2.
213. *ABRAHAM'S WELL IN ASHKELON: Travels of Rabbi Benjamin of Tudela.* Yaacob ben Nataniel (ed. Gruenhut), p. 5.
214. *WHERE WAS SEMIRAMIS BORN?:* Ovid, *Metamorphoses*, IV, 45.
215. *THE MIRACULOUS PILLAR OF ASHKELON:* Ibn Battuta, *Tuhfat an-nuzzar fi gharaib al-amsar wa'ajaib al-asfar*, I, 1853, p. 126. H. A. R. Gibb, *The Travels of Ibn Battuta*, I, 1958, p. 81.
216. *THE TREASURE OF ASHKELON: Travels of Lady Hester Stanhope*, III, 1846, pp. 158–59. *Narrative of the Life and Adventures of Giovanni Finati*, II, 1830, p. 130.
217. *WHERE DOES THE SHALLOT ORIGINATE?:* Yerushalmi, Sanhedrin 6:4. Plinius, *Naturalis Historia*, 5, 14. *A Spanish Franciscan's Narrative of a Journey to the Holy Land.*
218. *THE VALE OF THE ANTS:* 1 Kings 5:9, 13. "Maaseh ha-Nemala," *Beit ha-Midrash* (ed. Yellinek), V, p. 22. *Maaseh ha-Nemala we-Shelomo ha-Melech*, 1869. Koran, The Ant 27:16–18. Ibn Battuta, *Tuhfat an-nuzzar*, I, p. 126.
219. *WISDOM IN THE SOUTH:* Babli, Baba Bathra 158b. *Bereishith Rabba* 16:4.

220. *THE FLOWERY LANGUAGE OF THE JUDEANS:*
Babli, Eirubin 53a–b.
221. *THE HERMIT FROM THE SOUTH:* Babli, Nedarim 9b.
Tosefta, Nezirut 4:7. Yerushalmi, Taanith 3:4.
222. *THE INNKEEPER OF THE SOUTH:* Yerushalmi, Pesahim 5:3. *Bereishith Rabba* 92:6 (ed. Theodor), p. 1144.
Genesis 1:4.
223. *THE SYCAMORES IN THE LOWLAND:* 1 Chronicles
27:28. 2 Chronicles 1:15, 9:27. 1 Kings 10:27. Amos 7:14.
Tosefta, Shebiit 7:11.
224. *HOW DID THEY BORDER THEIR FIELDS?:* Babli,
Baba Bathra 56a; Beiza 25b. Yerushalmi, Peah 2:1.
225. *BEROR HAIL—THE HOME OF RABBI YOHANAN:*
Babli, Sanhedrin 32b. Deuteronomy 16:20.
226. *BEROR HAIL AND BURNI:* Babli, Sanhedrin 32b.
Jeremiah 25:10.
227. *BEIT GUVRIN IN THE END OF TIME:* Genesis 14:6,
27:39, 33:14. *Yalkut Shimoni, Vaishlah* 133.
228. *VILLAGES IN THE KING'S MOUNTAIN:* Numbers
2:32. Babli, Gittin 57a.
229. *THE DESTRUCTION OF THE KING'S MOUNTAIN:*
Ibid.
230. *WHY WAS IT CALLED GAZA?:* M. A. Meyer, *History
of the City of Gaza*, p. 5. Yakut, *Mujam al-Buldan*, III,
p. 799.
231. *SAMSON AND THE GATES OF GAZA:* Judges 16:3.
Babli, Sottah 10a.
232. *THE FATE OF SAMSON IN GAZA:* Judges 16:25–30.
Babli, Sottah 10a.
233. *WHAT IS THE ORIGIN OF GAUZE?:* C. Du Cange,
Glossarium Mediae et infimae Latinitatis, IV, 1844, p. 49.
J. D. Mansi, *Sacrum Conciliorum*, 24, 1279, p. 301.
234. *WHAT IS METHEG AMMAH?:* 2 Samuel 8:1. The version in 1 Chronicles 18:1 speaks of "Gath and its towns."
Yalkut Shimoni, 2 Samuel 287.
235. *ZENAN—HADASHAH—MIGDAL-GAD:* Joshua 15:37.
Micah 1:11. *Tanhuma, Tisa* 13 (ed. Warsaw), I, p. 120.
Shemot Rabba 40:4. Isaiah 65:11.

236. *KABZEEL—EDER—YAGUR:* Joshua 15:21. 2 Samuel 23:20. 1 Chronicles 11:22. Babli, Berachoth 18b. *Yalkut Shimoni, 2 Samuel* 165, 23. *Aruch ha-Shalem*, s. v. "Kabez."

237. *WHY WAS IT CALLED BEERSHEBA?:* Genesis 21:22–31, 26:30–33. *Targum Yerushalmi* to Genesis 21:31. Josephus, *Antiquities*, I, 12, 1. Eusebius Hieronymus, *Onomastikon. Pirke Rabbi Eliezer* 35. *Sifri, Deuteronomy* 8, 1866, p. 54a.

238. *ABRAHAM'S TAMARISK IN BEERSHEBA:* Genesis 21:33. *Midrash Tehillim*, 110 (ed. Buber), p. 233. *Yalkut Shimoni, Tehillim* 869.

239. *ABRAHAM'S CEDARS IN BEERSHEBA:* Genesis 32:29, 46:1. *Bereishith Rabba* 94:4.

240. *THE HOSPITALITY OF ABRAHAM IN BEERSHEBA:* *Aboth de-Rabbi Nathan* 1:7. *Bereishith Rabba* 54:5. Babli, Sottah 10 a–b. The commentary of Rashi to Genesis 21:22.

241. *THE FEAST OF SUKKOTH IN BEERSHEBA: Book of Jubileum* 16:20–31. Charles, *The Apocrypha and Pseudepigrapha*, II, p. 38.

242. *SAMUEL'S SONS IN BEERSHEBA:* 1 Samuel 8:1–3. Yerushalmi Sottah 1:4.

243. *THE MONUMENT TO ALLENBY IN BEERSHEBA:* This story was current at the time of the British conquest of the Holy Land.

244. *BEERSHEBA IN THE END OF TIME:* Yakut, *Mujam al-Buldan*, III, p. 34.

245. *ABRAHAM THE PATRIARCH IN GERAR: Bereishith Rabba* 52:1. *Agadath Bereishith* 25:1. Genesis 20:1.

246. *ARAD AND THE WAY OF ATHARIM:* Numbers 21:1. *Ba-Midbar Rabba* 19:20. Babli, Rosh ha-Shana 3a.

247. *THE ASCENT OF SCORPIONS:* Numbers 34:2–4. Joshua 15:3.

249. *THE SPIES IN THE NEGEV:* Numbers 13:17–18. *Tanhuma, Shaloah* 6 (ed. Warsaw), II, p. 68; (ed. Buber), II, p. 66.

250. *THE TRIBE OF SIMEON IN THE NEGEV:* Joshua 19:8–9. Genesis 49:7 and Rashi's commentary. *Bereishith Rabba* 88:7.

251. *ALEXANDER THE GREAT AND THE WISE MEN OF THE NEGEV:* Babli, Tamid 31b–32a. Genesis 1:1.
252. *THE LAND OF JOSEPH: EPHRAIM AND MANASSEH:* Deuteronomy 33:13. Babli, Berachoth 20a; Baba Bathra 118b. Genesis 48:15. *Bereishith Rabba* 97.
253. *THE FLAGS OF JOSEPH AND HIS SONS: Ba-Midbar Rabba* 82. Deuteronomy 33:17.
254. *SHILOH—CENTER OF THE TRIBES OF ISRAEL:* Joshua 18:1. Deuteronomy 12:9. Tosefta, Zebahim 13:6–8. Psalms 78:58–61. Babli, Zebahim 118b. *Ba-Midbar Rabba* 12. Ha-Parhi, *Kaftor Va-Perah* (ed. Lunz).
255. *THE PILGRIMS TO SHILOH:* 1 Samuel 1:3, 20. *Tana Devei Eliyahu* 8:4, 1912, p. 54.
256. *SHILOH AND GEREB:* Judges 18:13–14. Babli, Sanhedrin 103b.
257. *A COIN HONORING JOSHUA:* Deuteronomy 33:17. Babli, Eirubin 22b. *Bereishith Rabba* 39:11.
258. *TIMNATH HERES—THE CITY OF JOSHUA:* Judges 2:9. The commentary of Rashi to Deuteronomy 33:17.
259. *TIMNATH HERES—TIMNATH SERAH:* Ibid. Joshua 24:30.
260. *MOUNT GAASH NEAR TIMNATH HERES:* Joshua 24:30. Judges 2:8–9. Babli, Shabbath 105b. *Koheleth Rabba* 7:1.
261. *THE PRIESTLY PAIRS IN GOFNA:* Babli, Berachoth 44a. Yerushalmi, Taanith 4:8. *Eicha Rabba* 2:4.
262. *IN THE HOSTEL OF YASSUF: Joshua of the Samaritans,* 47.
263. *SAMARIA—CAPITAL OF THE KINGDOM OF ISRAEL:* Isaiah 7:9. 1 Kings 16:24. Babli, Sanhedrin 102b.
264. *THE PLACE OF THE FIRE:* 2 Kings 1:2–4, 9–10. A. Alt, "Eine Vergessenes Heiligtum des Propheten Elias," *ZDPV*, XLVIII, 1925, pp. 393–97.
265. *THE PIT OF JOSEPH IN SAMARIA:* Genesis 37:17, 24–28. Zakaria Kazwini, *Athar al-Buldan*, II, p. 18; III, p. 162; IV, p. 516.
266. *KING SAUL, BEZEK, AND TELAIM:* 1 Samuel 11:8, 15:4. Babli, Yoma 22b.

267. *SHECHEM AND SIMEON'S STANDARD:* Numbers
2:2. Genesis 34:25–27. *Ba-Midbar Rabba* 2:7.
268. *SHECHEM IS CALLED NABLUS:* Yakut, *Mujam al-
Buldan*, IV, p. 729.
269. *JACOB THE PATRIARCH IN SHECHEM:* Genesis
33:18–20. *Bereishith Rabba* 79:6.
270. *THE MOSQUE OF JACOB'S MOURNING:* This was
told by the keeper of the mosque in 1925. Genesis 37:31–
34.
271. *THE MIGHTY NIMROD IN SHECHEM:* Genesis 10:6–
10. Micah 5:5. Yakut, *Mujam al-Buldan*, I, p. 710.
272. *HOW MANY SPRINGS ARE THERE IN SHECHEM?:*
Abraham Rozanes, "Masaot Haabir," *Sinai*, 33, 1953
(Hebrew).
273. *THE WELL OF JACOB:* Genesis 32. John 4:3–26.
274. *THE FOUNTAIN OF SOCHER:* John 4:5. Leviticus
23:17. Yerushalmi, Shekalim 5:1. Babli, Sottah 49b; Minahoth 64b.
275. *THE WELL OF JOB: The Pilgrimage of Arnold von
Harff*, p. 226. *Itinerarium Burdigalense*, (ed. Geyer),
1898, "Aser, ubi fuit villa Job." *PPTS*, I, 1897, p. 18.
276. *MOUNT OF BLESSING AND MOUNT OF CURSE:*
Deuteronomy 11:29, 27:11–13. Joshua 8:30, 33–34. *Mase-
cheth Kutim* 18:2.
277. *MOUNT GERIZIM AND THE GREAT FLOOD: Bereishith Rabba* 32:10.
278. *MOUNT GERIZIM—THE ANCIENT MOUNTAIN:*
"Ernoul's Account of Palestine," *PPTS*, VI, 1896, p. 61.
Deuteronomy 27:1, 4, 8.
279. *MOUNT CAIN AND MOUNT ABEL:* Theodoricus, in
PPTS, V, 1896, p. 62. "Ernoul's Account of Palestine,"
PPTS, VI, 1896, p. 61.
280. *WHY WAS IT CALLED EBAL?:* Genesis 5:24. *Yalkut
Shimoni, Torah* 76; *Ezekiel* 367. "Book of Asatir" (ed.
Ben-Haim), *Tarbitz*, 14, 1943, p. 180.
281. *THE DOVE ON MOUNT GERIZIM:* Babli, Hullin 6a;
Abodah Zarah 27a. Tosefta, Abodah Zarah 3:13. Yeru-
shalmi, Shabbath 19:1.

282. *THE SPEAKING FOWL ON MOUNT GERIZIM: Joshua of the Samaritans,* 50. G. J. Juynboll, *Chronicon Samaritanum,* 1848.

283. *THE PRAYER OF THE SHARONITES:* Job 4:19. Deuteronomy 20:5. Mishnah, Sottah 8:3. Babli, Sottah 44a. Yerushalmi, Sottah 5:7.

284. *THE FORESTS OF SHARON:* This story was told by an Arab from Jaffa in 1925.

285. *THE SYCAMORE OF KEFAR SABA:* 1 Chronicles 27:28. 1 Kings 10:27. Tosefta, Nidah 8:5. Babli, Nidah 61a.

286. *THE BATTLE WITH THE SUN:* This was told by an Arab of the vicinity in 1926.

287. *THE TEST STONE IN SIDNA ALI:* I was present at a test of this kind which took place in 1925. C. W. Wilson, *Ordnance Survey of Jerusalem, Notes,* 1865, p. 41.

288. *SHEIK HILLU NEAR HADERA:* This legend was told by a bedouin near Hadera in 1925.

289. *THE RIVER OF THE CROCODILES:* Fettelus (Frettelus), in *PPTS,* V, 1897, p. 47. Pococke, *A Description of the East,* II, p. 47.

290. *THE SPRING OF MOUNT SINA: Itinerarium Burdigalense* (ed. Geyer), p. 19.

291. *THE DRUM AND ITS STICK: Sefer ha-Shana shel Erez-Israel,* II–III, 1926, p. 93.

292. *RAHASH STREET IN HADERA: Sefer Toldoth ha-Haganah,* 1955, p. 357.

293. *THE JEWISH NOTABLES OF CAESAREA:* Psalms 116:9. Babli, Ketuboth 17a; Moed Kattan 28b.

294. *THE JEWISH MARTYRS IN CAESAREA:* Yaacob ben Nataniel (ed. Gruenhut), p. 11.

295. *ROMAN SOLDIERS IN OLD CAESAREA: Tanhuma, Vayeshev,* 3, 1875, I, p. 46.

296. *ON THE COAST OF ANCIENT CAESAREA: Bereishith Rabba* 6:7. *Va-Yikra Rabba* 22:4.

297. *THE WAYS OF JUSTICE IN ANCIENT CAESAREA:* Yerushalmi, Shabbath 14:1. *Va-Yikra Rabba* 6:2. Babli, Gittin 45a.

298. *IN THE THEATERS OF ROMAN CAESAREA:*
Yerushalmi, Berachoth 4:2. Babli, Abodah Zarah 18b.
Eicha Rabba 17.
299. *THE RIVALRY BETWEEN CAESAREA AND JE-
RUSALEM: Eicha Rabba* 1. Babli, Megillah 6a.
300. *EKRON—CAESAREA:* Zephaniah 2:4. Babli, Megillah
6a.
301. *THE GOOD LIFE IN CAESAREA: Eicha Rabba* 3.
Koheleth Rabba 1:5. Ezekiel 27:17.
302. *WHO BUILT THE AQUEDUCT OF CAESAREA?:*
This was told by an Arab near Caesarea in 1925.
303. *HOW WAS CAESAREA RID OF ITS BAD SMELLS?:*
Fettelus (Frettelus), in *PPTS*, V, 1897, p. 47. M. de Vogüé,
Les Églises de la Terre Sainte, 1860, p. 430.